本书受中央高校基本科研业务费专项资金资助
(Supported by the Fundamental Research Funds for the Central Universities)

短语学
在篇章意义构建中的作用
——基于语料库的高频名词措词研究

李双玲／著

Phraseology in the Construction of Meaning in Discourse:
A Corpus-Based Study of the Phraseological Behaviour of High Frequency Nouns

西南财经大学出版社
四川·成都

图书在版编目(CIP)数据

短语学在篇章意义构建中的作用:基于语料库的高频名词措词研究/李双玲著.—成都:西南财经大学出版社,2018.11
ISBN 978-7-5504-3709-8

Ⅰ.①短…　Ⅱ.①李…　Ⅲ.①英语—短语—研究②英语—名词—研究　Ⅳ.①H314.3②H314.2

中国版本图书馆 CIP 数据核字(2018)第 204848 号

短语学在篇章意义构建中的作用:基于语料库的高频名词措词研究
Duanyuxue zai Pianzhang Yiyi Goujianzhong de Zuoyong:Jiyu Yuliaoku de Gaopin Mingci Cuoci Yanjiu
李双玲　著

责任编辑:王正好
助理编辑:周晓琬
封面设计:墨创文化
责任印制:朱曼丽

出版发行	西南财经大学出版社(四川省成都市光华村街 55 号)
网　　址	http://www.bookcj.com
电子邮件	bookcj@foxmail.com
邮政编码	610074
电　　话	028-87353785　87352368
照　　排	四川胜翔数码印务设计有限公司
印　　刷	四川五洲彩印有限责任公司
成品尺寸	170mm×240mm
印　　张	15.75
字　　数	530 千字
版　　次	2018 年 11 月第 1 版
印　　次	2018 年 11 月第 1 次印刷
书　　号	ISBN 978-7-5504-3709-8
定　　价	88.00 元

前 言

短语学或措词学（phraseology）通常被认为是一个可以概括各种多字词组（multi-word phrases）的术语。在过去的几十年，短语学的重要性已广泛地被语言研究者认可。许多语料库语言学家（如Sinclair，Hunston和Hoey）指出语言本身是具有很强的用语特征（phraseological nature）的，比如，英语用语里面经常出现的往往是惯用的多字词组和短语。措词或者用语的研究因而被应用于很多研究领域，如心理语言学、认知语言学、社会语言学、翻译和话语分析。

然而，许多过去对措词的研究主要集中在语言的形式或语法结构方面，而非篇章本身的意义构建方面（the construction of meaning）。比如，先前大多数对措词的研究把重心放在了对措词的定义（definition）或者措词的范围（scope）方面，或者重视对语词种类的区分（categorisation）及区分标准（criteria）等。除此之外，相对较少的研究侧重于研究措词和话语意义构建的关系，如措词与篇章里面的隐喻（metaphor）、评价（evaluation）和模糊用法（vague use）之间的关系。因此，本书旨在弥合这一研究上的差距并主要探讨措词和篇章意义的构建之间是否有联系、联系究竟是什么以及此联系对日后的研究和教学意味着什么。

本书中的研究主要基于语料库语言学的方法论，通过语料对措词进行分析。该研究方法具有许多优势：第一，语料库的研究是基于计算机的软件分析（computer-based），这意味着数据分析的速度和规模都是远远胜于传统的语言研究方法的；第二，语料库的研究基于真实的语言数据（authentic data），其分析结果展示的将是人类实际使用语言的特征，而非人类语言中可能出现的特征，也就是说，语料库语言学是采用实证主义的态度，与自然科学的学科研究类似，其分析建立在真实数据的基础上；第三，语料库的研究比传统语言分析更具有科学性（scientific approach）和客观性，对语料的分析不依赖于研究者的语感和经历，而是从数据的质和量上进行统计和分析，更加可靠。

具体而言，本书中的研究使用两个通用英语语料库来分析高频名词（如 time 和 thing）的语言特征：柯林斯英语语料库（BoE）以及英国国家语料库（BNC）。根据对高频名词的分析，本书试图探讨与高频名词相关的用法（如隐喻、评价和模糊用法）是否以及如何与高频名词的用语行为（phraseological behaviour）产生联系。结果表明，措词和这一系列与话语意义构建相关的用法是有着密切关联的。例如，研究发现 time 的隐喻用法（如 TIME IS MONEY 和 TIME IS MOTION）与围绕这个词的某些语词项（collocations and phraseologies）有着独特的联系；同样，thing 所表现的不同评价用法（evaluative usages）也往往体现在与这个词相联系的语言模式（patterns）上面。也就是说，研究的结果揭示了措词在话语意义构建上的重要性及在哪些方面有密切联系。

本书同时也侧重于措词在英语教学中的应用。尽管措词在语言学习中的重要性已被越来越多的人认可，措词在语言教学中的体现仍然是存在一些问题的。因此，本书还致力于考察措词在中国英语教学中的应用，希望能为日后语言课堂教学以及教学材料的设计提供一些见解。这部分的调查选用了两个语料库：由大学英语课本组建的教学语料库 CEC（Corpus of English Coursebooks）和学习者语料库 CLEC（Chinese Learner English Corpus）。对这两个语料库的研究着重于语料库中的语词项的选择（choice of phraseologies）以及对语词项用法（usage of phraseologies）的展示。结果表明这两个语料库中都出现了不同程度的对语词项的“过度表现”和“表现不足”的情况（‘over- and under-representation’）。对于部分语词项，这两个语料库甚至只展现了这些语词项比较罕见的用法。因此日后措词的教学可以多考虑以明确的教学用法（explicit teaching）和隐含教学方法（implicit teaching）结合的形式进行；日后的教学还可以多参考一些当前与教学相关的以语料库为平台的研究。

李双玲

2018 年 3 月

Acknowledgements

The publication of this book is surpported by the Fundamental Research Funds for the Central Universities. This book is based on the author's PhD thesis completed in 2015 at the University of Birmingham (the thesis title originally being *A Corpus-Based Study of the High Frequency Nouns time and thing: Investigating the Role of Phraseology in the Construction of Meaning in Discourse*). The book mainly keeps the research contents from the PhD thesis; it changes the organisation and format of the thesis and updates some of the contents where necessary. Therefore, as this book comes into reality, I would like to thank all the people who helped me making the thesis possible and my PhD life an enjoyable one.

First, I would like to express my profound gratitude to my lead supervisor Dr. Crayton Walker for his guidance and for sharing his expertise throughout the PhD life. I would also like to thank my second supervisor Dr. Paul Thompson forproviding detailed and encouraging feedback on the PhD thesis. Then, I want to thank Dr. Jeannette Littlemore for her insightful comments on the chapter on metaphor. I am also grateful to all the other wonderful staff and PhD fellows at the University of Birmingham for their encouragement, and to the kind colleagues here at the Southwestern University of Finance and Economics for their support. Lastly, my eternal gratitude goes to my family who have always provided unconditional love and support. I dedicate this book to them.

Conventions used in this book

Italics

a. used in the running text to indicate the words or phrases under analysis or discussion, e.g. the high frequency noun *time*, and the phrases *big time* and *at the same time*;

b. used in the running text to indicate examples from the corpus, e.g. the word *time* can denote the sense of 'actual time on a clock', as in this example *What time is it? Three–thirty.*

CAPITALS

used to indicate conceptual metaphors (e.g. TIME IS MONEY) and conceptual domains (e.g. TIME or MONEY).

small capitals

used to indicate lemma (all word forms of an item), e.g. spend as the lemma form of the verb *spend*, or make as the lemma form of the verb *make*.

"double quotation marks"

a. used to indicate citations from others' work, e.g. "studies on the actual treatment of phraseology in ELT material are rare" (Meunier and Gouverneur 2007: 121);

b. used to indicate terminology in this book, e.g. the term "phraseology" or the term "collocation".

'single quotation marks'

a. used to indicate a word or phrase which is used vaguely or broadly, e.g.

meaning at the 'discourse' level, or the 'semantic' role of phraseology in language use;

b. used to indicate concepts or meanings/senses, e.g. the concept of 'money' or 'spending money', or the sense of 'occasion' associated with the word *time*;

c. used occasionally to indicate a pattern and differentiate it from other words in the running text, e.g. the discussion of 'spend *time with* n.' in Section 6.2, or the patterns '*it* v-link *time to*-inf.' and '*at the time of* N' in Section 7.4.

目 录

PART ONE Phraseology and corpus linguistics

PART TWO
Phraseology and the construction of meaning in discourse

PART ONE
Phraseology and corpus linguistics

Chapter 1 What is phraseology?

1.1 Significance of phraseology

It is no exaggeration to say that phraseology occupies a central position in language use. This important role of phraseology has been recognised by many linguists (e.g. Sinclair 1991, 2004a; Hoey 2005; Granger and Meunier 2008; Römer and Schulze 2009; Stubbs 2009a; Moon 2010; O'Keeffe and McCarthy 2010; Hunston 2011; Granger *et al.* 2013). Advances in technology and an increasing use of corpus-based methods have also made the research on different aspects of phraseology more feasible and easier, e.g. automatic extraction of certain phraseological items or studies on phraseology using large quantities of data. Various academic disciplines such as discourse analysis, psycholinguistics, sociolinguistics and multilingualism have taken phraseology as a starting point to investigate features of language, mind and society (see Deignan 2005; Hoey 2005; Mahlberg 2005; McEnery *et al.* 2006; Granger and Meunier 2008; Murphy 2010; O'Keeffe and McCarthy 2010; Hunston 2011; McEnery and Hardie 2012; Granger *et al.* 2013; John and Laso 2013).

Phraseology is a pervasive phenomenon in language use (see Sinclair 1991, 2004a; Howarth 1996; Cowie 1998; Meunier and Granger 2008; McEnery and Hardie 2012). For example, Altenberg (1998) has suggested that over 80% of the words in the London – Lund corpus of spoken English are involved in recurrent word combinations (cf. Pawley 2007: 20). Greaves and Warren (2010: 221) further argue that if the "multiword units with constituency and or positional variation" (e.g. concgrams or collocational frameworks) are taken into consideration, the figure related to the phraseological nature of language could be "closer to 100 percent". Similarly, the current corpus-based analysis of *time* and *thing* suggests that these two words are associated with a strong phraseological tendency, i.e. they tend to occur in fixed phrases or patterns (cf. Sinclair 1991, 1996). Approximately 96% of the concordances of *time* in a random corpus sample of 500 lines contain recurring phraseological items; and around 79% of the concordances of *thing* in a 500-line corpus sample involve the occurrences of multi-word phrases. Thus, it can be reasonably argued that language itself exhibits a strong phraseological nature (see Sinclair 1991, 2004a; Cowie 1998; Wray 2002; Hoey 2005; Ellis 2008; Römer and Schulze 2009; Moon 2010; Stubbs 2011; Granger *et al*. 2013).

Phraseology can also reflect the linguistic features of a certain discourse. For instance, the phraseological items which occur frequently in conversational discourse may differ from those in academic writing (see Biber 2006; Biber and Conrad 2009; Charles *et al*. 2009; O'Keeffe and McCarthy 2010; John and Laso 2013; Sindoni 2013). Similarly, the phraseological features of lexical items in business-related discourse are somewhat different from those in newspaper articles. In other words, this relation between phraseology and genre makes it possible to analyse features associated with a certain discourse or compare two different genres based on the use of phraseology in texts (see Aijmer and Stenström 2004; Biber *et al*. 2004; Sinclair 2004a; Hoey 2005; Biber 2006; Biber and Conrad 2009; Römer and Schulze 2010; John and Laso 2013). Furthermore, a comparison of the use of phraseology can also be carried out across different languages, e.g. by using parallel corpora to explore the preference of phraseology in two languages (cf. Granger and Meunier 2008; Ji 2010; McEnery and Hardie 2012). In short, it is undeniable that phraseology is important in language use and that further research on phraseology would be beneficial, which is the main reason why the current investigation focuses on phraseology or the phraseological behaviour of lexical items.

1.2 Scope of phraseology

Increasingly, it has been widely recognised that language has a strong phraseological nature (see Sinclair 1991, 2004a; Hoey 2005; Granger and Meunier 2008; Römer and Schulze 2009; Stubbs 2009a; Moon 2010; O'Keeffe and McCarthy 2010;

Hunston 2011; Granger *et al*. 2013; John and Laso 2013). Sinclair (1991) in particular proposes the idiom principle which accounts for how language normally works and suggests that phraseology is central to language use. This principle states that "a language user has available to him or her a large number of semi-preconstructed phrases that constitute single choices, even though they might appear to be analysable into segments" (Sinclair 1991: 110). It suggests to some extent how the lexical or lexico-grammatical co-occurrence may be the default mode of language organisation and provides the theoretical basis for the current study.

However, there is still no clear consensus to date about either the definition or scope of phraseology (cf. Anderson 2006; Granger and Meunier 2008). In other words, the definition of this term varies from researcher to researcher. For instance, some traditional studies of phraseology have been restricted to idioms and fixed expressions (cf. Howarth 1996; Cowie 1998; Granger and Meunier 2008), while later studies (e.g. Sinclair 1991, 2004a; Hoey 2005; Meunier and Granger 2008; O'Keeffe and McCarthy 2010; Hunston 2011; McEnery and Hardie 2012; Hanks 2013) adopt a broader view and define phraseology as a cover term for all sorts of multi-word phrases.

In this book, I argue that the term "phraseology" refers to two aspects of multi-word sequences: 1) the analysis of the form, i.e. recurring multi-word phrases as well as sequences with paradigmatic choices (such as patterns and collocational frameworks); 2) the analysis of the use of these phraseological items (phraseological behaviour), e.g. the semantic and pragmatic uses of a phraseological item and the relation between this phraseological item and its co-texts. In the following sections, I will provide the rationale for my definition of phraseology, discuss the criteria for defining and describing a phraseological item, and introduce relevant terminology which is used in this book.

1.2.1 Phraseology and a phraseological item

A phraseological item involves two main types of lexical (or lexicogrammatical) co-occurrence: continuous or discontinuous multi-word phrases which are constructed by specific words, and a type of 'sequence' which involves paradigmatic choices of words or phrases (e.g. pattern and frame).

The first type of phraseological item, "recurring (dis) continuous multi-word phrases", is discussed under different labels, e.g. "lexicalised stems", "lexical phrases", "formulaic sequences", "lexical bundles", "n-grams", "lexical items", "multi-word expressions" (MWEs), and "multi-word units" (MWUs) (see Wray 2000: 465; Biber *et al.* 2004: 372; Meunier and Granger 2008; O'Keeffe and McCarthy 2010; McEnery and Hardie 2012). However, these labels for multi-word phrases are not used entirely synonymously by researchers, except for the more 'general' terms such as "multi-word sequences", "multi-word units" (MWUs) and "multi-word expressions" (MWEs).

For instance, Pawley and Syder (1983: 191) use the term "lexicalised stem" to refer to "a unit of clause length or longer whose grammatical form and lexical content is wholly or largely fixed", which covers longer sequences and highlights the criterion of "institutionalisation" and "lexicalisation" for a phraseological item. Nattinger and DeCarrico (1992) adopt the term "lexical phrases" to mean "prefabricated language chunks" or "conventionalised form/function composites that occur more frequently and have more idiomatically determined meaning than language that is put together each time" (Nattinger and DeCarrico 1992: 1), which emphasises the criteria of frequency and semantic non-compositionality for a phraseological item. Nattinger and DeCarrico's (1992) study is also normally associated with the application of multi-word phrases in the field of language teaching.

Wray (2000, 2002), writing from the perspective of psycholinguistics or clinicallinguistics, prefers the term "formulaic sequences" for the description of a wide range of multi-word strings which are "stored and retrieved whole from memory at the time of use, rather than being subject to generation or analysis by the language grammar" (Wray 2000: 465). Additionally, one positive aspect that has emerged from Wray's studies is the inclusion of discontinous sequences into the scope of formulaic language, which supports my definition of phraseology, i.e. a phraseological item can be a continuous multi-word sequence or a discontinous sequence. Biber *et al.* (2004) and Biber (2006), on the other hand, use the label "lexical bundles" to investigate recurrent sequences of words with a corpus-based approach, paying more attention to the use of phraseology in specific genres or across genres.

The term "lexical items" among the group of labels for recurring multi-word sequences is also worthy of more explanation. In this book, this term is used to refer to both single words and multi-word phrases as long as the word or phrase is used as an individual unit of meaning in context. This definition of "lexical items" follows Sinclair *et al.* (2004: 9) who suggest that "a lexical item" may not always be associated with "an orthographic word"; among many forms a lexical item can refer to (e.g. "morpheme"), the term "lexical item" also covers "a pair or group of words associated syntagmatically" such as a multi-word sequence. In other words, a lexical item can refer to either a word (e.g. *time* or *thing*) or a phrase (e.g. *at the same time* and *from time to time*).

The second type of phraseological item, as discussed earlier, involves a type of 'sequence' which is not entirely constructed by specific words and is associated with paradigmatic choices of lexical items, e.g. "pattern" (Hunston and Francis 2000) and "frame" (Renouf and Sinclair 1991). The main reason that I include this type of sequence within the scope of phraseology is that patterns and frames are also associated with lexical or lexicogrammatical co-occurrence. Generally speaking, patterns (e.g. '*it* v-link *time to*-inf.' and '*the* ADJ *thing to do*') describe the co-selection of lexical items and grammatical categories; and frames (e.g. '*a* (*n*) + ? + *of*') concern the co-occurrence of a fixed part of lexical items and a variable part of lexical or grammatical items. The above argument that patterns and frames can be included within the scope of phraseology is also supported by other researchers. For instance, Hunston (2011) has illustrated the relation between phraseology and evaluation using language patterns (e.g. '*it* v-link ADJ *to*-inf.' and '*a time of* N') as well as multi-word phrases. This suggests that it is possible to consider phraseology as a broad term to include patterns. Similarly, in Granger and Meunier (2008), frames (e.g. '*a* (*n*) + ? + *of*' and '*be* + ? + *to*') and patterns (e.g. 'ADJ N' and '*as* ADJ *as*') are examined under the scope of phraseology (cf. Granger and Paquot 2008: 39; Martin 2008: 51-66; Arnaud *et al.* 2008: 111-126; Wikberg 2008: 127-142). Furthermore, the categorisation of patterns and frames as types of phraseological item extends the scope of phraseology, which could be viewed as a better recognition of the significant role of phraseology in language use.

In addition to being an umbrella term for all types of multi-word sequences or sequences with paradigmatic choices, phraseology can also refer to various aspects of a phraseological item: e.g. the syntagmatic features of this item, the semantic and pragmatic uses of this item, and the textual and social functions of this item. Cowie (1994: 3168), for instance, defines phraseology as "the study of the structure, meaning and use of word combinations". His definition of phraseology includes at least three aspects of the study of word combinations: the form, semantic features and pragmatic use. Hunston also suggests that phraseology refers to more than just a collection of phrases or sequences: "it encompasses all aspects of preferred sequencing" (2002a: 138). Similarly, Thompson and Hunston argue that:

The term 'phraseology' can be used to describe not just the fact that many words frequently occur in phrases, but the more abstract tendency for words to co-occur non-randomly and for the selection of particular lexical items to alter the probability of other lexical and grammatical choices. (Thompson and Hunston 2006: 10)

In otherwords, Thompson and Hunston regard the features from the co-occurrence of words, e.g. the collocational or colligational behaviour of a lexical item, as a part of the study of phraseology.

To summarise the above discussion, it is argued in this book that the term "a phraseological item" refers to recurring multi-word phrases and sequences with paradigmatic choices (e.g. patterns and frames). The term "phraseology", on the other hand, involves the study of both the form and the use of a phraseological item. More specifically, the investigation of phraseology in this book concerns the syntagmatic features of a phraseological item, the semantic and pragmatic features of this item, and the discourse functions of this item.

1.2.2 Criteria for identifying a phraseological item

ccording to previous studies on phraseology, there are three generally-accepted criteria fordefining and describing a phraseological item: frequency, syntagmatic fixedness and semantic non-compositionality (see Sinclair 1991; Howarth 1996; Cowie 1998; Moon 1998; Hoey 2005; Anderson 2006; Granger and Meunier 2008; Gries 2008; Meunier and Granger 2008; Bolly 2009; Römer and Schulze 2009; Herbst *et al*. 2011; Maienborn *et al.* 2011). Before discussing these three criteria in more detail, it is important to note that each criterion should be perceived more as a dimension because each is not a binary feature but involves a continuum of features with different degrees. For instance, the criterion semantic non-compositionality describes not only the lexical items which are compositional or non-compositional, but also the items which are partially compositional or partially non-compositional (a further discussion of this criterion is provided below). These three criteria are represented in Figure 1.1.

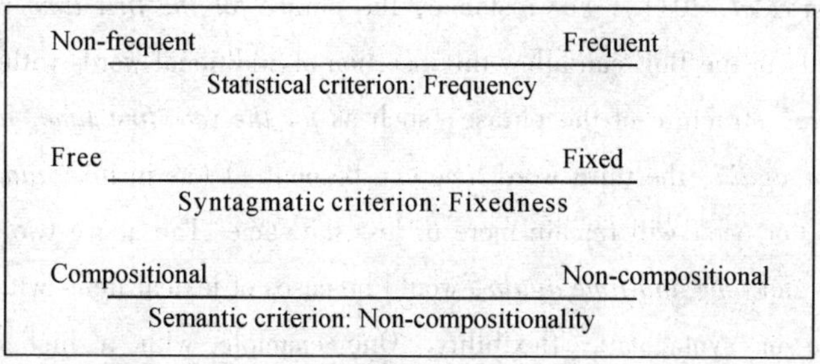

Figure 1. 1 **The three main criteria associated with a phraseological item**

The first dimension, frequency, is considered to be the statistical criterion for identifying a phraseological item (see Sinclair 1991; Hunston 2002a; McEnery *et al.* 2006; Gries 2008). Phraseological items can range on a continuum based on their occurrences in a corpus. Some of these can occur very frequently in a corpus, e.g. *for the first time* (110 times per million in the BoE) and *at the same time* (57 times per million in the BoE); while others may be less frequent, e.g. *time after time* (0. 85 times per million in the BoE) and *time flies* (0. 27 times per million in the BoE). It is thus up to the researcher to decide how many times a sequence needs to occur in the corpus to be counted as a phraseological item, but generally, if a sequence occurs more frequently in the corpus, it is more likely that this sequence will be regarded as a phraseological item. In these cases, the normalised frequency (e.g. the number of occurrences per million words) is often used instead of raw frequency so that the occurrences of a phraseological item can be compared across corpora. Other statistical measures, such as the t-score, can be used as supplementary criteria if the multi-word sequence occurs with a relatively low frequency. It has been suggested from the statistical point of view that the combinations with a t-score above 2. 4 (or sometimes even 3) can be regarded with confidence as strong co-occurrences (see Barnbrook 1996: 97; Hunston 2002a: 72; Hoover *et al*. 2014: 154).

The dimension of fixedness relates to the degree of syntagmatic variability or flexibility (see Burger 2007: 910; Granger and Meunier 2008). Several factors may contribute to different degrees of syntagmatic fixedness, e.g. the insertion of words into the combinations, the omission of components in the combinations, the substitution of components in the combinations and other alterations of components in the combinations (see Howarth 1996; Granger and Meunier 2008; Römer and Schulze

2009; Herbst *et al.* 2011). For instance, the phrase *for the first time* which occurs very frequently in the BoE can allow the insertion of additional words without interrupting the 'core' structure of the phrase, such as *for the very first time*. In the phrase *time and time again*, the third word *time* can be omitted (as in *time and again*) and the meaning (or use) will remain more or less the same. The above two phrases, *for the first time* and *time and time again*, would be cases of lexical items with a relatively lower degree of syntagmatic flexibility. One example with a higher degree of syntagmatic flexibility is the verb phrase *spend time*, as its variants can be *spent time*, *time is spent*, *spend some time* and *spend a lot of time*. In fact, it is argued that the majority of phraseological items are associated with some sort of syntagmatic flexibility, i.e. a lexical item may involve one canonical form and one or more variants (see Sinclair 1991). Examples which are fully syntagmatically fixed are rare. The phrases *from time to time* and *once upon a time* may be cases of this sort.

The third criterion which is often used for identifying a phraseological item is semantic non-compositionality which refers to the degree to which the meaning of a multi-word sequence cannot be derived based on the sum of its constituent words (see Moon 1998; Anderson 2006; Gries 2008; Meunier and Granger 2008; Römer and Schulze 2009; Aijmer and Altenberg 2013). Semantic non-compositionality is also sometimes referred to as semantic opaqueness or "non-predictability" (Gries 2008: 4). One type of phraseological item at the non-compositional end could be idioms because the meaning of idioms (especially 'pure' or 'typical' idioms) is usually hard to interpret on a word-for-word basis (cf. Howarth 1996; Cowie 1998; Moon 1998; Anderson 2006; Skandera 2007; Granger and Meunier 2008). Examples which are semantically non-compositional in this study could be *from time to time*, *big time* and *in time* whose meaning is associated with the entire unit rather than separate components of the unit. There are also examples which are partially compositional (or transparent). For instance, it could be argued that in the cases of *full time* and *part time*, the meaning of at least one part of the lexical item can be interpreted. The examples at the compositional end may be phrases like *a waste of time*, *for the first time* and '*the time has come for* n.'.

To illustrate the interactive relationship between the three criteria for the description of a phraseological item, two phrases *for the first time* and *from time to time* are used as examples. As can be seen from Figure 1.2, the phrase *for the first time* occurs frequently in the BoE; it is relatively fixed and semantically compositional. The phrase *from time to time*, as represented in Figure 1. 3, occurs less frequently than *for the first time*, but this phrase is syntagmatically more fixed than *for the first time* and it is relatively non-compositional.

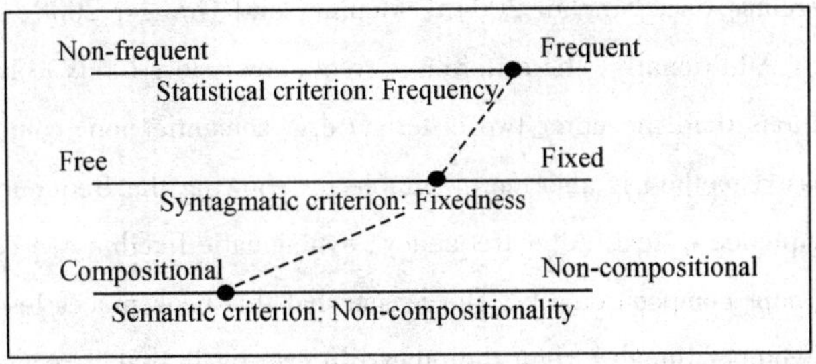

Figure 1. 2 **The three main criteria illustrated with the example *for the first time***

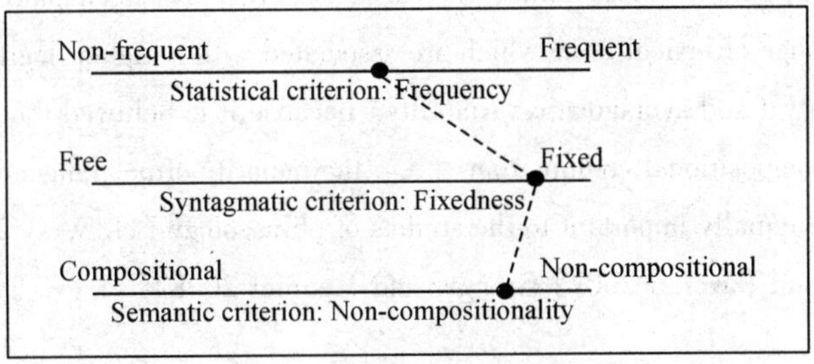

Figure 1. 3 **The three main criteria illustrated with the example *from time to time***

In other words, each phraseological item is associated with the three features to a different degree. In thecase of *from time to time*, it involves a high degree of syntagmatic invariability and semantic non-compositionality; it however occurs relatively less frequently (see Figure 1. 3). On the other hand, a sequence or a combination which is non-frequent, syntagmatically free and semantically compositional is not likely to be regarded as a phraseological item in this book.

Even though the three criteria or dimensions are represented as being parallel to each other in these figures (e.g. Figure 1. 3), it is argued in this book that there is an order in which these three criteria play a part in the determination of whether a sequence should be considered as a phraseological item. The criterion of frequency is prioritised before the other two criteria in this study since the frequent occurrences of an item in the corpus may highlight its importance in language use (see Sinclair 1991; McEnery *et al.* 2006; Gries 2008; Herbst *et al.* 2011). A sequence which occurs only twice in the BoE, for instance, may not be important enough to teach to students in language classrooms (see Sinclair 2004b; Meunier and Granger 2008; Aijmer 2009; Reppen 2010). Additionally, the criterion of frequency is less likely to involve subjective interpretations than the other two criteria (e.g. semantic non-compositionality). The corpus-based method is also more suitable for showing the frequency data of any multi-word sequence in text. After frequency, syntagmatic fixedness is considered and then semantic non-compositionality. The reason that this book places less emphasis on semantic non-compositionality than the other two criteria is that it recognises the significance of frequently occurring phraseological items which are compositional. Although traditional research on phraseology has mainly focused on the study of more fixed and opaque multi-word units, increased attention has been paid recently to a much wider range of lexical units which are associated with a higher degree of semantic compositionality (and syntagmatic variability) because it is believed that these semantically more compositional combinations (e.g. the majority of n-grams analysed by Biber 2006) are equally important to the studies of phraseology (cf. Wray 2002; Schmitt 2004; Biber and Barbieri 2007; Granger and Meunier 2008).

1.3 Relevant terminology

In the investigation of phraseology in previous studies (e.g. Howarth 1996; Cowie 1998; Lewis 2000; Hunston and Francis 2000; Hunston 2002a; Barnbrook *et al.* 2013), other terms are often mentioned. The following sections introduce four commonly discussed terms, namely, collocation, colligation, pattern, and frame.

1.3.1 Collocation and colligation

Among the various terms used in the study of phraseology, "collocation" is probably one of the most controversial and slippery terms because different scholars have used it to refer to slightly different groups of phraseological items (cf. Sinclair 1991; Howarth 1996; Cowie 1998; Lewis 2000; Sinclair *et al.* 2004; Hoey 2005;

Nesselhauf 2005; Barnbrook *et al.* 2013). According to Handl (2008: 50), the use of the term "collocation" can "stretch on the continuum between free word combinations and fully fixed idioms or compounds", which indicates the 'looseness' of "a collocation".

Despite the lack of consensus about this term, most researchers have agreed on a few of the features which are exhibited by a collocation, e.g. its frequent occurrences and a certain degree of syntagmatic variability and semantic compositionality (cf. Howarth 1996; Handl 2008; Barnbrook *et al.* 2013). In other words, in this book a collocation is regarded as a phraseological item and it is used broadly to refer to frequently occurring combinations which may be compositional or non-compositional.

It should be noted that the term "collocation", however, is sometimes referred to differently from "a collocation". A collocation usually refers to a sequence of two or more words, e.g. *spend time* and *part time*. On the other hand, collocation can be used to describe the phenomenon of co-occurrence of two (or more) words (see Sinclair 1991; Sinclair *et al.* 2004; Hoey 2005; Lindquist 2009). For instance, when the word *time* exhibits the sense of 'occasion', it can co-occur frequently with words such as *first*, *second*, *next* and *last*. This co-occurrence of the word *time* with words like *first* and *second* is relevant to the phenomenon of collocation. In this case, *time* is regarded as the node word and the words which co-occur with *time* (e.g. *first* and *second*) are referred to as collocates of *time*. It is also possible to consider the above features exhibited by the word *time* as collocational features or "collocational behaviour" (see Sinclair *et al.* 2004; Hoey 2005; Walker 2011; Barnbrook *et al.* 2013).

Additionally, collocation in this study is not limited to the co-occurrence of words. Instead, it is argued that the phenomenon of collocation can be extended to the co-occurring features of lexical items, i.e. collocation can refer to the co-occurrence of two lexical items (cf. Sinclair 1991; Sinclair *et al.* 2004; Hoey 2005; Walker 2011; Barnbrook *et al.* 2013). The analysis of *that sort of thing*, for instance, shows that this lexical item co-occurs frequently with the word *and*, as in *and that sort of thing*. To some extent, it is argued that this co-occurrence of *that sort of thing* with the word *and* may also be regarded as collocation (or collocational features of *that sort of thing*). Another example is the sequence *the big time*. The analysis of this sequence shows that it tends to co-occur with *hit* and *make*, as in *hit the big time* and *make the big time*. This tendency of co-occurrence of *the big time* with *hit* (or *make*), similarly, is considered in this book as a type of collocational feature of *the big time*.

Related to collocation in this study is the term "colligation", or, in the case of collocational behaviour, "colligational behaviour" (see Sinclair 1991, 1996, 2004a; Stubbs 2009a). Collocation or collocational behaviour describes the co-occurrence of features at the lexical level; while colligation or colligational behaviour refers to the co-occurrence of features at the syntactic (or lexical-syntactical) level (see Sinclair 1991; Römer 2005; Lindquist 2009; Stubbs 2009a). In other words, collocation is related to the frequent co-occurrence of one lexical item and another lexical item whereas colligation involves the frequent co-occurrence of a lexical item and grammatical categories (cf. Hoey [2005: 43] for a broader definition of colligation). In the case of the sequence *and that sort of thing*, for example, the current study shows that it tends to co-occur with noun phrases and verb phrases. This feature may be referred to as the colligational behaviour of *and that sort of thing*.

1.3.2 Pattern

As mentionedearlier, "a pattern" is regarded as a phraseological item which describes the co-selection of lexis and grammar (see Hunston and Francis 2000; Hunston 2002a, 2002b; Hunston 2011; McEnery and Hardie 2012). More specifically, "a pattern" in the current study refers to a sequence which contains specific lexical item (s) and at least one 'slot' which involves paradigmatic choices of lexical items. What is more, the lexical items which fit the 'slot' in a pattern are often grammatically and/or semantically related (see Hunston and Francis 2000).

For instance, the sequence '*spend time* v-ing' is considered as a pattern in this study because, firstly, it is associated with a type of lexicogrammatical co-occurrence, i.e. the co-occurrence of specific lexical item (s) and a group of "word types or clause types" (Hunston 2002b: 169); and, secondly, this sequence contains one 'slot' which involves paradigmatic choices of related clause type ('v-ing'). In this case, the words or phrases which fit the slot 'v-ing' in the pattern are at least grammatically similar (e.g. *working*, *reading* and *watching movies*). Equally, the sequence '*it* v-link *time to*-inf.' is referred to as a pattern because it involves paradigmatic choices of word types or clause types. In this pattern, two 'slots' are involved: 'v-link' which refers to link verbs such as *is*, *was* and *may be*; and '*to*-inf.' which refers to *to*-infinitive clauses such as *to change*, *to act* and *to take a closer look*. Another example, '<place> + *time*', is also regarded as a pattern in this study because the lexical items which occur at the slot '<place>' in this sequence are mainly words which express similar meanings: describing a place, e.g. *Brisbane*, *New York*, *London* and *British*. In other words, the lexical items which fit the 'slot' in the pattern '<place> + *time*' are at least semantically related.

This definition of "pattern" in this book is more or less consistent with Hunston and Francis (2000) or Hunston (2002a, 2002b). In these studies, "a pattern" is similarly viewed as a language phenomenon which relates to both lexis and grammar (or breaks the sharp division between lexis and grammar) and involves paradigmatic choices of lexical items. For example, Hunston (2002b: 169) defines a pattern as "a sequence of grammar words, word types or clause types which co-occur with a given lexical item", which is somewhat similar to the definition of pattern in this book. One difference, however, is that the current study uses the term "pattern" slightly more broadly than Hunston and Francis and includes more sequences which describe lexico-grammatical co-occurrence. For instance, the sequences such as '<place> + *time*', '*the* ADJ *thing to do*' and '*at the time of* N' were not analysed in Hunston and Francis's (2000) study of patterns, but these sequences are regarded as patterns in the current study because they fit the definition as discussed earlier. By adopting a broader definition of pattern, the current study also contends that patterns are more common and important in language than previously believed.

In this study a pattern can also be described by the three criteria associated with a phraseological item. For instance, Gries (2008: 7) suggests that patterns involve several features: 1) they are "lexically partially filled"; 2) they "require the insertion of additional lexical material"; 3) they "allow for syntactic variation". In other words, the two criteria, semantic non-compositionality and syntagmatic fixedness, are regarded as features of a pattern. The other criterion, frequency, is not mentioned by Gries (2008); but this criterion is equally important for the definition of a pattern. It is argued in this book that a pattern can only be identified if the sequences which fit the pattern occur relatively frequently (see Hunston and Francis 2000; Hunston 2002b; Mahlberg 2006).

1.3.3 Frame

The term "frames" in this study is also viewed as a type of phraseological item which is "an alternative" to the combinations constructed by specific individual words in a language (cf. Hunston 2002a: 50). To be more specific, a frame is defined as a discontinuous sequence which contains a paradigmatic choice of lexical items (cf. "collocational frameworks" in Renouf and Sinclair 1991). For instance, the sequence '*the time is* + ? + *minutes past/before the hour*' is regarded as a frame because it involves a variable lexical 'slot' where words such as *seven*, *nineteen* and *twenty* can be inserted.

This definition of "frame" in the current study mainly follows Renouf and Sinclair (1991) who have suggested that a frame or a "collocational framework" is composed of a fixed part of lexical items and a variable 'slot' which can be filled by a group of words (cf. Butler 1998; Marco 2000; Vincent 2013). However, the definition in this book concerns frames which include at least three words (e.g. '*the time is* + ? + *minutes past/before the hour*'). Traditionally, researchers have investigated the frames composed of generally three or four words, e.g. '*a* (*n*) + ? + *of*' which includes the fixed part of two grammatical words (the article *a* (*n*) and the preposition *of*) and a variable part where words such as *couple*, *lot*, *number* and *indication* can be inserted (see Renouf and Sinclair 1991; Francis 1993; Stubbs 2007b; Granger and Meunier 2008). The current study argues that the term "frame" could cover a broader scope of sequences, e.g. longer sequences such as '*the time is* + ? + *minutes past/before the hour*'.

Another point about the term "frame" which is worth mentioning is that even though patterns and frames are similar in the way that they both involve paradigmatic choices of lexical items, a frame is different from a pattern with regard to the type of lexical items which fill the variable 'slot'. The lexical items which are associated with a 'slot' in a pattern as defined in the current study can involve phrases and clauses (e.g. '*it* v-link *time to*-inf.') while it is mainly individual words which fill the 'slot' in a frame (e.g. '*a* (*n*) + ? + *of*'). Additionally, the lexical items which fit a pattern are considered to be either grammatically and/or semantically related; on the other hand, the group of lexical items which fill the 'slot' in a frame may be less closely related, e.g. *couple*, *lot*, *number* and *indication* which fit the frame '*a* (*n*) + ? + *of*'. Similarly, regarding the above-mentioned example '*the time is* + ? + *minutes past/before the hour*', although the items which fit this frame appear to be largely numbers (e.g. seven, nineteen and twenty), they may not be categorised into the same grammatical or semantic group as those for a pattern like '*it* v-link *time to* -inf.'.

To sum up the discussion on the terminology of phraseology, Table 1.1 again presents the definitions and examples for the above-mentioned terms. It is also important to emphasise that the above description in Table 1.1 is based on my definitions of "a phraseological item" and "phraseology". To reiterate, "a phraseological item" in this book is used as an umbrella term which refers to different types of recurring multi-word phrases and discontinuous sequences which contain paradigmatic choices of lexical items (including "patterns" and "frames"). The identification and description of a phraseological item are usually associated with three criteria: frequency, syntagmatic fixedness and semantic non-compositionality. The term "phraseology", on the other hand, encompasses the study of both the form of phraseological items (e.g. various types of multi-word sequences) and their use (i.e. the syntagmatic, semantic, pragmatic and textual features of a phraseological item).

Table1.1 The terminology related to phraseology used in this book

Terminology	Definition	Example
Collocation	Collocation is a phenomenon which describes the frequent co-occurrence of one lexical item with another lexical item; A collocation is a sequence of two or more words of which the components co-occurrence frequently with each other.	*spend time*; *part time*; *and that sort of thing*; *hit the big time*
Colligation	Colligation is a phenomenon which describes the frequent co-occurrence of a lexical item and grammatical categories.	N/NP + *and that sort of thing*
Frame	A frame is a phraseological item which includes a fixed part and a variable part; the lexical items which fit the variable part are often single words.	'*a* (*n*) + ? + *of*'; '*be* + ? + *to*'
Lexical item	A lexical item can refer to both a single word and a multi-word phrase as long as they function as individual units of meaning in context.	*time*; *at the same time*
Multi-word units / phrases / expressions	Multi-word units / phrases / expressions are more 'general' terms for frequently occurring sequences; these terms are used more or less synonymously in this book.	*full time*; *from time to time*; *for the first time*

Table1. 1(continued)

Terminology	Definition	Example
Pattern	A pattern is a phraseological item which contains at least one 'slot' where related lexical items can be inserted; the lexical items which fit the 'slot' are often word types or clause types.	'*it* v - link *time to* -inf.'; 'the ADJ *thing to do*'; '*at the time of* N'

Chapter 2 Corpus-based approach to phraseology

2.1 The corpus approach in the investigations of phraseology

The current investigation adopts a corpus-based approach to investigate the relation between phraseology and the construction of meaning. This is mainly because a corpus-based method is particularly suited to research on phraseology, which has been shown in many previous studies (e.g. Sinclair 1991, 2004a; McEnery *et al.* 2006; Stubbs 2007b, 2009b; O'Keeffe and McCarthy 2010; McEnery and Hardie 2012; John and Laso 2013). As argued by Granger and Meunier (2008: xvi), the use of a corpus-based method could be "the main reason for the rapid increase in interest in phraseology".

One of the main advantages of adopting a corpus-based method is that using computer software is an efficient way to examine the phraseological features of lexical items, e.g. collocational and patterning features (see Sinclair 1991, 2004a; Hunston 2010; McEnery and Hardie 2012; Barnbrook *et al.* 2013). Concordance tools can better reveal patterning features of a lexical item whereas these features may not be easily detected with pure manual analysis or intuition (see Sinclair 2004a; O'Keeffe *et al.* 2010; McEnery and Hardie 2012). The LookUp software from the BoE, for instance, enables the researcher to observe the frequent collocates of any lexical item and explore the phraseological behaviour associated with this lexical item. Similarly, Stubbs (2007c: 131) has asserted that a corpus method can "demonstrate order where previously only randomness or idiosyncracy were visible, and therefore open up research topics which were previously inconceivable".

Secondly, the corpus-based method can normally incorporate large quantities of data. As argued earlier, only a limited number of studies (e.g. Sinclair 1991, 2004a; Deignan 2005, 2008a; Hoey 2005; Mahlberg 2005; Hunston 2011; Cutting 2013) have intensively investigated the relation between phraseology and the construction of meaning in discourse; and studies which are based on a large quantity of data appear to be even fewer. In fact, the review of previous studies on phraseology indicates that there are just a small number of studies which have focused on phraseology using large corpora (e.g. Schmid 2000; Sinclair *et al.* 2004; Hoey 2005; Moon 2010; Hunston 2011; Walker 2011; Barnbrook *et al.* 2013). As suggested by Granger and Meunier (2008: xx), "corpus [linguistic] studies describing phraseological expressions in larger computer corpora are undeservedly little known". Therefore, it is beneficial for the current study to investigate phraseology with larger corpora such as the BoE.

2.2 Research questions

The current research aims to answer two main research questions:

1. What is the role of phraseology in the construction of meaning in discourse?
2. How is phraseology represented in English teaching inChina?

The first research question (Question 1) is addressed by investigating whether and how phraseology is related to four phenomena which are important to the construction of meaning in discourse - polysemy, metaphor, evaluation and vague use. In other words, seeking answers to Question 1 means seeking answers to the following two sub-questions:

1.1 Are the four phenomena-polysemy, metaphor, evaluation and vague use-associated respectively with phraseology or the phraseological behaviour of lexical items?

1.2 If so, how is each phenomenon associated with phraseology or the phraseological behaviour of lexical items?

These two specific questions (Questions 1.1. and 1.2) concern respectively the 'whether' part and the 'how' part of the relation between phraseology and the four phenomena which are important to the construction of meaning. In the case of polysemy, for example, Question 1. 1 relates to whether polysemy is associated with the phraseological behaviour of lexical items (e.g. the word *time* and the phrase *at the same time*); and Question 1. 2 looks at how exactly polysemy or the polysemous nature of a lexical item is associated with the phraseological behaviour of this lexical item. Similarly, in the case of metaphor, Question 1. 1 focuses on the examination of whether metaphor, or more accurately the linguistic metaphors associated with *time*, is related to phraseology or is realised by phraseological items rather than single words; and then Question 1. 2 concerns the investigation of how phraseology may play a role in metaphorical use. To answer Question 1 (or Questions 1. 1 and 1. 2), two reference corpora of general English, the Bank of English (BoE) and the British National Corpus (BNC), are used.

The second research question (Question 2) relates to the representation of phraseology in English teaching in China. Two corpora are used for this part of the study: a pedagogic corpus compiled of English course-books used in Chinese universities (CEC) and a learner corpus which contains university students' essays (CLEC). Four sub-questions are relevant to Question 2, as shown below.

2. 1 Are the frequently occurring phraseological items which are associated with the four phenomena in the BoE presented in the pedagogic corpus (CEC)?

2. 2 How are these phraseological items represented in the pedagogic corpus (CEC)?

2. 3 Are the frequently occurring phraseological items which are associated with the four phenomena in the BoE presented in the learner corpus (CLEC)?

2. 4 How are these phraseological items used in the CLEC?

These specific sub-questions focus on the representation of phraseology in pedagogy in terms of two aspects: the selection of phraseology and the presentation of phraseology. Forinstance, to answer Question 2. 1, the current study explores the selection of phraseological items in the pedagogic corpus (CEC), by investigating whether the frequently occurring phraseological items in the reference corpus (e.g. the BoE) are actually presented in the pedagogic corpus (CEC). To address Question 2. 2, the current study examines the presentation of the uses of phraseological items, e.g. whether the frequent uses of one phraseological item as shown in the reference corpus are presented in the pedagogic corpus. Questions 2.3 and 2.4 then consider these two aspects of phraseology in the learner corpus (CLEC). By seeking answers to these four specific questions, this study hopes to provide some insights for course-book writers and teachers regarding approaches and techniques that can be used to teach phraseology to learners.

2.3 Corpora

As mentioned earlier, four corpora are used in the current study. To reiterate, the BoE and the BNC are used in order to address Research Question 1 (the role of phraseology in the construction of meaning in discourse). A pedagogic corpus (CEC) and a learner corpus (CLEC) are used to address Research Question 2 (the representation of phraseology in English teaching in China). The following sections will describe the four corpora respectively and provide justifications for choosing these corpora.

2.3.1 Bank of English (BoE) as the main reference corpus

The Bank of English (BoE) is one of the largest general English corpora held at the University of Birmingham, and consists of approximately 450 million tokens. Its large size is the main reason for using it as the main reference corpus in this study. A large corpus can provide better opportunities to analyse longer sequences of words, it is thus more beneficial to use a large corpus to observe the phraseological behaviour of a lexical item. This point has been similarly suggested by many corpus linguists (e.g. Sinclair 1991, 2004a; Hunston and Francis 2000; O'Keeffe and McCarthy 2010) who argue that the study of phraseology in any systematic way needs to be based on a corpus which should be as large as possible.

Take the word *time* as an example. As shown in Table 2.1, there are 705,866 occurrences of the noun *time* in the BoE, which provides ample language examples for analysis.

Table 2. 1 The frequency data for *time* and its extended sequences in the BoE (including the sequence *the best time of the year*).

Lexical item	Freq (BoE)
time	705,866
time of	27,031
time of the	7,155
time of the year	819
best time of the year	17
the best time of the year	12

However, the occurrences of the extended sequence associated with*time* reduce very quickly as the sequence becomes longer. It can be seen from Table 2. 1 that for each increased component of the sequence, the number of occurrences of the extended sequence is reduced by one digit. The sequence *the best time of the year* has only 12 hits in the BoE. If a smaller reference corpus were used for this study, for instance a corpus of 100 million tokens, the number of occurrences of this sequence *the best time of the year* could be four times fewer, which would be inadequate for use in any analysis or argument.

Similarly, as shown in Table 2. 2, the search for another formulaic sequence, *the next time I saw him*, returns 10 hits when using the BoE. Therefore, it would not be possible to observe the linguistic features of this sequence with other smaller reference corpora in a thorough manner. For instance, in the BNC which is a 100-million-token corpus, no occurrence of the sequence *the next time I saw him* can be found.

Table 2. 2 The frequency data for *time* and its extend sequence *the next time I saw him* in the BoE

Lexical item	Freq (BoE)
time	705,866
next time	5,180
the next time	1,738
the next time I	226
the next time I saw	28
the next time I saw him	10

The BoE contains data which are drawn largely from British English texts. Around 70% of the texts in the BoE represent British English, 20% represent American English, and the remaining 10% represent other types of English such as Australian and Canadian English. Additionally, the BoE consists of more written data than spoken data. Approximately 85% of the texts in this corpus are written data mainly collected from newspapers and magazines and also from academic and non-academic books. The other 15% of the texts in the BoE are spoken data, e.g. radio broadcasts and informal conversations. Table 2. 3 shows a more detailed picture of the construction of the BoE (see Barnbrook *et al*. 2013: 214).

The concordance tool for the BoE is the LookUp software which is part of the package for the BoE. In other words, the data for the BoE were indexed to be accessed and analysed using this software. LookUp provides basic functions to analyse data, e.g. showing the contexts in which a word or phrase occurs and displaying the collocational profiles of this item. These corpus techniques for using the BoE will be described in detail later.

2. 3. 2 British National Corpus (BNC)

The BoE is sometimes criticised because its contents tend to be more journalistic (see Table 2. 3) and it mainly contains texts from the 1980s; however, it is used as the main reference corpus in this study because it is the largest reference corpus so far in the UK. To triangulate the results obtained from the BoE, another reference corpus, the BNC, is also used in this study.

Table 2. 3 The construction of the BoE

(based on Barnbrook *et al*. 2013: 214)

Subcorpus	Description	Origin	Text	No. of tokens
times	The Times	UK	news	51,884,209
sunnow	Sun & News of the World	UK	news	44,756,902
brmags	British magazines	UK	magazine articles	44,150,323
brbooks	British books	UK	non-academic books	43,367,592
oznews	Australian news	Australia	news	34,940,271
usbooks	American books	US	non-academic books	32,437,160
guard	Guardian	UK	news	32,274,484

Table2. 3(continued)

indy	Independent	UK	news	28,075,280
npr	National Public Radio	US	radio broadcasts	22,232,422
brspok	British spoken	UK	spoken texts	20,078,901
bbc	BBC radio	UK	radio broadcasts	18,604,882
strathy	Strathy	Canada	mixed texts	15,920,137
econ	Economist	UK	news	15,716,140
usnews	American newspapers	US	news	10,002,620
wbe	Business	UK	business-related texts	9,648,371
newsci	New Scientist	UK	magazine articles	7,894,959
usacad	American academic books	US	academic books	6,341,888
brephem	British ephemera	UK	leaflets, letters, ads, etc.	4,640,529
usephem	American ephemera	US	leaflets, letters, ads, etc.	3,506,272
usspok	American spoken	US	spoken texts	2,023,482

The BNC is a 100-million-token corpus and consists of texts which are generally more 'contemporary' than those in the BoE (many of the texts in the BNC originated in the 1990s). The BNC is often regarded as a more 'balanced' general English corpus because it contains texts from a wide range of sources and genres. Among its contents, around 90% of the texts are written and are extracted from newspapers, published academic journals, general books, students' essays, etc. The remaining 10% of the texts comprise spoken data, e. g. informal conversations which happened in different situations and more formal interactions such as business and government meetings.

To access this corpus, I use the BNC web which is an online interface for the BNC. The programme offers powerful corpus-analysis tools, such as searching for a lexical item, showing the collocates of a lexical item and displaying the distributional information of this lexical item (e.g. the preference of this lexical item for occurring in spoken data or in a certain genre).

2.3.3 Corpus of English Course-books (CEC)

The CEC is a pedagogic corpus of around 6.9 million tokens and contains data drawn from 80 English course-books currently used in universities inChina (cf. Willis

1993 for the definition of "a pedagogic corpus"). The course-books that I chose for the CEC range from year 1 to year 4 of the undergraduate study because I attempted to compile a corpus which covers different levels of pedagogic materials for college courses. A detailed list of these course-books can be found in Appendix 1.

The English course-books chosen for the CEC are mainly general English course-books rather than specific (such as Business English and Medical English). The reason for using general English books is that the results from the pedagogic corpus would be more comparable to those observed in the BoE or BNC which are both general English corpora. In their prefaces many of these course-books claim that their objective is to teach students a more comprehensive set of English skills: vocabulary, grammar, reading, writing, listening, speaking and translation. The texts they include also cover various genres (e.g. essays, novels, newspaper articles, speeches, poems, songs and even jokes), and are associated with diverse topics related to society, literature and philosophy, etc. This variety in genre and topics can be seen as a positive feature of the design of course-books. Additionally, it indicates that the compiled pedagogic corpus is more or less balanced in terms of the selection of texts.

Wordsmith Tools 6 (Scott 2013) is utilised to analyse the pedagogic corpus. This software includes three main corpus-analysis tools: Concord, Keywords and Wordlist. Concord is a concordancing tool which shows the concordance lines (the linguistic context) of the word or phrase searched for. The Keywords and Wordlist tool respectively present the list of key words or all types of words in the researcher's data ranking by frequency or other statistical criteria. More details about how to install and use this corpus tool can be found on the website http: //www. lexically. net/wordsmith/ index. html.

2. 3. 4 Chinese Learner English Corpus (CLEC)

The learner corpus (CLEC) chosen for this study is a 1. 2-million-token corpus of written texts by Chinese learners which was compiled by Shichun Gui and Huizhong Yang in 2002. The corpus contains essays written in English by Chinese learners at various stages of education: middle school students (st2), lower level non-English major college students (Band 4, st3), higher level non-English major college students (Band 6, st4), lower level English major college students (junior, st5) and higher level English major college students (senior, st6). Since the pedagogic corpus is based on college level course-books, the essays written by college learners in the CLEC (st3, st4, st5 and st6), which amount to 987,498 tokens, are analysed in this study. The Wordsmith software is again used as the concordance tool for this corpus.

2.4 Research techniques

This sectiondescribes the research techniques utilised in the current investigation: sample analysis, collocational analysis, and corpus techniques such as how to search for multi-word phrases, collocations and patterns in a corpus and how to sort the concordances.

2.4.1 Sample analysis

Sample analysis is used in the first stage of the study: investigating the relation between phraseology and the fourphenomena which are important to the construction of meaning - polysemy, metaphor, evaluation and vague use. Sample analysis refers to the technique of analysing a feature or phenomenon (e.g. the polysemous nature of *time*) with a corpus sample composed of 500 randomly selected concordance lines, which is a sufficient sample size to reveal relatively detailed results. The next step after sample analysis is usually to further examine the results observed with the corpus sample using the whole corpus.

The main reason for using sample analysis is due to the high frequency nature of *time* and *thing*. Take the word *time* as an example. As the most commonly used noun in the BoE, the word *time* occurs in 705,866 instances (1,569 times per million words). Therefore, it would not be possible to manually process all the concordance lines of *time* at once to observe its phraseological behaviour. In this case, an initial analysis of this word with a corpus sample is more practical. Sample analysis allows the researcher to reduce the data down to a manageable size. This technique has been used in many corpus studies on high frequency words (see Mahlberg 2005; O'Keeffe *et al.* 2007; Moon 2010).

Another reason for using sample analysis relates to the investigation of the four phenomena (polysemy, metaphor, evaluation and vagueness). The investigation of any of these four phenomena or features inevitably requires a level of human interpretation. In the case of polysemy, investigating this phenomenon involves the researcher in determining how many senses are associated with a lexical item or identifying which sense is associated with a lexical item in a given example. This process, however, cannot be done by computers or any software as yet. Therefore, it is more feasible to use a corpus sample to analyse the meaning associated with a lexical item. The investigation using the sample can reveal different senses which are associated with a lexical item (e.g. the word *time* or the phrase *at the same time*); this will make possible a further and detailed examination of these senses associated with this item in the whole corpus.

Similarly, regarding the study of metaphor, a corpus sample of 500 random lines provides a starting point for the researcher to identify linguistic metaphors of *time*, as it is not possible to use computers to reliably identify or extract these. In the identification process, the definition of metaphor by CMT (a cognitive phenomenon of understanding one thing in terms of another) and the Metaphor Identification Procedure (MIP; Pragglejaz Group 2007) are referred to. In relation to the latter, only the relevant principles are consulted, e.g. a lexical unit associated with *time* is identified as metaphorical if the lexical unit in the given context conveys a meaning which is less 'basic' (or 'concrete' / physical) and contrasts with the basic meaning of the lexical unit (see Pragglejaz Group 2007: 3; Dorst and Kaal 2012: 53). Then after sample analysis, the identified linguistic metaphors of *time* using the corpus sample can be further examined in the whole corpus.

2.4.2 Collocational analysis

Collocational analysis is another research technique which is adopted in the current investigation. Since the results from sample analysis are mainly based on the features observed from 500 concordance lines, it ispossible that some less frequently occurring phraseological items associated with a lexical item will not appear in the corpus sample even though the sample size is relatively large. Collocational analysis can thus be used to observe frequently occurring phraseological items and complement the results from sample analysis (see Hunston 2010).

Collocational analysis mainly involves examining the 'collocational profile' of a lexical item to investigate its phraseological behaviour. More specifically, I use the picture function (or picture profile) provided by the LookUp software. The picture function shows an overview of the collocates to the left and right of the node within a span of 3 to 6 ranking by either frequency, mutual information or t-score. The node in this case can be either a word or multi-word sequence.

Table 2. 4 shows the picture function for the word *time*. The collocates which occur in different positions of the node word *time* are sorted in this table according to raw frequency (the picture function by frequency is the default in this study).

Table 2. 4 The picture function for *time* in the BoE with its collocates in each column sorted by frequency

the	for	the	the	time	to	the	the	the
and	at	at	first	time	and	a	to	to
to	a	a	this	time	in	was	a	a
a	the	of	a	time	the	and	and	of
it	and	by	same	time	of	i	of	and
in	to	all	of	time	for	to	in	in
of	in	for	long	time	i	it	was	i
for	it	it	that	time	he	time	it	was
<p>	was	in	some	time	<p>	is	is	that
was	<p>	and	in	time	when	in	s	it

On a first look, the overview of these collocates, i.e. collocates at different positions of*time* in Table 2. 4, may not be easy to interpret, but the picture function is one of the most useful ways to explore more fixed and longer sequences. For instance, as shown in Table 2. 4, the second most frequent collocate of *time* to its left is *first*. To explore extended phrases or sequences related to *first time*, firstly the concordance lines of *first time* need to be obtained by using the 'expanding-context' function: the lower case 'x' command (the results as shown below).

1	important meeting, because it was the	first time	that the representatives of
2	It got worse and worse until the	first time	he assaulted me. It happened
3	Centre. I understand this is the	first time	the U of A Senate has held
4	BM's profits were to fall for the	first time	in years. But Akers was caught
5	World Cup going toAfrica for the	first time	This led everyone to believe

6	fanfare. That was 1988. It was the	first time	the French film industry had
7	in the short straight. A winner	first time	out over course and distance
8	played the Ashcroft card for the	first time	in the Eddisbury by election

Then the combination (*first time*) as the new node is used to show the new overview of the collocates (see the picture function of *first time* in Table 2.5).

Table 2.5 The picture function for *first time* in the BoE with the collocates in each column sorted by frequency

it	for	the	first time	in	the	years
this	was	a	first time	since	a	the
and	is	for	first time	i	had	a
that	s	very	first time	the	his	had
<p>	not	my	first time	that	has	has
is	be	his	first time	he	ve	to
not	the	of	first time	a	have	of
will	<p>	right	first time	and	was	life
was	and	that	first time	that	he	been
the	it	<p>	first time	<p>	i	and

As can be seen from the list of collocates to the left of *first time* in Table 2.6, the most frequent word preceding *first time* is *the*. Thus a similar procedure can be repeated for the sequence *the first time*, which leads to the overview of the collocates of *the first time* (see Table 2.6).

Table 2.6 The picture function for *the first time* in the BoE with the collocates sorted by frequency

the	it	for	the first time	in	the	years
it	this	was	the first time	since	a	the
in	and	is	the first time	i	had	a
to	that	s	the first time	the	his	had
this	<p>	not	the first time	that	has	has
and	not	be	the first time	he	ve	life
a	<p>	<p>	the first time	a	have	been
<p>	not	t	the first time	this	was	to
of	is	and	the first time	and	he	of
was	will	t	the first time	we	my	and

As shown in Table 2. 6, it is not difficult to see that *for the first time* occurs the most frequently among all the other combinations of *the first time* with its left collocates, which establishes that the co-occurrence of *first* with *time* appears very often in the extended phrase *for the first time*. Consequently, using this technique of collocational analysis (or picture functions), any frequently occurring phraseological items which do not occur in the corpus sample can be observed.

2. 4. 3 Corpus techniques using LookUp

This section discusses several corpus or concordance techniques which can be used in the process of searching for phraseological items or analysing the contexts of these phraseological items. Since the BoE is used as the main reference corpus, the illustration of the corpus techniques will be based on the LookUp software.

Word-for-word search. Searching for a lexical item word for word with the BoE is comparatively easy, since if the exact word or phrase is entered at the query page, the software will return the concordance lines of this item. For instance, to search for the phrase *time and time again*, putting in 'time+and+time+again' as the query will suffice. (The components of a sequence are connected by the '+' symbol as the rule of the query function for the LookUp software.)

Lemma search. The lemma of an item represents all word forms of this word, usually written in small capitals (cf. Hunston 2002a: 17-18; Hanks 2013: 26). The lemma search, therefore, allows the researcher to obtain the concordance lines of not just one word form of an item but all forms of this item. This technique is particularly useful for searching for verb collocations of *time*. For instance, it is observed with the corpus sample (S_{BoE_time}) that *spend time* occurs frequently and hence it will be necessary to check the frequency data of this collocation and analyse its contexts. Yet, obtaining the concordances of *spend time* is not enough because the real language use of *spend time* involves the occurrences of other forms of *spend*, e.g. *spends* and *spent*. By using the lemma search - 'spend@ +time', the returned concordance lines will include all word forms of *spend*, as in *spend time*, *spends time*, *spending time* and *spent time*.

Variation search. Another technique related to the above query for verb collocations or any other combinations is the variation search. This allows for any of the components of the sequence to occur in flexible positions in relation to each other. Again taking 'spend *time*' as an example (spend as the lemma of the based form *spend*), the co-occurrence of spend with *time* in real language includes more than just the occurrence of two items adjacently to each other. Other words can occur between the two items, as in combinations like 'spend *some time*', 'spend *more time*' and 'spend *too much time*'. By entering 'spend@ +0, 2time' at the query page, the software can then return the concordance lines which include the co-occurrence of spend and *time* and allow up to two 'slots' to appear between the two items (e.g. the above-mentioned three combinations). This flexible-position search can also apply to multiple-word sequences (or frames). For instance, it is observed that these similar sequences, *for the first time in life*, *for the first time in my life* and *for the first time in his life*, occur in the BoE sample. Instead of conducting multiple searches respectively for each sequence, by entering the query language 'for+the+first+time+in+0, 1life', the software will return all instances of all the above sequences.

Tag search. The last important technique which is often used in the search of lexical items is to use tags in the query language. Since the BoE is POS tagged (words in the texts selected for the BoE are tagged in terms of their part of speech), a mixture of grammatical items and lexical items (e.g. patterns) can be searched in the LookUp software as well. For instance, two-word noun phrases associated with *time* can be searched for in the BoE by putting in 'NN+time' or 'time+NN' at the query page (NN stands for any common singular noun). The returned results may include phrases like *part time*, *injury time*, and *question time* which are results for 'NN+time' or phrases like *time limit* and *time management* for 'time+NN'. Additionally, this technique is not limited to searches for two-word combinations. By searching for 'it+is+time+for+NN', for instance, the software returns the concordances of the sequences like *it is time for action* or *it is time for change*.

Sorting concordances. The above corpus techniques are related to the search for lexical items while this technique involves manipulating concordance lines to analyse the contexts of a lexical item. The display of the returned concordance lines is often in the KWIC view (Key Word in Context) with the lexical item in each line aligned in the centre. The KWIC view allows repeated patterns of the lexical item to be detected more easily and quickly. This lexical item, be it a word or multi-word phrase, is also referred to as the node in this study (see Sinclair *et al*. 2004: 10). These concordance lines can be sorted alphabetically by collocates of the node in a certain position. The sorting function helps to reveal frequent collocates of the node or potential collocational features of the node.

For instance, the concordance lines shown in Figure 2. 1 below are sorted by the right collocates of *at the time of the* (also referred to as +1 collocates of the node).

9 Because of gusty winds **at thetime of the accident** investigators will
10 same road in Bishop Auckland **at thetime of the allegations** , were totally
11 contained civilian workers **at thetime of the attack** , American military
12 off duty in Oxford Street **at thetime of the blast** but immediately went to
13 what was going on around them **at thetime of the bomb** , they could grasp that
14 by the parties, at a price set **at thetime of the children's deaths** , doctors
15 by the parties, at a price set **at thetime of the contract** . Such Underlying
16 was no refueling going on **at thetime of the crash** . The military cargo
17 uniform from the Kells shop **at thetime of the explosion** . He said
18 The windows were closed **at thetime of the incident** . Maria A. Bennett
19 6. Was the home furnished **at thetime of the** loss or damage; If NO, when was
20 in the Pleine Fougeres area **at thetime of the murder** ." Caroline, from
21 and head of Humberside's CID **at thetime of the offence** . He was caught on his
22 Petersburg. And in any case, **at thetime of the** story it was still the Tsar's
23 of this doubt was known **at thetime of the trial** . Two of the forensic

Figure 2. 1 **Fifteen random concordance lines of *at the time of the* from the BoE which are sorted by the** +1 **collocates of *at the time of the***

By using the sorting function, it is easier to see which collocates tend to co-occur with this sequence. As shown in Figure2. 1, the majority of the +1 collocates of *at the time of the* are nouns and many of them also appear to be related to negative events.

PART TWO
Phraseology and the construction of meaning in discourse

Chapter 3 Phenomena important to the construction of meaning

3.1 Introduction

The central role of phraseology in language use has gained an increasing recognition by many researchers (e.g. Sinclair 1991, 2004a; Meunier and Granger 2008; Römer and Schulze 2009; Stubbs 2009a; Moon 2010; Hunston 2011; Granger *et al.* 2013), and the study of phraseology has also been applied to many areas of research, e.g. psycholinguistics, cognitive linguistics, sociolinguistics, translation, discourse analysis and language teaching (cf. Skandera 2007; Granger and Meunier 2008; Ji 2010; O'Keeffe and McCarthy 2010; McEnery and Hardie 2012; John and Laso 2013). However, based on a general review of previous studies, it seems that much of the research work on phraseology (especially in the early studies) has concentrated more on the form of language than the construction of meaning in discourse.

For instance, one of the major objectives for many previous studies on phraseology has been to define and examine the scope of phraseology, e.g. to establish what can be considered as a phraseological item and what cannot (cf. Arnaud and Béjoint 1992; Cowie 1994, 1998; Howarth 1996; Granger and Meunier 2008). Howarth (1996: 33-47), for example, has examined the scope of "word combinations", proposing criteria such as fixedness, semantic non-compositionality and institutionalisation to identify these phraseological items. Later Gläser (1998: 125-128) has tried to define "a phraseological unit" using seven potentially characteristic features: "lexicalisation", "common usage", "reproducibility", "syntactic and semantic stability", "idiomaticity", "connotations" and "expressive, emphatic or intensifying functions in a text". More recently, Gries (2008: 4) has provided six parameters for defining a phraseological item, which are: the nature of the elements involved in a phraseological item, the number of elements involved in the item, the occurrences of the item, the permissible distance between the elements involved in the item, the degree of lexical and syntactic flexibility, and the role of semantic non-predictability in the definition of a phraseological item. Similarly, Granger and Paquot (2008: 27-35) have focused on "disentangling the phraseological web" in order to deal with the highly variable scope of phraseology and the vast and confusing terminology associated with it, e.g. by distinguishing the methodological approaches to phraseology and the criteria for defining it in relation to semantics, morphology, syntax and discourse.

Other previous studies have also been devoted to establishing a system of classification for phraseology, e.g. categorising different types of phraseological items and providing the criteria for these categorisations (cf. Nattinger and DeCarrico 1992; Howarth 1996; Cowie 1998; Granger and Meunier 2008; Gries 2008; Handl 2008). For instance, Nattinger and DeCarrico (1992: 38 - 44) have categorised phraseological items (or "lexical phrases" in their term) into four groups based on the form of phraseological items and their functions: "polywords" (e.g. *for the most part* and *by the way*), "institutionalised expressions" (e.g. *how are you*), "phrasal constraints" (similar to frames, e.g. *a* + ? + *ago*), and "sentence builders" (e.g. *Not only X but also Y.*). Focusing on "fixed expressions", Moon (1992: 13-14) has divided phraseological items into three main groups: "anomalous collocations" (e.g. *at large* and *by and large*), "formulae" (e.g. proverbs, slogans and catchphrases) and "metaphor" (so-called pure idioms, e.g. *kick the bucket*). Howarth (1996: 33-47), on the other hand, has discussed four main types of phraseological items: "free collocations", "restricted collocations", "figurative collocations" and "idioms".

Further Altenberg (1998: 101 - 120) has analysed "recurring word combinations" and classified these items into three broad categories from a more grammatical perspective: "full clauses" (including independent clauses such as *thank you very much* and dependent clauses such as *as you know*), "clause constituents" (including multiple clause constituents such as *and you know* and single clause constituents such as *and so on*) and "incomplete phrases" (e.g. *out of the* and *a sort of*). Carter (1998: 67) in his book on vocabulary have also distinguished several types of "fixed expressions", e.g. "idioms" (including "compound idioms" such as *spick and span*, "full idioms" such as *to rain cats and dogs*, and "semi-idioms" such as *dead drunk*), "proverbs" (e.g. *a watched pot never boils*), "catchphrases" (e.g. *that's another fine mess you got me into*), "idiomatic similes" (e.g. *as sober as a judge*) and "discoursal expressions" (including "social formulae" such as *how do you do*, "connectives" such as *once upon a time*, and "conversational gambits" such as *guess what*). Willis (2003: 144) has similarly made a distinction between four subcategories of "lexical phrases": "polywords" (e.g. *according to* and *so to speak*), "frames" (e.g. *whatever ... are necessary* and *are not ... but ...*), "sentences and sentence stems" (e.g. *how do you do* and *would you like ...*) and "pattern" (e.g. N + *between*). Meanwhile, focusing on phraseology in Esperanto, Fiedler (2007) has classified phraseological units into "nominations" (e.g. *acid rain*), "proverbs" (e.g. *the one who likes his bed won't gain profit*), "sayings" (e.g. *to sweep sth. under the carpet*), "quotes" (e.g. *to be or not to be*), "binomials" (e.g. *step by step*), "stereotyped constructions with functional verbs" (e.g. *to draw conclusions*) and "communicative formulae" (e.g. *it's about time*).

It would thus seem that a large number of early studies on phraseology appear to pay more attention to the relation between phraseology and the form of language rather than the relation between phraseology and the use/meaning of language. Although these studies have provided the foundation for further studies to investigate the linguistic phenomena related to phraseology, e.g. rigorous typologies of phraseological items and the criteria for describing and categorising phraseological expressions, these studies may be most beneficial in the early stage of research on phraseology.

New research should concentrate more on the 'semantic' role of phraseology in language or the 'semantic' use of phraseology in discourse. For instance, it would be worthwhile exploring the interaction between phraseology or the phraseological behaviour of lexical items and other phenomena in language use like metaphor, metonymy, evaluation and vagueness, because the results from this type of studies could reveal the role of phraseology in the construction of meaning in discourse.

This is also a less frequently explored area, as only a few studies (e.g. Sinclair 1991, 2004a; Deignan 2005; Hoey 2005; Mahlberg 2005; Hunston 2011; Cutting 2013; Hanks 2013) have examined this area more intensively. Additionally, many of these studies have focused on one such phenomenon. For instance, Deignan (2005,

2008a) explored the relation between phraseology and metaphor; Hunston (2011) showed the importance of phraseology in evaluative use; and Cutting (2013) revealed the close connection between phraseology and vague use. Few researchers have attempted to expand the investigation of phraseology to the 'generic' level of construction of meaning, i.e. to bring together the studies on the relation between phraseology and meaning in general.

Therefore, the current study will further investigate the significant role phraseology plays in the construction of meaning in discourse. More specifically, it will concentrate on the relation between phraseology and phenomena which are important to the construction of meaning, namely polysemy, metaphor, evaluation and vague use. The reason for focusing on these four phenomena is that they are all central to the construction of meaning in discourse (see Channell 1994; Hunston and Thompson 2000; Dirven and Pörings 2002; Nerlich *et al.* 2003; Sinclair 2004a; Hoey 2005; Mahlberg 2005; Knowles and Moon 2006; Hunston 2011; Cutting 2013). What is more, they are also phenomena which can often be associated with the use of the two high frequency nouns, *time* and *thing*. For instance, the results from the current analysis show that the word *time* and phrases such as *at the same time* are often 'polysemous'; many phraseological items, e.g. '*spend time* v-ing' and '*waste time on* n.', can involve a metaphorical use; some language patterns, e.g. '*the* ADJ *thing* (*that*-cl.) *is*' and '*the* ADJ *thing to do*', can reflect an evaluative sense; and the sequences such as *that sort of thing* and *that type of thing* are related to a vague use.

This chapter then aims to introduce the above-mentioned four phenomena and provide the theoretical basis for the current investigation. These four phenomena-polysemy, metaphor, evaluation and vague use-will be discussed individually in the following sections. The discussion of each phenomenon will include its theoretical background, the definition adopted in this book, the significance of studying this phenomenon and other important aspects which are relevant for the current study.

3.2 Polysemy

The study of polysemy, asstated by Nerlich *et al.* (2003: 3), is "of fundamental importance for any semantic study of language and cognition". Therefore, an exploration of the phenomena important to the construction of meaning cannot be regarded as complete without analysing polysemy. In the following sections, I will first provide a definition of polysemy, and discuss some potential problems associated with analysing it. Then, I will focus on the association between polysemy and context which has been discussed in previous studies and justify the current investigation of the relation between polysemy and the phraseological behaviour of lexical items.

3.2.1 Polysemy and monosemy

This book considers "polysemy" to be a semantic phenomenon whereby a lexical item (i.e. a word or a phrase) is characterised by two or more related but distinct senses (see Nerlich *et al.* 2003; Riemer 2005, 2010). The term "sense" is used in the definition of polysemy in preference to the term "meaning" because it is argued that "sense" can refer to the situation where two or more meanings of a lexical item are regarded as related and 'close' (cf. Sinclair 1991; Nerlich *et al.* 2003; Hoey 2005; Saka 2007; Hanks 2013) whereas the term "meaning" is used in this book mainly in terms of the more 'general' concept of a lexical item.

It should be noted that the term "monosemy" describes a different semantic phenomenon whereby a lexical item is associated with a single sense (cf. Riemer 2010: 135; Cruse 2011: 322; Löbner 2013: 45-47). However, lexical items which are related to monosemy are rare (cf. Aronoff and Rees-Miller 2003: 358), and they tend to be those more specialised lexical items like terminological items which occur less frequently in language.

The majority of lexical items, in particular high frequency words, are usually polysemous (see Goddard 1998: 19; Aronoff and Rees-Miller 2003: 358; Aitchison 2012: 174). For instance, Butterfield (2008: 70) asserts that "[n]ot only are many words 'polysemous'; the words speakers use most are the most polysemous of all". Similarly, Stahl and Nagy (2006: 107) argue that, "the more common a word, the more likely it is to have multiple ... meanings". This implies that high frequency nouns like *time* in this study, are associated with a highly polysemous nature, and hence it is feasible and desirable to analyse the relation between polysemy and the phraseological behaviour of high frequency words.

3.2.2 Considerations for the analysis of polysemy: meaning and subjectivity

The above-mentioned definition of polysemy (a word having more than one distinct sense) seems to be straightforward, yet problems arise when applying this definition to the analysis of real data. First, this definition is largely based on our understanding of meaning. In other words, one significant question which may arise when analysing polysemy is what can be considered as the meaning of a lexical item. Second, the study of polysemy may require a researcher to distinguish related senses associated with a word or categorise different senses associated with a word. This process however is likely to be influenced by the researcher's language background or life experience, i.e. to a certain extent the analysis of polysemy will be subjective (cf. Hoey 2005 for a discussion on how primings are individual and unique for each language user).

A satisfactory answer to the first question about meaning would require an entire chapter or even a book to fully describe because it is so complex. Therefore the following only presents the definition of meaning used in this book in order to avoid a lengthy and perhaps confusing discussion. To put it simply, the current study limits the meaning of a lexical item to its contextualised use. That is to say, the meaning of a word or a sequence of words (e.g. a multi-word unit) is demonstrated by how this item is used in context (see Sinclair 1996; Renouf and Bauer 2000; Hoey 2005; Mahlberg 2005; Baptista and Rast 2010; Moon 2010; Hanks 2013). This view of meaning first became widely known when Firth (1935, 1957) argued that the meaning of a word mainly involves how it combines with other words in actual use, as illustrated by the famous quote "you shall know a word by the company it keeps" (Firth 1957: 11). This contextualised approach to meaning has been adopted and applied by the majority of neo-Firthian linguists and/or corpus linguists. For instance, Channell (2000) adopts the label "pragmatic meaning", indicating meaning is more than just semantics and comprises other aspects of meaning associated in the context like connotation or prosody. Sinclair (1996) uses the term "units of meaning" to suggest that the meaning of words can only be accurately revealed by considering the context in which they appear. Without the context (linguistic or social), it can be argued that words have no meaning at all (see Nida 1997; Baker and Hacker 2008; Vallée 2010) or only have "meaning potential" rather than meaning (Hanks 2013). Moon (1987: 87) goes on to argue that "meaning is the product of context". Therefore, the study of polysemy in the current investigation will be based on the understanding that the meaning of a lexical item is, or is associated with, its contextualised use.

The analysis of polysemy may also be affected by a researcher's language background or life experience. In other words, the interpretation of meaning inevitably involves subjective judgement (see Nerlich *et al.* 2003; Löbner 2013), even though context is often used as the main criterion to distinguish meaning, since meaning is context-dependent (as argued above). For instance, one researcher could consider two related senses of a lexical item as being distinct based on his/her intuition or language background whereby another researcher could regard these two senses as two aspects of one single sense. Using one of the examples analysed by Hoey (2005), the word *tea* can be associated with three distinct senses: 'the drink', 'the leaves for the drink', and 'the meal'; however, the first two senses may often be regarded as a single sense because they are closely related to each other and sometimes the distinction between these two senses becomes blurred in real examples (see Hoey 2005: 108).

It is thus inevitable that analysing polysemy will involve a degree of subjectivity (cf. Nerlich *et al.* 2003; Hanks 2013). In such case, it may not be meaningful if the sole purpose of a study on polysemy is to determine how many senses are associated with a lexical item or to categorise the different senses of a lexical item. The current study avoids this dilemma. Instead of attempting to categorise senses of *time*, this study mainly seeks to explore the relation between polysemy and phraseology, or more specifically, the relation between different senses of *time* and the phraseological behaviour of this word. For instance, it is admitted that there can be different versions of categorisation in terms of the meaning associated with *time* other than the one in the current study (e.g. Evans 2005). Similarly, it is acknowledged that in the discussion of different senses of *time* in this study, there may be overlapping or blurring areas between some senses, e.g. the two senses associated with *time*: 'a particular time point' and 'a period of time'. These two senses cannot always be distinguished from each other as clearly as would be expected, and some examples of *time*, e.g. *this time of year*, could exhibit either of the two senses in different contexts.

3. 2. 3 Polysemy and phraseology

Even though different researchers may categorise the multiple senses associated with a lexical item differently, the majority of them (e.g. Moon 1987; Sinclair 1991; Nerlich *et al*. 2003; Deignan 2005; Hoey 2005; Hanks 2013) agree that there is a relation between meaning and context (or between polysemy and context). Moon (1987), for instance, has shown that context has a disambiguating role in meaning. More specifically, she argues that regarding the meaning of a lexical item, "context restricts interpretation and thereby resolves ambiguity" (Moon 1987: 87).

There are many aspects of context which can disambiguate different senses associated with a lexical item. Barnbrook *et al*. (2013) suggest that collocation, as at least one aspect of context, can make a significant contribution to inform the interpretation of meaning. Moon (1987: 87) states that "in particular through syntax and collocation, and an interplay of these", the context "gives clear signals of meaning". Here she emphasises both the role played by collocates of a word and by the syntax related to this word in the disambiguation of meaning.

In addition, Sinclair (1991) talks about the more general patterning features of a word in relation to the interpretation of meaning. He demonstrates with examples like *yield* that each meaning or sense of a word can be associated with a "distinctive patterning" (Sinclair 1991: 65; also cf. Sinclair 2004a: 3). Similarly, Deignan (2005: 217) focuses on the literal and figurative senses of a word such as *blossomed* and reveals that the patterning features can restrict the senses of a word.

Hoey (2005), in one of the most comprehensive studies on context and meaning, has investigated a range of features associated with a word (or features "primed" for a word), e.g. collocation, colligation, semantic association and pragmatic association; and he argues that all these features contribute to disambiguating the usages of a lexical item. For instance, in the case of *consequence*, Hoey (2005: 82-88) has illustrated that *consequence* with the sense of 'importance' (primed for most language users) systematically differs from *consequence* with the sense of 'result' regarding its collocational, colligational and patterning features.

The current research thus contends that all the above-mentioned aspects, e.g. the collocational, colligational and patterning features of a word, can play a part in the disambiguation of the multiple senses associated with this word. These aspects are also included in the phraseological features of a lexical item in this study. In other words, this book argues that it is the various types of phraseological features of a word that tend to differentiate the senses of this word. For instance, it will be demonstrated in subsequent sections that it is not only the collocational features but also patterning features, frames, and other phraseological phenomena that determine and disambiguate the senses of a polysemous word such as *time*.

Furthermore, this book argues that the disambiguating role of phraseology in meaning not only applies to polysemous words such as *time*, but also applies to 'polysemous' phrases. For example, two multi-word phrases, *at the same time* and *big time*, will be analysed to investigate the association between their multiple senses (or uses) and the phraseological behaviour associated with these phrases. The results from the current analysis show that the use of a 'polysemous' phrase is closely connected with its phraseological or patterning features, or in other words each use of a 'polysemous' phrase is associated with particular phraseological features exhibited by this phrase.

3.3 Metaphor

Metaphor is analysed in this study because as stated earlier in this chapter, this phenomenon is important to the construction of meaning in discourse (see Dirven and Pörings 2002; Knowles and Moon 2006; Radden *et al*. 2007; Steen 2007; Panther *et al*. 2009), even though it is often defined from a cognitive perspective (see Lakoff and Johnson 1980a/2003). In the following sections, I will outline some of the main contemporary theories and strands of research on metaphor and metonymy, and then justify the approach adopted in the current study. First, I will review the Conceptual Metaphor Theory which has been recognised as the most widely accepted cognitive model and also one of the most authoritative theories (cf. Lakoff and Johnson 1980a/2003; Lakoff 1993; Gibbs 2008; Kövecses 2010). Relevant terminology in the Conceptual Metaphor Theory will be discussed, along with the strengths and weaknesses of this model. Second, I will briefly introduce Conceptual Blending Theory because it is often considered to be a more contemporary cognitive model than Conceptual Metaphor Theory. However, by showing the differences between these two cognitive models, I will also explain why I choose not to use Conceptual Blending Theory in the current study. Third, I will discuss the research on metaphors in discourse where the selection and use of metaphors are not simply based on conventional metaphorical mappings but also influenced by many contextual factors, in particular linguistic contextual factors such as the phraseological patterning of language. As the fourth point, I will present another cognitive mechanism which is closely related to metaphor-metonymy. In the final section, I will justify the corpus-based approach to metaphor which is adopted in the current study and provide in more detail the reasons why I mainly refer to the conceptual metaphor model for the investigation of metaphoric use.

3.3.1 Conceptual Metaphor Theory (CMT)

The Conceptual Metaphor Theory (also commonly referred to as the Contemporary Theory of Metaphor) was initially proposed by Lakoff and Johnson (1980a) and further described and developed in Lakoff (1993), Lakoff and Johnson (1999, 2003) and Kövecses (2010). This 'contemporary' view of metaphor has been widely accepted among linguists, in particular among cognitive linguists (e.g. Barcelona 2003; Kövecses 2010; Gibbs 2011; Gonzálvez-García *et al.* 2013). According to this view, metaphor is no longer perceived as a literary or stylistic device to embellish speech and writing; instead, it is defined as a systematic model of concepts which is pervasive in both language and thought (see Deignan 2005; Littlemore 2009; Kövecses 2010; Gibbs 2008, 2011; Gonzálvez-García *et al.* 2013). In other words, the Conceptual Metaphor Theory (henceforth CMT) proposed by Lakoff and Johnson (1980a, 1980b, 1999, 2003) recognises the significance of metaphor and its ubiquity in everyday life and language use.

More specifically, CMT proposes that in essence metaphor is "understanding and experiencing one kind of thing in terms of another" (Lakoff and Johnson 2003: 5). The 'thing' that is to be understood is often an abstract concept which is referred to in CMT as the "target domain" (or known to others as "topic"); the other concrete 'thing' which is used to understand the abstract concept is referred to as the "source domain" (or "vehicle"); and this phenomenon of conceptualising one domain in terms of another is called "conceptual metaphor" (see Lakoff and Johnson 1980a/2003; Deignan 2005; Littlemore 2009; Kövecses 2010).

One example frequently used by CMT is the conceptual metaphor ARGUMENT IS

WAR (see Lakoff and Johnson 2003; Knowles and Moon 2006; Stefanowitsch and Gries 2006; Kövecses 2010). The usual format of conceptual metaphor is 'A IS B', with A being the target domain and B being the source domain (cf. Steen 2007; Littlemore 2009; Kövecses 2010). It is often the case that both the conceptual metaphor and domains are written in capitals.

ARGUMENT IS WAR
Your claims are *indefensible*.
He*attacked every weak point* in my argument.
His criticisms were*right on target*.
I*demolished* his argument.
I've never *won* an argument with him.
(Lakoff and Johnson 2003: 4)

Based on this example, Lakoff and Johnson (1980a/2003) argue that the existence of this conceptual metaphor is demonstrated and realised by the use of a large number of relevant linguistic expressions. Those italicised words such as *indefensible*, *attack* and *won* which are associated with the WAR domain are systematically employed in connection with the ARGUMENT domain (see Lakoff and Johnson 2003: 7). It is thus considered that these linguistic expressions lexically realise the conceptual metaphor ARGUMENT IS WAR; and they are referred to as "linguistic metaphors" or "metaphorical expressions" (see Lakoff and Johnson 1980a/2003; Littlemore 2009; Kövecses 2010).

There are also "systematic correspondences" (Lakoff and Johnson 2003: 246) across the two domains, that is the way elements in the WAR domain correspond to elements in the ARGUMENT domain. For example, 'the physical attack in a war' corresponds to 'the verbal attack in an argument', and 'win a war' corresponds to 'win an argument'. This set of correspondences is called "metaphorical mapping" or "conceptual mapping" (cf. Lakoff and Johnson 2003; Kövecses 2010).

Regarding "conceptual mapping", it is important to note that the set of mappings between the source domain and the target domain is only partial. In other words, only a part of the source domain can be mapped onto the target domain. Cognitive linguists (e.g. Lakoff 1993; Lakoff and Johnson 2003; Kövecses 2010) give two major reasons for this partial mapping. First, it relates to the "highlighting" feature of metaphor: when a source domain applies to a target domain in a metaphor (e.g. ARGUMENT IS WAR), only certain aspects of the source are highlighted, e.g. the issue of the content of an argument and the control of the argument; the other aspects of the source domain on the other hand remain hidden, e.g. the construction of the argument or the progress of the argument. Kövecses (2010: 138) also uses the term "meaning focus" to argue that "[e] ach source is associated with a particular meaning focus (or foci) that is (or are) mapped onto the target" and the elements outside the meaning focus of the source domain will not be mapped onto the target domain. Put simply, it would not be practical if all the constituent elements of the source domain are mapped onto the target domain, because that means the two domains (or concepts) have the same content or structure which would make the two domains eventually the same (cf. Kövecses 2010: 91). Secondly, according to the "Invariance Principle" (or "Invariance Hypothesis") proposed by Lakoff (1993: 215), the mapping of elements from the source domain to the target domain only 'accepts' the elements from the source which would not conflict with the inherent structure of the target. Similarly, Kövecses (2010: 131) suggests that "the invariance principle blocks the mapping of knowledge that is not coherent with the schematic or skeletal structure of the target concept" (cf. Grady *et al.* 1996 for problems with the invariance principle and for an alternative explanation using "primary metaphors"). To take the metaphor LIFE IS A JOURNEY as an example, it is possible to walk back as well as forward; however, when a decision is made in life, it is not possible for us to be able to 'go back'. In other words, the two directions of 'forward' and 'back' in a physical journey cannot usually be mapped onto decision-making in life (cf. Kövecses 2010: 131).

The main advantage in adopting the CMT to investigate metaphor, as discussed earlier, is that this view highlights the central role of metaphor. CMT not only indicates the pervasive nature of metaphor in everyday life but also suggests that metaphor influences how people think, speak and act (see Lakoff and Johnson 2003; Deignan 2005; Gibbs 2008; Littlemore 2009; Kövecses 2010). To some extent, CMT can be considered as a cognitive or conceptual explanation for the metaphorical part of language use, e.g. how metaphorical language actually reflects mental constructions and how we refer to abstract concepts through more concrete and experientially motivated concepts (cf. Barcelona 2003; Kövecses 2010; Gibbs 2011; Gonzálvez-García *et* al. 2013).

Additionally, CMT proposes that the cognitive model of conceptual metaphors which people use to construct their thoughts is systematic. More specifically, conceptual metaphors are related rather than isolated from each other and they can be organised hierarchically (it should be noted that the same can be said about conceptual metonymies). As Kövecses (2010: 149) suggests, conceptual metaphors "make up larger systematic groupings, that is, metaphor systems". In this system, "the 'lower' mappings in the hierarchy inherit the structures of the 'higher' mappings" (Lakoff 1993: 222). This systematicity or hierarchical organisation would imply that one notion can be construed in terms of several conceptual metaphors (and conceptual metonymies). Using the concept of 'time' as an example, it can be understood by other more concrete concepts such as 'space', 'object', 'container' and 'force' (see Pérez Hernández 2001). These four mappings (e.g. TIME IS SPACE or TIME IS AN OBJECT) can be considered as the high-level "generic metaphor" (see Pérez Hernández 2001: 66; Kövecses 2010: 45). Under each generic metaphor, there may be more specific subtypes of metaphorical mappings. For instance, metaphors like TIME IS MONEY, TIME IS A RESOURCE and TIME IS A COMMODITY can be categorised under the high-level generic metaphor TIME IS AN OBJECT since the three concepts, 'money', 'resource' and 'commodity', can be reasonably argued to be subcategories of an object (cf. Pérez Hernández 2001: 68-69). Thus it could be argued that this proposition of metaphor systems by conceptual metaphor theorists makes it possible to conduct a more systematic analysis of one concept, for example in the case of the current study: the concept of 'time'.

The CMT, however, is not without its critics. The major challenge CMT faces from a corpus-linguistic perspective is its empirical validity (e.g. Deignan 2005, 2008b; McEnery and Hardie 2012; Li 2014). McEnery and Hardie (2012: 186) assert that "at its inception much work in CMT was based on intuition and the analysis of invented examples". Similarly, Deignan (2005, 2008b) and Knowles and Moon (2006) have also criticised CMT for a lack of empirical support from naturally-occurring data. These criticisms of CMT would suggest that it is beneficial to conduct corpus-based investigations of real language data to complement CMT.

In addition to the 'intuitive' method adopted by traditional conceptual metaphor analysts which has been challenged, the extent to which CMT can explain real language use also raises doubts. For instance, Deignan (2005, 2008b) demonstrates that there are more dynamic and restricted linguistic features to metaphor than CMT suggests with its one-to-one conceptual mapping. Take the animal lexis in her study as an example. The mapping of animal lexis from the source domain to the target domain can take on different grammatical roles (Deignan 2005: 152-155). These items which are shown to be predominantly nominal in the source domain seem to take the form of verbs and adjectives when used metaphorically to describe human behaviour and attributes. For instance, the animal lexis such as *horse* and *squirrel* are used only as verbs when they are associated with a metaphorical use, as in the examples '*I was horsing around with Katie*' and '*as consumers squirrel away huge sums for the down-payment on a home*' (ibid.: 153). This finding from Deignan (2005) that real language use may be more complicated than CMT suggests is also supported by the current corpus-based analysis. For example, it was found that the metaphor TIME IS MONEY is often associated with verb phrases; that the word *time* is normally used as the grammatical subject when it is associated with the metaphor TIME IS MOTION; and that some phraseological items related to a metaphorical use, e.g. *have the time of my life* and *take your time*, may exhibit more complex features at the linguistic level.

The other problems in CMT which have been highlighted mainly lie in its theoretical assumptions, e.g. the relationship between metaphor and metonymy (Barcelona 2003), the classification of metaphor types and constraints on metaphor (Ruiz de Mendoza Ibáñez and Pérez Hernández 2011) and the extent to which the conceptual metaphor model can be used to explain unconventional and novel expressions in real discourse (Cameron 2007; Fauconnier and Turner 2008; Kövecses 2010). The latter problem of CMT, in particular, has been discussed in many studies. It could be argued that this problem is the main reason for the increasing attention paid to the Conceptual Blending Theory. For instance, as Kövecses (2010: 291-292) asserts, "in real discourse, unconventional and novel linguistic metaphors can emerge not only from conventionally fixed mappings between a source and a target domain but also from mappings initiated *from the target* to the source" (italics original). In this case, the CMT model may not fully explain the cognitive phenomenon behind these linguistic metaphors; the Conceptual Blending Theory on the other hand may provide a better explanation for the cognitive processes of such linguistic metaphors (cf. Fauconnier and Turner 2002, 2008).

3.3.2 Conceptual Blending Theory (CBT)

The introduction of Conceptual Blending Theory is included in the review of metaphor in thisbook because Blending Theory is often considered to be a more 'contemporary' model than CMT (cf. Fauconnier and Turner 2002, 2008; Deignan 2005; Gibbs 2008; Littlemore 2009; Kövecses 2010). This section will thus describe Conceptual Blending Theory (henceforth CBT), but also show why CBT is not used in the current investigation of metaphor by comparing the differences between CBT and CMT.

CBT (or the Network Model) is proposed by Fauconnier and Turner (2002, 2008) and views metaphor as a more dynamic or 'online' process than CMT (Littlemore 2009: 104). Rather than analysing metaphor in terms of two domains (a source domain and target domain), this network model (CBT) explains the metaphorical process through the concept of "mental spaces". Mental spaces can be compared with domains in the CMT, but domains are relatively stable pre-existing knowledge structures while mental spaces are temporary structures. For instance, Fauconnier and Turner (2002: 40) define mental spaces as "small conceptual packets". As CBT suggests, the mental spaces consist of two or more "input spaces", a "blended space" and a "generic space" (see Fauconnier and Turner 2002, 2008). The input spaces are mental spaces which are structured by domains but are more specific than domains. By fusing the conceptual structures from the input spaces, the blended space is formed as a new mental space. The blended space, to some extent, allows the formation of the emergent structure of its own which may be impossible in the input spaces. The generic space, as a third type of space in the network model, is the mental space which captures the structure that the input spaces share.

Take the sentence *steam was coming out of his ears* as an example. CMT would consider this example as a linguistic realisation of the metaphor ANGER IS A HOT FLUID IN A CONTAINER, with the source domain as 'a container with hot fluid inside' and the target as 'anger or a person getting more and more angry' (cf. Kövecses 2010: 273). The association between this example and the conceptual metaphor may not be wrong, but the blending phenomenon in this example is not entirely reflected by the two-domain model (cf. Fauconnier and Turner 2002: 300; Kövecses 2006: 284). The problem in this conceptualisation is that no 'steam' can be found in the target domain (ANGER) and no 'ear (s)' can be found in the source domain

(CONTAINER).

The complexity in the above metaphorical process can be better accounted for using the blending theory (CBT). Two input spaces can be observed in this case: 'a container with hot steam coming out' and 'an angry person with ears'. The blended space can fuse the structures from these two input spaces and form an emergent structure of 'an angry person with steam coming out of his ears', which allows the 'steam' and 'ear (s)' to be present at the same time (see Kövecses 2010: 273–274). The generic space, on the other hand, captures the shared structures of the two input spaces: the 'vessel' (container or person), the 'content' (heat or anger), and 'the intensity may lead to potential danger' (e.g. the intensity of the heat in the container leads to the heat of the fluid and the intensity of anger in a person leads to the state of being more angry). The above blending phenomenon is represented in Figure 3.1 (cf. the basic diagram of conceptual blend in Fauconnier and Turner 2002: 46).

In short, the major difference between CMT and CBT is that the CBT has replaced the two-domain model of conceptual metaphors in CMT with a more complex network model of multiple mental spaces (cf. Steen 2007; Kövecses 2010). The two-domain model for metaphor in CMT can to some extent account for many cases of metaphorical behaviour, in particular the use of highly conventional conceptual metaphors with static schematic structures; and CBT, on the other hand, may provide a deeper understanding of the processes underlying metaphor, especially those complex metaphorical processes where there might be incompatible elements between the input spaces (or vaguely between the source and target domains) and this incompatibility can only be resolved in the blended space (cf. Fauconnier and Turner 2002, 2008; Steen 2007; Kövecses 2010). According to Kövecses (2010: 272–274), CBT may provide more "precise" and "refined" analysis of metaphor and "handle certain problems" which can not be entirely solved with CMT (cf. Steen 2007: 51).

However, while it is acknowledged that CBT may account for conceptual blending in a more effective manner, this complex network model is not used as the main reference of metaphor theories in the current investigation because this book does not attempt to explain or describe cognitive phenomena at the theoretical level. As discussed in an earlier section, the first objective of the current analysis is to explore the relation between phraseology and several phenomena which are important to the construction of

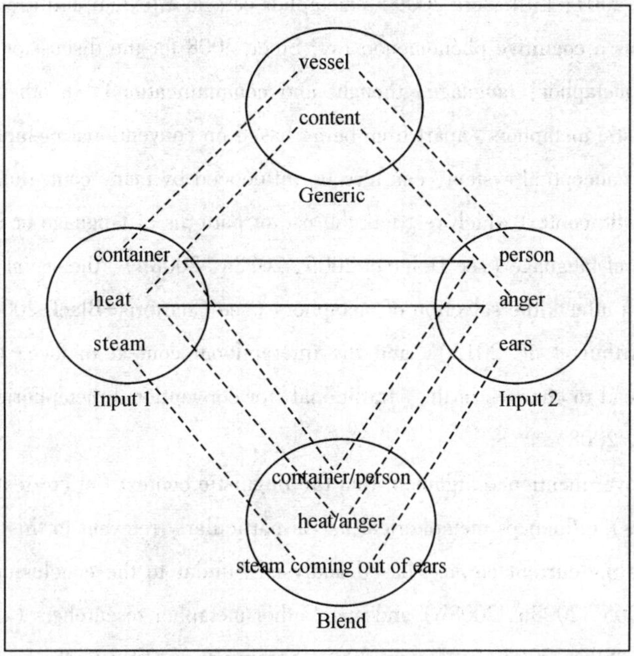

Figure 3.1 **The blend for *steam was coming out of his ears***

(**based on Fauconnier and Turner** 2002: 46 **and Kövecses** 2010: 273-274).

(**The solid lines represent the cross-space mapping between the inputs and the dotted lines indicate the connections between elements of mental spaces.**)

meaning in discourse; and in the case of metaphor, the current study mainly seeks to investigate more empirically the patterning or phraseological features which are associated with metaphorical use. Therefore, CMT qualifies as the theoretical model for this study (the rationale for primarily adopting the model of CMT will be provided in more detail in an subsequent section).

3.3.3 Context-induced metaphors

In the above two sections, I have introduced two contemporary theoretical models of metaphor which can explain metaphorical use from a cognitive perspective. In this section, I will show another important factor in metaphorical use in discourse: context.

As suggested by many empirical studies of linguistic metaphors (e.g. Charteris-Black 2004; Deignan 2005, 2008b; Stefanowitsch and Gries 2006; Cameron 2007,

2008; Steen 2007; Littlemore 2009), metaphor can be a textual and social phenomenon as well as a cognitive phenomenon (cf. Steen 2008 for the discussion of three dimensions of metaphor: language, thought and communication). In other words, the use of linguistic metaphors, apart from being based on conventional metaphorical mappings in the conceptual system, can also be influenced by many contextual factors, e.g. the linguistic context which restricts the use of patterns of language or requires certain patterns of language (see Deignan 2005, 2008a, 2008b), the social and cultural context which affects the selection of metaphors (see Charteris-Black 2004; Kövecses 2010; MacArthur *et al.* 2012), and the interactional context in face-to-face talk which may lead to changes in the 'traditional' or conventional metaphorical use (Cameron 2007, 2008).

The above-mentioned argument that the linguistic context (or co-texts of linguistic metaphors) influences metaphorical use is particularly relevant to this study and is supported by the current corpus-based analysis. Similar to the conclusions drawn by Deignan (2005, 2008a, 2008b) and many other metaphor researchers (e.g. Cameron 2007, 2008; Steen 2007; Littlemore 2009; Semino *et al.* 2013), the results from the current investigation suggest that the use of metaphorical expressions can extend beyond the restrictions imposed by fixed mappings between a source domain and a target domain. More specifically, the current study reveals that the relation between metaphorical use and the phraseological patterning of language can be equally important (cf. Deignan 2005, 2008a, 2008b).

This finding of the current study is reflected in two aspects. First, phraseology as a significant carrier of meaning (Sinclair 1991, 2004a) can play an essential part in the construction of metaphorical meaning (cf. Deignan 2005; Stefanowitsch and Gries 2006; Littlemore 2009). That is to say, phraseology and meaning (or metaphorical meaning) are closely connected. For instance, it was found that the linguistic metaphors of *time* associated with TIME IS MONEY are a more or less 'systematic' group of phraseological items: largely verb phrases such as '*spend time* v-ing', '*spend time with* n.', '*waste time on* n.' and '*make time for* n.'. Second, the choice of linguistic metaphorical expressions in a discourse can be influenced by its co-texts so that the patterning of language appears natural and the pragmatic meaning of the whole discourse is not interrupted (cf. Deignan 2008b; Littlemore and Low 2006; Kövecses 2010). For example, the analysis of the semi-fixed phrase '*it takes time ...*' suggests that the co-texts of this phrase (e.g. the modal verbs, adjectives and the to-infinitive clauses which co-occur with it) consistently contribute to the sense associated with this phrase, i.e. that a specific type of work which is to be completed is time-consuming. In other words, the choice of this linguistic metaphor ('*it takes time ...*') depends significantly on its co-texts (or phraseological behaviour) so that the pragmatic sense of the discourse can be consistent.

3.3.4 Metonymy

Apart from analysing metaphorical use of lexical items, metonymy is also investigated in the current study because metaphor and metonymy are two related phenomena (cf. Dirven and Pörings 2002; Barcelona 2003; Radden 2005; Kövecses 2010). Therefore, this section will discuss metonymy and provide the relevant theoretical basis for this part of the investigation.

Corresponding to metaphor, metonymy is also normally described as a cognitive phenomenon. One example which is frequently used to illustrate metonymy is *I'm reading Shakespeare*, where *Shakespeare* the person stands for his work, i. e. THE AUTHOR FOR THE WORK (Kövecses 2010: 172). In this case, the two concepts in the metonymic mapping ('person' and 'his work') are related and 'close' to each other in conceptual space so that they are more likely to be associated with one domain. In other words, metonymy is often defined as conceptual mappings within a single domain. For instance, Kövecses gives the following definition for metonymy:

> Metonymy is a cognitive process in which one conceptual entity, the vehicle, provides mental access to another conceptual entity, the target, within the same domain, or idealized cognitive model (ICM). (Kövecses 2010: 173)

It can be seen from this definition that a main difference between metaphor and metonymy is whether the conceptual mapping 'takes place' across two domains or within one domain. Other differences between the two cognitive phenomena can involve their basis. For example, it has often been argued that metaphor is based on a pre-existing similarity between two concepts (or domains) while metonymy is usually based on the relationship of contiguity between two concepts (see Dirven and Pörings 2002; Forceville and Urios-Aparisi 2009; Littlemore 2009). Yet this 'similarity vs. contiguity' point has not been fully supported, mostly because the notion of 'similarity' (or 'contiguity') itself is used in a vague and superficial way (cf. Barcelona 2003; Steen 2007; Kövecses 2010; MacArthur *et al.* 2012). The 'two domains versus one domain' difference, among all the other differences between the cognitive mechanisms, is probably one of the least controversial points (see Gibbs 1994; Barcelona 2003; Kövecses 2010).

Even so, the definition (or understanding) of domain can still be a problematic factor in distinguishing between metaphor and metonymy (see Barcelona 2003; Haser 2005; Kövecses 2010; Benczes *et al.* 2011). Generally, it may be considered that the two entities involved in a metaphor are more distinct or 'distant' from each other and could be considered to belong to two different domains, whereas the two entities involved in a metonymy are closely related to each other such that they are considered to belong to the same domain (cf. Kövecses 2010). The 'distance' between two entities, however, still remains a subjective matter. For instance, the concept of 'human beings' may be perceived as one domain, but it can be argued that this concept is profiled in relation to several different domains, e.g. physical objects, living entities and volitional agents (see Croft 1993; Dirven and Pörings 2002; Croft and Cruse 2004; Haser 2005).

This problem regarding domain has been partially addressed by a few cognitive linguists (e.g. Croft 1993; Panther and Radden 1999; Barcelona 2003; Haser 2005; Geeraerts 2006; Benczes *et al.* 2011) who employ the term "domain matrix" instead of domain when referring to entities such as 'human beings'. The notion of domain matrix refers to "the totality of knowledge structures which are activated in multiple domains as the conceptual background of a particular meaning" (Barcelona 2003: 62). In the case of 'human beings', a domain matrix may represent the "combination of domains simultaneously presupposed by [this] concept" (Croft 1993: 340) which to some extent solves the dilemma. Furthermore, the two domains involved in metaphorical mappings cannot form a domain matrix since they are not closely related. Therefore, using this term, metonymy can be further defined as mappings within a single domain matrix with metaphor as mappings across two 'separate' domains (or two domain matrices).

While it is necessary to distinguish metaphor and metonymy in the current study, it is not appropriate to regard metaphor and metonymy as two distinct phenomena because many conceptual metaphors (especially those with experiential groundings) derive from conceptual metonymies or have a metonymic basis (see Dirven and Pörings 2002; Barcelona 2003; Radden 2005; Geeraerts and Cuyckens 2007; Goatly 2007; Kövecses 2010). For instance, the metaphor ANGER IS HEAT (e.g. realised by *boil with anger* and *breathe fire*) would be relevant to the metonymy EFFECT FOR CAUSE because it can be argued that anger to some extent causes increased body heat (see Kövecses 2010: 184). Similarly, as Barcelona (2003: 47) argues, metaphors such as SADNESS IS DOWN, MORE IS UP and NEGATIVE IS DARK would at least have some sort of metonymic motivation: for example, the metaphor SADNESS IS DOWN (e.g. realised by *she walked with drooping shoulders*) can be motivated by the metonymy DOWNWARD BODILY POSTURE FOR SADNESS; the metaphor MORE IS UP (e.g. realised by *speak up* or *keep your voice down*) can be related to the metonymy VERTICALITY FOR QUANTITY. In the case of TIME, the conceptual metaphor TIME IS MOTION may also be argued to be motivated by metonymy. More specifically, it can involve the metonymic relationship of CAUSE AND EFFECT. For instance, Kövecses (2010: 186) suggests that in the metaphor of TIME IS MOTION, "it is the target domain of time that enables movement", or in other words "[w]ithout time, there is no movement".

There are generally three common metonymic mappings: PART FOR WHOLE (e.g. *England* for 'Great Britain'), WHOLE FOR PART (e.g. *America* for 'United States') and PART FOR PART (e.g. *we're reading Shakespeare* where the author stands for his work). Each generic metonymic mapping involves many subcases of metonymies. Take, for example, the mapping of PART FOR WHOLE. This metonymy has also been traditionally referred to as "synecdoche" (see Knowles and Moon 2006: 37; Littlemore 2009: 110; Kövecses 2010: 179). Subcases of the metonymy PART FOR WHOLE can be: PART OF A THING FOR THE WHOLE THING (e.g. body parts such as *hand*, *head* or *leg* for 'the whole person'), THE MATERIAL CONSTITUTING AN OBJECT FOR THE OBJECT (e.g. *wood* for 'the forest'), PART OF AN EVENT FOR THE WHOLE EVENT (e.g. *mother is cooking potatoes* for 'the whole preparation of food' such as cleaning and peeling the potatoes and boiling the potatoes), and MEMBER OF A CATEGORY FOR THE CATEGORY (e.g. *aspirin* for 'any pain-relieving tablet) (see Kövecses 2010: 179-181).

The discussion in this section has indicated the important role of metonymy in figurative use and the close relation between metaphor and metonymy. To sum up: 1) metaphor and metonymy are both systematic cognitive models which are pervasive in everyday life; 2) metaphor is defined as conceptual mappings across two domains (or domain matrices) while metonymy is defined as mappings within the boundaries of a single domain or domain matrix; 3) metaphor and metonymy are not separate cognitive phenomena but rather are related and can interact with each other in real language use.

3.3.5 The approach to metaphor in this study: CMT and corpus linguistics

The investigation of metaphor (and metonymy) in the current study refers to CMT as the theoretical basis for three reasons. First, CMT is a well-established model. It is one of the most widely accepted cognitive models of metaphor and this model proposes that metaphor is a cognitive phenomenon as well as a linguistic one (see Deignan 2005, 2008b; Gibbs 2008; Kövecses 2010). CMT also suggests that conceptual metaphors are related and can be organised hierarchically, which makes it possible to analyse a notion (e.g. the concept of 'time') relatively more systematically.

The second reason for adopting CMT as the theoretical model, rather than CBT, relates to the objective of this study. This study aims to investigate the metaphorical phenomenon more empirically at the linguistic level in order to reveal the phraseological or patterning features of language. In this case, the suggestions proposed by CMT, e.g. abstract concepts are understood in terms of concrete concepts and metaphorical expressions realise the conceptual metaphors at the linguistic level, may be more measurable than CBT. Additionally, since I do not attempt to explain complex cognitive or conceptual processes underlying metaphorical expressions at the theoretical level, this study does not require frequent reference to a comparatively more complex model such as the CBT.

Another reason for referring mainly to CMT in this study relates to the usage or purpose of this model in the current investigation. The major use of the theoretical model is to identify and categorise linguistic metaphors of *time*, for which CMT is considered to be more suitable than CBT. The CMT has proposed a refined and widely recognised definition of metaphor which can aid the identification of linguistic metaphors, especially those with conventional metaphorical mappings in the corpus data (the Metaphor Identification Procedure used by the Pragglejaz group (2007) is also occasionally referred to). Previous research in CMT has also provided a relatively comprehensive list of conceptual metaphors of TIME which can be used as the basis for the categorisations of linguistic metaphors of *time* in this study. The CBT, on the other hand, focuses largely on providing a precise explanation of the conceptual processes of metaphorical (or non-metaphorical) expressions.

The corpus - based method is adopted in the analysis of metaphor (and metonymy) because the current study aims to reveal the empirical aspect of metaphorical/metonymic use of language. As Deignan (2005, 2008a, 2008b) suggests, the corpus approach can show the patterning features of language which are essential to metaphorical use and yet often neglected by traditional conceptual metaphor theorists (cf. Stefanowitsch and Gries 2006; Philip 2011). The patterning features of language or phraseological behaviour of a certain metaphorical expression can also be better examined with a corpus-based approach than the traditional approach (see Sinclair 1991, 2004a; Hunston 2010; McEnery and Hardie 2012). Furthermore, traditional metaphorical analysis has often been criticised for drawing conclusions based on a small amount of data. This limitation can be largely compensated for by an investigation based on a large corpus of naturally-occurring data.

3.4 Evaluation

Evaluation is also considered as aphenomenon which is important to the construction of meaning in discourse, and therefore it will be investigated with regard to its relation to phraseology. This study adopts the definition of evaluation proposed by Hunston and Thompson (2000: 5) who use this term as "the broad cover term for the expression of the speaker or writer's attitude or stance towards, viewpoint on, or feelings about the entities or proposition that he or she is talking about" (cf. Hunston 2011). The following sections will describe evaluation in detail with regard to the terminology associated with evaluation, the frequent evaluative items in text, different types of evaluative uses, and the reasons for adopting a corpus-based approach to investigate evaluative use.

3.4.1 Evaluation as an umbrella term for speakers' stance and attitude

As suggested by Hunston and Thompson (2000: 2) and Hunston (2011: 10), existing studies of evaluation have used a broad range of terminology to refer to slightly different overlapping areas of evaluation, e.g. "connotation" (Lyons 1977), "affect" (Besnier 1993), "attitude" (Halliday 1994), "appraisal" (Martin 2000; Martin and White 2005), "stance" (Conrad and Biber 2000), "metadiscourse" (Hyland and Tse 2004) and "sentiment" (Asher *et al.* 2009). The term "evaluation" is used because this study does not attempt to distinguish different areas of evaluation but to explore the relation between the broad category of evaluation and phraseology. In this case, the term "evaluation" may be one of the most neutral terms in the studies of evaluative language and can be used as an umbrella term to refer more broadly to all subcategories of evaluation (see Hunston and Thompson 2000; Tognini-Bonelli and Del Lungo Camiciotti 2005; Hunston 2011). Additionally, an advantage in adopting the term "evaluation", according to Hunston and Thompson (2000: 5), is that it allows a "syntactic and morphological flexibility", highlights the "user-orientation" attribute (e.g. 'it is the user who evaluates') and "allows us to talk about the *values* ascribed to the entities and propositions which are *evaluated*" (italics original; also see Hunston 2011 for the use of the term "evaluation").

3.4.2 Evaluative items in text

Among the significant number of evaluative items which have been identified in normal discourse, the most common or typical evaluative items discussed in previous studies include adjectives such as *good*, *bad* and *wonderful* which can be considered as "evaluative even out of context" (Hunston 2011: 13). Some nouns, verbs and adverbs can also exhibit an evaluative sense in context. For instance, some researchers on evaluation (e.g. Hunston and Thompson 2000; Hunston 2011) have listed nouns like *success*, *failure* and *tragedy* which can indicate a strong evaluation in discourse (cf. Francis 1986 on anaphoric nouns). Similarly, the verbs such as *succeed*, *fail* and *win*, and the adverbs like *unfortunately* have also been included in the list of evaluative items (see Hunston and Thompson 2000; Hunston 2011).

In addition to the above single words which can show evaluative senses in text, another category of evaluative items concerns patterns or phraseological units (see Sinclair 1991, 2004a; Hunston and Sinclair 2000; Hunston 2011). This group of evaluative items, however, has received much less attention than evaluative words (especially adjectives) in previous studies on evaluation (see Hunston 2011). Sinclair (1991, 1996, 2004a) is one of the few researchers who have investigated evaluation exhibited by phrases and multi-word units. More specifically, he focuses on the evaluative use of lexical items which are normally referred to using the label "semantic prosody" or "discourse prosody". For example, the analysis of the co-texts of *the naked eye* suggests that it is often associated with a semantic prosody of 'difficulty' and the analysis of *true feelings* reveals that this phrase is often associated with a prosody of 'reluctance' (Sinclair 2004: 30-36). This relation between evaluation and phraseology has also been studied intensively by Hunston and Sinclair (2000) and Hunston (2011). They assert that grammatical frames or patterns such as '*it* v-link ADJ *to*-inf.' and '*it* v-link ADJ *that*-cl.' are normally associated with an evaluative use. The recognition of the category of phraseological items as evaluative language may have far-reaching effects because it broadens the scope of evaluative studies. Additionally, the establishment of the relation between evaluation and phraseology justifies the investigation in the current study as to whether this relation exists in the case of *time* and *thing*, or more importantly how an evaluative use can be exhibited by the phraseological items associated with the two words.

3.4.3 Different types of evaluative uses

As suggested earlier, some words such as *good* and *wonderful* denote an evaluative meaning while some items such as *the naked eye* and *true feelings* are associated with an evaluative sense through the co-texts of these items. In other words, the evaluative meaning can be exhibited either by the lexical items themselves or associated with their co-texts. Based on this criterion, there are two broad types of evaluative uses. The first type of evaluative use involves the group of lexical items which explicitly convey an evaluative sense, i.e. explicit evaluation (cf. "inscribed evaluation" in Martin 2004: 289). Examples are evaluative words like *wonderful* and *success* and phraseological items such as '*the most important thing* (*that*-cl.) *is/was*' and '*it is a good thing*'. Hunston and Thompson (2000: 14) also refer to these lexical items as "attitudinal lexis" which are associated with an evaluative sense even out of context (cf. Mahlberg 2005: 149-150 for the discussion of the cases where the "core meaning" of lexical items is clearly evaluative).

The second type of evaluative use involves the group of lexical items such as *the naked eye* and *true feelings* which are associated with an evaluative meaning through their co-texts. This type of evaluative use is often referred to as "evoked evaluation" by Martin (2004: 289) or "implicit evaluation" by Hunston (2011: 55-65). Researchers such as Louw (1993), Sinclair (2004a) and Stubbs (2007a, 2009b) focus on "semantic prosody" (or "discourse prosody") which relates to this type of evaluative use although there is a complicated relationship between semantic prosody and evaluation (see Stewart 2010 for a detailed and critical discussion of "semantic prosody"). Louw (1993), Sinclair (2004a) and Stubbs (2009b) consider semantic prosody as a phenomenon which concerns evaluative meanings (more often favourable or unfavourable) that are associated with the co-texts of a lexical item (cf. Fellbaum 2007: 10; Hunston 2011: 55-56). Sinclair (2004a) and Stubbs (2007a, 2009b) also suggest that semantic prosody is a type of attitudinal or discourse function associated with a lexical item which "describes the speaker's communicative purpose" (Stubbs 2009b: 22; cf. Lindquist 2009: 59). In the current analysis, the phrase *the whole thing* can be included in the second type of evaluative use, i.e. implicit evaluation, because even though this phrase appears to be 'non-evaluative', it was found that this phrase tends to occur in a negative semantic environment. For instance, the co-texts of this phrase, especially the adjectives which are used to describe *the whole thing* are often associated with a negative sense (e.g. *the whole thing is nonsense*, *the whole thing is stupid* and *the whole thing is rubbish*). Another example could be the pattern '*at the time of the* N'. The current analysis using both the BoE and the BNC shows that the nouns in this pattern seem to be largely negative words, such as *attack*, *murder* and *accident*.

In other words, the distinction between the above two broad categories of evaluative use (explicit evaluation and implicit evaluation) is based on whether the evaluative meaning is exhibited by the lexical item or associated with the co-texts of this item. Additionally, different evaluative uses can be distinguished according to the kind of evaluative meanings or values exhibited in text. For instance, Hunston and Thompson (2000: 25) propose four evaluative parameters, "Good-bad", "certainty", "expectedness" and "importance", which relate to different aspects of evaluation. These four parameters could to some extent serve to reflect different types of evaluative uses, e.g. the evaluative use which emphasises the 'good–bad' aspect of entities, the evaluative use which emphasises 'certainty' or 'uncertainty', and the evaluative use which highlights 'importance' or 'unimportance'. It is also necessary to point out that there can be an overlap of evaluative parameters in a specific evaluative use exhibited in real discourse (cf. "evaluative interplay" in Bednarek 2006: 58). For example, an expression which involves the evaluative sense of 'importance' is likely to be associated with the evaluative sense of 'good' as well (e.g. *it is the most important thing* and *the important thing is* ...).

The four parameters proposed by Hunston and Thompson (2000) indicate the existence of at least four types of evaluative uses (see Table 3.1), if the interplay of parameters is not considered for the moment. The first type of evaluative use which highlights the 'good' or 'bad' aspect of entities (see Table 3.1) has been frequently discussed in previous studies. The reason for this is that the sense of 'good' or 'bad', or of 'positive' or 'negative', may be one of the most common senses associated with evaluation (see Hunston and Thompson 2000: 22). Bednarek (2006) also uses the term "emotivity" to describe this aspect of evaluation because it can show the speaker's "approval" or "disapproval" when things are evaluated in terms of "how good and bad they are" (Bednarek 2006: 19). There are many examples of this type of evaluative use, including *it is a good thing*, *this is the best thing that ever happened to me*, *the most wonderful thing about you is* ... and *the worst thing about it was* ... .

Table 3.1 **The major types of evaluative uses based on the evaluative values exhibited by phraseological items (based on work by Hunston and Thompson** 2000 **and Bednarek** 2006)

	Evaluative meaning/value	Explanation	Example
1	'good–bad'	The positive or negative aspect of an item is highlighted.	*It is a good thing*; *the worst thing about it was*...
2	'certainty'	The evaluative meaning relates to how certain the writer/speaker is about a piece of information.	*one thing is certain*; *one thing is for sure*

Table3. 1(continued)

	Evaluative meaning/value	Explanation	Example
3	'expectedness'	The evaluative meaning relates to how obvious a piece of information is to the reader/hearer.	*one thing is clear*; *one thing is absolutely clear*
4	'importance'	The importance of an item ishighlighted.	*the most important thing is*; *it is the most important thing*
5	'difficulty'	The evaluative meaning relates to how difficult an action or event is.	*the simplest thing to do*; *the hardestthing to do*
6	'morality'	The morality of an event or action ishighlighted.	*do the right thing*; *do the honourable thing*
7	'rationality'	The evaluative meaning relates to how rational an action or event is.	*the sensible thing to do*; *the smart thing to do*

The second type of evaluative use highlights the sense of 'certainty' of an entity (see Table 3. 1). As Hunston and Thompson (2000: 23) suggest, this type of evaluation relates to "how certain the writer is of each piece of information" (cf. the evaluative parameter of "reliability" in Bednarek 2006: 42). They state that the evaluative use which emphasises the sense of 'certainty' is usually indicated by "modal auxiliaries and other signals of modal meaning such as *unlikely* and *probably*" (Hunston and Thompson 2000: 23). The analysis in this study also reveals that sequences such as *one thing is certain* and *one thing is for sure* can be associated similarly with this type of evaluation.

The third type of evaluative use which highlights the sense of 'expectedness' (see Table 3. 1) concerns how obvious a piece of information is to the reader, or whether it is expected by the reader (see Hunston and Thompson 2000: 23). The phraseological items such as *one thing is clear* and *one thing is absolutely clear* may be associated with the sense of 'expectedness'. This evaluative use ('expectedness') is related to, or can overlap with, the second type of evaluative use ('certainty') because these two evaluative senses are often regarded as close to each other. For instance, when Hunston and Thompson (2000: 23) discuss the use of the adverb *clearly* in their example - *clearly, the results from the two hospitals are unlikely to be the same* - they suggest that this word can be associated with the senses of both 'certainty' and 'expectedness'.

The fourth evaluative use highlights the sense of ‘importance’ (see Table 3.1). According to Hunston and Thompson (2000: 24), this may have a “text-oriented function”, that is, lexical items associated with the evaluative sense of ‘importance’ may direct the reader “towards the main point of the text”. This evaluative use is “typically signalled through adjectives and adverbs such as *important* and *significantly*” (ibid.). In the current investigation, it is suggested that the patterns such as ‘*it* v-link *time to*-inf.’ and ‘*it* v-link *time that*-cl.’ can be related to this type of evaluative use.

Other types of evaluative use can involve the sense or value of “desirability”, “possibility”, “evidentiality” and “humorousness” (Lemke 1998: 33-37; Bednarek 2006: 42). In the current analysis of evaluation, it was also found that senses like ‘difficulty’, ‘morality’ and ‘rationality’ can also play a part in evaluative use. For instance, sequences like *the simplest thing to do* or *the hardest thing to do* can be related to the evaluative sense of ‘difficulty’; the items *do the right thing* and *do the honourable thing* can be related to the evaluative sense of ‘morality’; and sequences such as *the sensible thing to do* and *the smart thing to do* may be associated with a sense of ‘rationality’ (see Table 3.1). These three evaluative senses revealed by the current study also indicate that it is valuable to adopt a corpus-based method to investigate evaluation.

3.4.4 Corpus-based approach to evaluation

Hunston (2011: 166-167) presents some of theimportant roles a corpus-based method can play in the study of evaluative language, as listed below:

1) Corpus investigation allows a researcher to establish that a given word or phrase has a typical evaluative use or polarity.

2) Corpus investigation permits quantification of evaluative meaning in one set of texts over another, by counting the occurrences of given forms.

3) Corpus investigation permits mapping of meaning elements onto form elements where these coincide consistently.

4) Corpus investigation allows a researcher to observe consistency in co-text in meaning as well as in form.

(Hunston 2011: 166-167)

Relevant to the current study, the corpus-based method can reveal how the patterning features of language areimportant to evaluation. For instance, the corpus-based analysis will suggest in a subsequent chapter that many language patterns are associated with an evaluative use. What is more, the results show that the use of these patterns can reflect different evaluative senses or values. In other words, the use of a corpus-based approach can greatly assist the researcher to discover the relation between phraseology and evaluation. Similarly, Hunston (2011) summarises the advantage of corpus linguistics as follows: "[m]any phrases as well as individual words are associated with evaluative meaning; this makes the approaches associated with corpus linguistics particularly suitable for studying evaluation" (Hunston 2011: 171).

3.5 Vagueness

Another phenomenon which contributes to the construction of meaning in discourse is vague use. Therefore, in the following sections, I will provide the theoretical background for investigating this phenomenon. More specifically, I will firstly show the significance of studying vague language and the definition of vague language adopted in this study; and then I will discuss two other aspects of vague use where the corpus-based analysis reveals more complex or unexpected features: the categorisation of vague language and the genre in which vague use can be 'normally' found.

3.5.1 Significance of studying vague language

Overthe last few decades the vague use of language has been established as common and desirable in discourse (see Channell 1994; Cutting 2007, 2013; Murphy 2010). For instance, many researchers (e.g. Crystal and Davy 1975; Carter and McCarthy 1997; Ädel and Reppen 2008) have argued that it is one of the most important characteristics of conversational language. Drave (2002: 26-27) also shows that vague language can tailor conversational contributions to the perceived informational needs of the other participant, e.g. by filling lexical or knowledge gaps, emphasising or withholding certain information, and conveying tentativeness. In addition, vague use is considered to be of great social significance (see Fairclough 2003; Jucker *et al.*

2003; Cutting 2007; Fernandez and Yuldashev 2011). Cutting (2007: 8) refers to it as a "marker of social cohesion" because it can indicate shared knowledge among the interlocutors, mark a sense of in-group membership, and maintain (and further enhance) the ongoing relationship (also see Ädel and Reppen 2008: 10). McEnery *et al*. (2006) similarly suggest that it serves various pragmatic or social functions, e.g. "serving as politeness strategies, softening implicit complaints and criticisms, and providing a way of establishing a social bond" (ibid.: 106).

3.5.2 Definition of vague language used in this book

The definition of 'vague language' adopted in this book is mainly based on Channell (1994) in which she states that:

> an expression or word is vague if: A. it can be contrasted with another word or expression which appears to render the same proposition; B. it is 'purposely and unabashedly vague'; C. its meaning arises from the 'intrinsic uncertainty' (ibid.: 20).

To paraphrase Channell's first requirement for vague language, the precondition for the existence of vague language is that vague use can be contrasted with 'precise' use, i.e. not all language use is vague. This understanding of vague language is different and should be distinguished from the logical approach to vagueness which is adopted in particular in the area of philosophy. For instance, Russell (1923) has claimed from the philosophical perspective that all language is more or less vague, even logical words like *or* and *not* (also see Williamson 1994; Ongley and Carey 2013). Following this view, Smith (2008: 4) has asserted that vagueness is ubiquitous and "[o]utside mathematics, virtually all of our language is vague, to a greater or lesser extent". This view, however, despite its appreciation of vagueness in language, seems to be somewhat extreme and will not prove to be very useful for the analysis of vague language in the current study. Therefore, this study follows Channell's definition of vague use, or more specifically her understanding of meaning which is that the meaning of language can be vague as well as precise.

The second and third requirements in Channell's definition may be easier to understand. The third requirement (point C) which states that vague expressions need to be intrinsically vague, to some extent limits the vague nature to the linguistic expression itself rather than other external factors for the cause of vagueness, e. g. the speaker's own habits of language, misinterpretations by the interlocutor (s), or a lack of background information about the conversation. This point or requirement adds a level of stability and 'precision' to the understanding and analysis of vague language.

The second requirement (point B) indicates that vague use is deliberate. However, this point has not been supported by all researchers. For instance, Cutting (2007: 7) argues that "not all vague language use is intentional": the speakers may be tired or in a hurry to find the right word, or sometimes they may not process the conversation properly. Similarly, among the reasons given by Crystal and Davy (1975) for using vague language (see below), the majority of the reasons (i.e. the first three reasons) are not indications of the purposeful use of vague language.

a. memory loss: the speaker forgets a word, or it may be 'on the tip of his tongue';

b. no accurate word or not knowing the word: there is no word in the language for what s/he wants to say, or s/he does not know the appropriate word;

c. no need for precision: the conversation does not require precision, and an approximation or characterisation will do;

d. purposeful use: the choice of vague lexical items is conducive to maintain the informal atmosphere of the situation.

(Crystal and Davy 1975: 112)

In another list of reasons for using vague language provided by Jucker*et al.* (2003), as shown below, there are also unintentional reasons such as lack of knowledge or an inability to access the expression mentally.

a. the language user does not know a lexical item or is not able to access it;
b. the language user knows the name of an entity but prefers not to use it;
c. the language user intends to invite collaboration or tries to establish a bond.

(Jucker*et al.* 2003: 1750)

Therefore, Channell's (1994) definition of vague language needs to be adapted in order to ensure a broader applicability. In the current study, the vague lexical items associated with *thing* or *time* in the current analysis refer to the expressions that can show intrinsically the sense of imprecision or uncertainty which can be used either deliberately or unavoidably, e.g. when a speaker cannot be precise, when s/he does not know how to be precise, when s/he does not need or want to be precise.

3.5.3 Categorisations of vague language

The categorisation of vaguelanguage in previous studies (e.g. Carter and McCarthy 1997; Ädel and Reppen 2008; Murphy 2010; Anderson 2013) has often been conducted by examining all vague expressions in the researcher's data and classifying these vague expressions based on the types of vague uses (e.g. approximation of quantities or vague reference to a set of items). Of the previous studies which contribute to the categorisations of vague language, Channell (1994) is the one which is often quoted because her framework of different categories of vague language has been considered as possibly the most comprehensive and systematic (see Stenström *et al.* 2002; Cutting 2007; Koester 2007; Carroll 2009). In Channell's (1994) framework, vague language is classified into five categories, as listed in Table 3.2.

The first three categorises in Channell's framework are vague approximators which concern quantities and amounts, such as *about*, *approximately*, *some* and *many*. The fourth category involves multi-word sequences beginning usually with *or* and *and*, as in *or something like that* and *and things like that*, which Channell (1994: 131) labels as "vague category identifiers" (cf. "vague category markers [VCMs]" in Ädel and Reppen [2008: 10-11] and Murphy [2010: 85-91]; and "general extender" in Cutting [2013: 191]). The fifth category comprises placeholder words such as *thingy* and *whatsitsname*.

In some of the later studies, these five categories of vague language proposed by Channell (1994) have been regrouped and referred to under different labels. For instance, Cotterill (2007: 99) recategorises Channell's framework into three areas: "vague additives" which include approximators like *about* and *approximately* and vague category identifiers like *and stuff like that*; "vagueness through lexical choice" which refers to placeholder words like *thingy* and *whatsit* and vague quantifiers like *tons of*; and "vagueness by implicature" which involves examples like *Sam is 6 feet tall* and *Sam has $10,000 in his savings account* where the vagueness is implied through round numbers.

Table 3.2 **Channell's** (1994) **categories of vague language**

(**cf. Stenström** ***et al.*** 2002: 88; **Koester** 2007: 41)

	Category	Example
1	Approximating quantities with numbers and approximators	*about*, *around and round*, *approximately*, *n or m*, *n or so*
2	Approximating quantities with round numbers	*Sam is six feet tall*; *Sam has* $10,000 *in his savings account*; *Odessa has a population of one million*
3	Approximating quantities with non-numerical vague quantifiers	*bags* (*of*), *loads* (*of*), *lots* (*of*), *masses* (*of*), *oodles* (*of*); *a bit of*, *a load of*, *a lot* (*of*), *a mass of*, *a scrap* (*of*), *a touch of*; (*a*) *few*, *some*, *several*, *many*, *umpteen*; *always*, *often*, *sometimes*, *occasionally*, *seldom*, *never*
4	Vague category identifier	*or something/anything* (*like that*); *and things*; *and things like that*
5	Placeholder words	*thingy*, *whatsitsname*, *watnot*, *whosit*, *whatsit*

Further to Channell's (1994) framework, the system of classification of vague language proposed by Wang (2005) is also comprehensive and has often been cited (see Cotterill 2007: 99). Different from Channell's categories, Wang (2005) classifies vague language according to pragmatic functions. As can be seen from Table 3.3, there are five categories in her system: 'impression' indicators (e.g. *a lot* and *approximately*), 'unspecificity' indicators (e.g. *at six-ish*), 'fuzziness' indicators (e.g. *sort of* and *kind of*), 'etcetera' indicators (e.g. *and things like that*) and 'uncertainty' indicators (e.g. *maybe*).

Table 3.3 **Wang's** (2005) **categories of vague language** (**cited in Cotterill** 2007: 99)

	Category	Example
1	'Impression' indicators	Vague quantifiers (*a lot*, *many*); Approximators (*approximately*, *about*, *roughly*)
2	'Unspecificity' indicators	*after* 10 *o' clock*, *at six-ish*
3	'Fuzziness' indicators	Approximators (*sort of*, *kind of*)

Table3. 3(continued)

	Category	Example
4	'Etcetera' indicators	Additives (*and so*, *and things like that*)
5	'Uncertainty' indicators	Vague adverbs (*maybe*, *probably*)

Compared to Channell's framework, this categorisation does not include round numbers which may imply vagueness (category 2 in Table 3.2) or placeholder words such as *thingy* and *whatsit* (category 5 in Table 3.2). However, the system proposed by Wang (2005) involves other vague items which have not been included in Channell's framework, for instance, the 'unspecificity' indicators (e.g. *at six-ish*) and the 'fuzziness' indicators (e.g. *sort of* and *kind of*). Additionally, Wang's (2005) study shows that it is possible to categorise vague language based on different criteria.

A relatively more recent categorisation of vague language is provided by Cutting (2013: 190-191). As can be seen from Table 3.4, there are three categories of vague language: "semantically empty noun", "vague modifier" and "general extender", and each category can be further divided (see Cutting 2013: 190-191).

Table 3.4 **Cutting's** (2013) **categories of vague language**

Category	Description	Example
1. Semantically empty noun		
1.1 General noun	superordinate noun	*thing*, *place*, *person*
1.2 Colloquial general noun	placeholder words	*thingy*, *thingymagig*
1.3 General nominal cluster	'question word + verb + noun or pronoun'	Did you see the; *what do you call it*? You could ask *what's-her-face*
2. Vague modifier		
2.1 Vague quantifier	numerical or non-numerical approximators	*about*, *roughly*, *lots of*, *a number of*
2.2 Vague epistemic modifier	adjectival or adverbial expression used as a hedging device	*a bit*; *sort of*
3. General extender	vague category marker	*or something*; *and so on*

As noted in Table 3. 4, three subcategories can be found under the label "semantically empty noun": "general noun" such as *thing* and *place*, "colloquial general noun" such as *thingy*, and "general nominal cluster" such as *what's-her-face*. The second and third subcategories in Cutting's framework are related to placeholder words in Channell's categories (Table 3. 2). The first subcategory "general noun", on the other hand, has not been covered in either Channell's or Wang's system, although Carter and McCarthy (1997: 16) have similarly considered general nouns as a subcategory of vague language. The inclusion of this subcategory as vague language, however, may occasionally be problematic because general nouns such as *thing* are largely context-dependent and therefore the vague use of general nouns can only be identified in specific contexts. For instance, the current investigation shows that not all expressions which involve the word *thing* exhibit a vague use, e.g. the two phrases *for one thing* and *first thing in the morning* which are relatively more lexicalised. Furthermore, it is not appropriate to consider sequences such as *it is the right thing to do* and *family is the most important thing in my life* as vague expressions because here their evaluative use may be prioritised before the other uses (including vague use).

The second category in Cutting's framework, "vague modifier", comprises two subcategories: "vague quantifier" such as *about* and *lots of* which is similar to the approximators and vague quantifiers in Channell's categorisation (Table 3. 2), and "vague epistemic modifier" which may be related to the 'fuzziness' indicators in Wang's system (Table 3. 3). The third category, "general extender" (Table 3. 4), seems to include similar vague items to "vague category identifier" in Channell (1994) and "etcetera indicators" in Wang (2005).

To summarise, Channell's (1994) framework is one of the most comprehensive categorisations of vague language and includes vague quantifiers, approximators, vague category identifiers, placeholder words and round numbers which imply vagueness. Wang's (2005) system is based on the criterion of the pragmatic functions of vague language, which adds 'unspecificity' indicators (e.g. *at six-ish*) and 'fuzziness' indicators (e.g. *sort of* and *kind of*) to the above categorisation of vague items. Cutting (2013) further includes more items in her categories of vague language, e.g. general nouns, although it has been argued above that this inclusion may sometimes be problematic.

Even though each of these three frameworks appears to be comprehensive and covers a large number of vague expressions, the current investigation shows that there may still be more vague items than suggested by these frameworks, for example, the pattern 'N *thing*' and phrases such as *from time to time* and *once upon a time*. This finding suggests that vague use may be more 'common' than previously thought and it would be beneficial for further studies on the categorisation of vague language to conduct or refer to corpus-based research with large quantities of data or with specialised data (e.g. legal documents or business discourse).

3.5.4 Genre and vague use

Many previous studiesof vague language have shown that vague use is often found in informal discourse (e.g. Crystal and Davy 1975; Carter and McCarthy 1997; Ädel and Reppen 2008; Gee and Handford 2012; Cutting 2013). The main reasons for this are listed as follows:

1) vague use is one of the most important features ofinformal conversations in terms of vocabulary and grammar (see Carter and McCarthy 1997; Jucker *et al*. 2003; Ädel and Reppen 2008; Anderson 2013);

2) vague use can help the speaker to realise a list of communicative functions, e.g. making approximations, withholding certain information, projecting shared knowledge and indicating in-group membership (see Section 3.4.1; cf. Channell 1994; Drave 2002; Cutting 2007);

3) many vague items such as placeholder words (*thingy* and *whatsisname*) tend to occur more frequently in informal discourse (cf. Channell 1994; Carter and McCarthy 1997; Cutting 2013).

As a consequence, many researchers who have looked at vague language have used largely informal discourse as their data (e.g. Carter and McCarthy 1997; Jucker *et al*. 2003; Ädel and Reppen 2008; Anderson 2013; Harvey and Koteyko 2013).

A few researchers, on the other hand, also argue that vague use can be found in a broader range of genres. Koester (2006, 2010), for instance, focuses on business-related discourse and shows that vague language can occur in those relatively more formal genres as well as informal discourse. More specifically, Koester (2006, 2010) suggests that vague use can be found frequently in professional talks or written workplace interactions. Similarly, Handford (2010) analyses the language of business meetings and concludes that vague language is very common in this type of discourse.

Cotterill (2007) has also investigated the relation between vague use and more formal genres. She shows that despite the characteristics of precision and clarity which are often assumed to exist in the legal system, vague language can appear in the British courtroom. Other studies of vague use in legal documents also include Henkin (2005) which involves the use of vague lexical items in the drafting of engineering contracts and Steadman (2013) which explains the 'reasonable' amount of vagueness in legal documents.

Consistent with these studies, the current investigation of phraseology associated with *thing* and *time* aims to discover whether vague use can be found in more formal texts as well as informal texts. The phraseological item *the vision thing*, for instance, occurs largely in newspaper and magazine articles. The phrase *from time to time* which is associated with vague use occurs mainly in business-related discourse; this phrase is also frequently found in legal documents such as constitutions, legislations and laws.

3.6 Summary

In this chapter, I have introduced four phenomena which are important to the construction of meaning in discourse: polysemy, metaphor, evaluation and vague use. For each phenomenon, I have given the definition adopted in this study and shown the significance of investigating it. Other important aspects of these phenomena which are relevant to the current investigation have also been described.

For instance, with regard to polysemy, I have discussed two potential problems in terms of analysing this phenomenon: the understanding of meaning and the subjectivity which is likely to be involved in distinguishing different senses associated with a lexical item. It is explained that the current study considers the contextualised use of a lexical item as its meaning, and uses context as the main factor, in order to distinguish two senses associated with a lexical item. It is also argued that there is a close connection between polysemy and phraseology, which will be further illustrated with the analysis of *time* and phrases such as *at the same time* and *big time* in the subsequent chapter.

Regarding metaphor, I have introduced the contemporary theories on metaphor and metonymy, and provided justifications for choosing the Conceptual Metaphor Theory as the theoretical reference point for my research and for using a corpus-based method to explore the more empirical aspects of metaphorical or metonymic use.

In the case of evaluation, I have discussed different kinds of evaluative items in text and the potential types of evaluative uses which as two important aspects of evaluation will be further investigated in the current analysis.

Lastly, in terms of vague use, it is suggested that there may be more vague expressions than indicated in previous frameworks of vague language and that vague use can be found in informal discourse as well as more formal discourse, which to some extent provides the theoretical grounds for discussing these aspects in the subsequent chapters.

Chapter 4 Polysemy and phraseology

This chapter explores the relation between polysemy and phraseology. First, I will focus on the word *time* and illustrate its polysemous nature by showing the major senses that are associated with it using a randomly selected sample of 500 concordance lines from the BoE (S_{BoE}). Second, these senses will be discussed in detail in terms of their associations with the phraseological behaviour of the word *time*, e.g. how each sense of *time* may be related to a particular phraseological feature. Then the relation between polysemy and phraseology will be further investigated by looking at two 'polysemous' phrases-*at the same time* and *big time*. It will be demonstrated that the meaning of a phrase can also be strongly associated with its patterning features.

4.1 Polysemy: time

Many contemporary English dictionaries, e.g. the Collins English Dictionary (2010) and the Oxford English Dictionary (2012), list more than two distinct senses of the word time, which suggests that time is normally considered as a 'polysemous' word. Similarly, Evans (2005: 52) has classified the meaning of time into multiple senses although her approach is more conceptual than empirical (see Appendix 2). Thus the following section will describe the major senses associated with time using the BoE sample and briefly discuss each of these senses. Then in Section 4.1.2, I will discuss the fuzzy boundaries between these senses which are often regarded as an inevitable problem in any study of polysemy.

4.1.1 Major senses exhibited by time in the BoE sample

The analysis of time using the BoE sample (S_{BoE_time}) reveals that it is indeed a polysemous word which is associated with eight major distinguishable senses, as shown in Table 4. 1 below.

Table 4. 1 The eight major senses of *time* observed in the BoE sample

	Sense	Short version	%	Example
$time_1$	'actual time on a clock'	clock	2. 6	*What time is it? Three-thirty.*
$time_2$	'a particular time point'	point	30. 1	*by the time I went to Sheffield Uni*
$time_3$	'a period of time'	period	21. 9	*there was a time when women were*
$time_4$	'occasion'	occasion	24. 8	*it wasn't the first time that I found*
$time_5$	'time as money'	money	6. 1	*valuable time is spent discussing*
$time_6$	'time as a resource'	resource	12. 5	*that gave him time to initiate a plan*
$time_7$	'time as a commodity'	commodity	1. 0	*hoped to buy some time for you*
$time_8$	'time as a person'	person	1. 0	*time waits for no man*

For convenience, I have provided the shortened version of the eight senses for the following discussion in this chapter, e.g. 'clock' as the short version of the sense 'actual time on a clock' ($time_1$ in Table 4. 1) and 'point' as the short version for the sense 'particular time point' ($time_2$ in Table 4. 1).

The first sense, $time_1$ ('actual time on a clock' or 'clock'), is generally considered to be the 'intuitive' and more 'basic' sense of *time*, as in the example provided in Table 4. 1 '*What time is it? Three-thirty*'. This sense of *time* is also normally listed as the first or second sense in many dictionaries such as the aforementioned COBUILD Advanced Learner's English dictionary (2005) and the Oxford Advanced Learner's Dictionary (2010). However, somewhat unusually, this 'clock' sense has a very low frequency of 2. 6% in the corpus sample (Table 5. 1). This unexpected finding agrees with Sinclair's (1991: 112) study on the word *back*. He argues that "[t]he commonest meanings of the commonest words are not the meanings supplied by introspection" (Sinclair 1991: 112; also see Barnbrook 2007: 187) because he found that it is much less frequent for *back* to denote the sense of 'the posterior part of the human body' than the adverbial sense of 'towards the original place' as in the expressions *come back* or *go back*. In the case of $time_1$ ('clock'), this 'intuitive' sense turns out to be an infrequent sense associated with the word *time*.

The next two senses, $time_2$ and $time_3$, are regarded as relatively close senses of *time* such that in a few cases it is difficult to distinguish between them (see Section 4.1.2 for further discussion of fuzzy boundaries between senses). $Time_2$ refers to 'a particular time point' (or 'point'), as in the examples *by the time I went to Sheffield University* and *a final decision was made at the time*. $Time_3$ describes 'a period of time' (or 'period'), as in the examples *there was a time when women were really responsible* and *fundamentalism has been an important part of American life for a long time*. In other words, it can be considered that $time_2$ highlights the 'momentary' sense and $time_3$ emphasises the 'durational' aspect of time. Both $time_2$ ('point') and $time_3$ ('period') are frequent senses of *time* observed in the BoE sample, accounting for respectively 30.1% and 21.9% of the concordance lines (see Table 4.1).

$Time_4$ ('occasion') is also a frequent sense of *time*. The analysis using the BoE sample suggests that 24.8% of the concordance lines are associated with this sense, as in the two examples *it wasn't the first time that I found...* and *every time I go to the hairdresser's they threaten not to bleach it* (Table 4.1). In comparison to the previous three senses of *time* which are generally perceived as cognitively 'core' or 'close' to the concept of time, $time_4$ involves the concept of 'occasion' or 'opportunity' and is thus relatively more distinctive.

The other four senses, $time_5$, $time_6$, $time_7$ and $time_8$, are regarded as more metaphorically-associated, being analogous respectively to 'money' (as in the example *valuable time is spent discussing why...*), 'a resource' (*that gave him time to initiate a plan*), 'a commodity' (*to buy some time for you*) and 'a person' (*time waits for no man* and *time stood still*), as shown in Table 4.1. These four metaphorically-associated senses, however, do not appear as frequently as the more 'literal' senses of *time*. They account for only 20.6% of the concordance lines in the BoE sample ($time_5$: 6.1%, $time_6$: 12.5%, $time_7$: 1.0%, $time_8$: 1.0%); by contrast, $time_2$, $time_3$ and $time_4$ account for 76.8% of the concordance lines in the sample. To some extent, this significant difference between more literal senses and metaphorically-associated senses regarding the proportion challenges some of the previous findings from lexicographers, as many of them have argued that in most cases figurative senses are more frequent than literal ones (also see Deignan 2005: 118; Sardinha 2008: 142). It would seem that in the case of *time*, their argument may not be valid.

4.1.2 Fuzzy boundaries between senses

When analysing polysemy or a polysemous word, the boundaries between senses are inevitably fuzzy (see Nerlich *et al.* 2003). Similarly, regarding the multiple senses associated with *time*, it is also observed that there are overlapping areas between some senses. The 'particular time point' sense ($time_2$) and the 'period of time' sense ($time_3$), for instance, cannot always be distinguished from each other as clearly as would be expected. Although most of the frequently occurring language examples of *time* which exhibit $time_2$ or $time_3$ can usually be classified properly based on the difference between these two senses, in a small number of examples it is not easy to determine which of the two usages is exhibited.

One example is the sequence *this time of year* which in different contexts is associated with either the 'point' sense or the 'period' sense, depending mainly on its collocates and the researcher's interpretation. For instance, in example 1 below, it is possible to argue that this sequence exhibits the 'point' sense rather than the 'period' sense because the preposition *at* precedes the sequence *this time of year* and there is the occurrence of *it's time ...* (as in *it's time FIFA halted internationals*). The co-texts of *this time of year* in example 1 below imply that this sequence is more likely to be associated with the 'particular time point' sense. In the remaining three examples, however, it can be argued that the sequence *this time of year* exhibits either of the two senses ('point' or 'period') and the decision as to which is appropriate appears to be more of a matter of subjective interpretation.

1 Simpson reckons it's time FIFA halted internationals around the world at this time of year as players have so many club commitments.

2 Most of us around this time of year are thinking about our Christmas gift list, and wondering what to buy family and friends.

3 The tiny sovereign state the size of Oxfordshire, squeezed between France, Germany and Belgium, is a cosy place, and quiet this time of year.

4 In the interest of safety, Latigo scrapped a plan to have the cattle ford the Yellowstone River, which is high for this time of year.

Similarly, the two noun phrases, *question time* and *lunch time*, can be regarded as examples of either the 'point' usage or the 'period' usage in different contexts. As shown in the following concordances, the two phrases seem to be associated with the 'point' sense in examples 5 and 6 whilst in examples 7 and 8 it is more reasonable to argue that they exhibit the 'period' sense because they are preceded by the preposition *during*.

5 there was little doubt that British Prime Minister John Major would have to discuss the case at today's parliamentary **question time**.

6 It's 12 o'clock. It's **lunch time**; so let's eat.

7 The prime minister made his announcement during **question time** at the House of Commons.

8 principal Lee Cheshire used the public address system to call for a moment of silence from his students during **lunch time**.

Even though cases of this kind are relatively rare in the current analysis, the fuzzy boundaries between the multiple senses of a lexical item still remain an issue to be resolved in any study of polysemy (cf. Nerlich *et al.* 2003; Hanks 2013).

Another type of fuzziness in the distinguishing of multiple senses is related to the interpretation of a phraseological unit, more specifically, how the researcher determines the beginning and the end of a phraseological unit. A relevant example is the sequence *spend a long period of time*. It can be difficult to decide whether the complete unit of this sequence is *a long period of time* or rather a variation of the verb phrase *spend time*. It can be argued that the former unit, *a long period of time*, is associated with the 'period' sense ($time_3$) while the latter, *spend time*, relates to the 'money' sense ($time_5$). In the current analysis, the sequence *spend a long period of time* is categorised under $time_5$ ('money') due to the metaphorical association of the entire sequence, yet it might be just as acceptable to state that this sequence exhibits the 'period' sense ($time_3$).

4.2 Polysemy and phraseology: time

Section 4.1.1 has shown the eight major senses associated with the word *time* using the BoE sample. The following sections will discuss these using the whole BoE corpus in relation to the phraseological behaviour of the word *time* in order to illustrate the relation between meaning and phraseology. In Section 4.2.1, I will present an overview of the eight senses and their associated phraseological features. Then in Sections 4.2.2 to 4.2.5, I will discuss the first four senses of *time* (time$_1$, time$_2$, time$_3$ and time$_4$) using the BoE and demonstrate how each sense is related to the phraseological behaviour of *time*. The other four metaphorically-associated senses of *time* are not discussed here because they will be analysed specifically in the metaphor chapter; besides, the discussion of all the eight senses might have become rather repetitive.

4.2.1 Senses of time and its phraseological behaviour

In Table 4.2, the eight senses of *time* are again listed along with their associated phraseological items.

Table 4.2 **The eight main senses of *time* found in the S_{BoE} and the associated phraseological items**

	Sense	Phraseologicalitems	Example
time$_1$	clock	a) frame: *the time is + ? + minutes past/before the hour*	*The time is 19 minutes past the hour; The time is 7 minutes before the hour*
		b) phrase: *what time*	*What time is it?*
time$_2$	point	a) prepositional phrase	*at the time (of); by the time; at that time; by that time*
		b) Patterns: *it* v-link *time to*-inf. *it* v-link *time that*-cl. *it* v-link *time for* n.	*It is time to take a closer look at the; it is time that voters took responsibility for; It was time for a change*
time$_3$	period	a) phrases associated with 'a period of time'	*a (long) period/length of time; (for) a long time; at a time (when)*
		b) co-occur with evaluative adjectives	*good / difficult / wonderful + time*
time$_4$	occasion	a) co-occur with numerals	*first / one / second / third + time; for the first time in my life I've got peace*
		b) co-occur with 'sequence' words	*this / last / next + time; But this time things were different.*
time$_5$	money	verb phrases	*spend / waste / save / make / lose + time; valuable time is spent discussing why ...*
time$_6$	resource	verb phrases	*have / take / give / find + time; that gave him time to initiate a plan*

Table4. 2(continued)

	Sense	Phraseologicalitems	Example
$time_7$	commodity	verb phrases	*buy time*; *time is running out*; ... *hoped to buy some time for you*
$time_8$	person	other phrases	*Time waits for no man*; *Saturday, time stood still*

As can be seen, in each sense *time* seems to be associated with particular phrases or patterns. For instance, *time* with the 'clock' sense ($time_1$) tends to occur in the frame '*the time is* + ? + *minutes past/before the hour*' and the phrase *what time*; *time* with the 'point' sense ($time_2$) appears frequently in prepositional phrases, e.g. *at the time* and *by the time*, and patterns, e.g. '*it* v-link *time to*-inf.' and '*it* v-link *time that*-cl.'.

Additionally, the phraseological features exhibited by *time* in one sense are not likely to overlap with those exhibited by this word in another sense. For example, the phraseological items associated with the first four senses of *time* in the BoE sample all appear to be different from each other. Even though $time_5$ ('money'), $time_6$ ('resource') and $time_7$ ('commodity') are exhibited mainly by verb phrases, each sense is related to a particular group of verb phrases. The verbs associated with $time_5$ ('money') are *spend*, *waste*, *save*, *make* and *lose*; the verbs associated with $time_6$ ('resource') are *have*, *take*, *give* and *find*; and the verb phrases for $time_7$ ('commodity') tend to be *buy time* and *time is running out* (see Chapter 5 for a detailed analysis of these metaphorical senses).

This association between different senses of *time* and its phraseological behaviour at the macro level confirms the inseparable relation between meaning and form – a theme which has been repeatedly suggested and substantiated by corpus linguists (see Sinclair 1991; Hunston and Francis 2000). At the micro level, this association coincides with Moon's (1987) point that context has a disambiguating role in meaning. More specifically, the phraseological features of *time* disambiguate its senses, that is, different senses of *time* are associated with unique phraseological patterns. This finding is consistent with Sinclair (1991: 53-65) who, based on a small scale study, shows that each meaning or sense of a word can be associated with a distinctive patterning of that word. The same point has also been articulated by Hoey (2005) in his priming theory for a polysemous word. He contends that the collocational and colligational features of a lexical item (which are "primed" for most language users through our experience or encounters with this lexical item) will systematically differentiate its senses or uses (Hoey 2005: 81–108). The results from the current investigation of *time* further support the important role of context in the disambiguation of meaning. It is shown that various aspects of the phraseological behaviour of a polysemous word, e.g. collocational, colligational and patterning features, can contribute to determining and disambiguating the multiple senses of this word (cf. Deignan 2005; Mahlberg 2005; Hanks 2013).

4.2.2 $Time_1$: 'actual time on a clock' and phraseological features of time

Among the four senses to be discussed, $time_1$ ('clock') is the least frequent sense in the BoE sample. Nonetheless, its association with the phraseological behaviour of the word *time* is considered to be rather strong, as has been shown in Table 4.2 above. In Table 4.3, the phraseological features associated with $time_1$ ('clock') are again presented in more detail using the whole BoE corpus. Based on the data in this table, it can be reasonably argued that *time* with this 'clock' sense occurs in unique syntagmatic structures.

Table 4.3 shows that the most frequent language form of *time* with the 'clock' sense is the frame: '*the time is + ? + minutes before/past the hour*'. It was found that this frame occurs largely in the texts which date from the 1990s and that these texts originate mainly from the npr/US subcorpus (National Public Radio, USA). In other words, this frame occurs mainly in radio broadcasts from the 1990s. One explanation for this is that people listening to the radio at that time would have appreciated constant reminders of the time, especially if they were driving their cars during the morning commute. This speculation is partially supported by the co-texts of '*the time is + ? + minutes before/past the hour*', as this frame is frequently followed by the sequences like *this is Morning Edition* or *Good morning* which both indicate that this frame was usually being used in the morning (see examples 9 and 10 below).

What is also interesting about the usage of this frame is that it often appears at the junction between different programmes in the radio scripts. As can be seen from both example 9 and example 10, '*the time is + ? + minutes before/past the hour*' is used between two separate programmes, as though to act as the mark of the starting of a radio programme or another piece of news.

Table 4.3 Phraseological items associated with $time_1$ ('clock')

Phraseologicalitems	Freq	Freq per mil.	Example
1) frame: *the time is + ? + minutes past/before the hour.*	2,536	5.64	*The time is 21 minutes past the hour. The time is now 19 minutes past the hour. The time is seven minutes before the hour.*
2) phrase: *what time*	1,862	4.14	*What time is it? What time are we going sailing? I do not know what time it was when I woke up.*
3) pattern: <place> +*time*	522	1.15	*Brisbane time* (Freq: 148), *New York time* (100), *London time* (74), *British time* (71), *Pacific time* (56), *Moscow time* (37), *Washington time* (36),
4) collocation: tell + *time*	147	0.33	*I didn't learn how to tell time until the sixth grade. Carl May was surprised that the lad could tell the time from a handed watch.*

9 ... the House Energy and Commerce Committee chaired by John Dingell, a powerful opponent of the bill, also from Michigan. I'm Elizabeth Arnold at the Capitol. Renee Motagne, host: **The time is 21 minutes before the hour**. This is Morning Edition, I'm Renee Motagne. Jury selection enters its second day today in the trial of a Cincinnati art museum and its director. The Cincinnati Contemporary ...

10 ... Hussein may find it impossible to stand at the eye of the storm without seeking shelter from one side or the other. InAmman, Jordan, I'm Alan Tomlinson reporting. Edwards: **The time is 29 minutes past the hour**. Bob Edwards, host: Good morning, I'm Bob Edwards. Running for re-election next month, the mayor of Rancho Cucamonga, California, Dennis Stout is facing a challenge from a ...

The second type of syntagmatic structure associated with $time_1$ contains the phrase *what time*, as in the examples *what time is it* and *what time are we going sailing* (see Table 4.3). This phrase is also one of the commonest sequences deemed to be necessary if not indispensable in most English language teaching classrooms. The number of occurrences of this phrase in the pedagogic corpus (CEC), for instance, is nearly three times as many as those in the BoE (11.6 times per million in the CEC vs. 4.1 times per million in the BoE). Considering this phrase is not among the most frequent phraseological items, nor is $time_1$ the most frequent sense of *time*, the considerable attention paid to it in English course-books is a questionable practice. Further discussion of the criteria for selecting lexical items in pedagogic materials will be provided in the subsequent chapters.

The remaining two phraseological items associated with $time_1$ (as listed in Table 4.3) are less frequent than the above-mentioned items. The third phraseological item is a pattern '<place> + *time*' which involves combinations that include a 'place' noun (or occasionally adjective) and *time*. Frequent words which co-occur with *time* in this pattern are *Brisbane*, *New York*, *London* and *British*. The last phraseological item noted in Table 4.3 is a verb phrase: tell (*the*) *time*. This item is also one of the few verb phrases which are associated with the four more 'literal' senses of *time* ($time_1$ to $time_4$), as the majority of the verb phrases (e.g. *spend time*, *waste time*, and *have time*) appear to exhibit more metaphorically-associated senses ($time_5$ to $time_8$).

The association between $time_1$ ('clock') and these unique phraseological features can also be explained from a cognitive perspective. As has been discussed in Section 4.1.1, $time_1$ relates to a more concrete aspect of time and can thus be perceived to some extent as more physically existent, for example, to be 'seen', 'told' or 'measured'. As a consequence, the structures of *time* with the 'clock' sense may involve this more concrete nature. For instance, it explains the phenomena that the actual time can be viewed and reported, as in the first type of structure: *the time is...*; that time can be measured and asked about, as in the second type: *what time...*; and that time can be described, as in the third type: *tell* (*the*) *time* and the fourth: *New York time* and *London time*.

4.2.3 $Time_2$: 'a particular time point' and phraseological features of time

As shown in Table 4.2, time with the 'particular time point' sense occurs mainly in prepositional phrases and patterns in the BoE sample (S_{BoE_time}). These phraseological items are again presented in Table 4.4 with the frequency data from the whole BoE corpus. It can be seen that these phrases and patterns which appear frequently in the corpus sample also occur frequently in the whole corpus.

It can be seen from Table 4.4 that the prepositional phrases with the 'point' usage include primarily *at the time* (*or at the time of/when*), *by the time*, *at that time*, *at any* (*other*) *time and by that time.* These prepositional phrases also share similar syntagmatic features which are related to the 'point' sense. Firstly, many of them contain determiners like the and that which are largely associated with a specific reference. Secondly, they tend to involve prepositions like at or by which are more likely to be associated with the 'point' sense than the 'period' sense ($time_3$).

The four mainlanguage patterns associated with $time_2$ ('point') in the BoE are: 'it *v-link* time to-*inf.*', 'it *v-link* time that-*cl.*', 'it *v-link* time for *n.* to-*inf.*' *and* 'it *v-link* time for *n.*', as shown in Table 4.4. 'v-link' in these patterns refers mainly to link verbs like is, was and combinations of modal verbs and be such as may be and can be. Among the four patterns, the first one occurs most frequently in the BoE (at least three times more than the other patterns with $time_2$). Examples for these patterns are also given in Table 4.4. It can be seen that these four patterns share the sense of 'particular time point'. In addition, it seems that the use of these language patterns in context would imply a similar pragmatic or discourse function: calling for immediate action at that time moment, e.g. it is time to take a closer look or it was time for a change.

Table 4.4 The phraseological items associated with $time_2$ ('point')

Phraseological items	Freq	Freq per mil.	Example
1) prepositional phrases			
at the time (*of/when*)	32,862	73.03	*... a final decision was made at the time*; *... he was asleep at the time of the attack...*
by the time	15,470	34.38	*And by the time he was 29, Nash was a tenured professor at MIT...*
at that time	7,807	17.35	*At that time I was doing the tutorials in abnormal psychology at the clinic...*
at any (*other*) *time*	6,580	14.62	*The bank may at any time in the future obtain consumer reports to...*
by that time	1,424	3.16	*... but by that time the question was of only academic interest*
2) patterns with *time*			

Table4. 4(continued)

Phraseological items	Freq	Freq per mil.	Example
it v-link *time to*-inf.	3,768	8. 37	*It is time to take a closer look at the ...*;
it v-link *time that*-cl.	1,131	2. 51	*it is time that voters took responsibility for ...*
it v-link *time for* n. *to*-inf.	1,038	2. 31	*It is time for researchers to get to know ...*
it v-link *time for* n.	941	2. 09	*It was time for a change*

4. 2. 4 Time$_3$: 'a period of time' and phraseological features of time

The results similarly show that time$_3$ ('period') is related to unique phraseological features of *time*. As can be seen from Table 4. 5, the first group of phraseological items associated with this sense mainly contains the phrases or combinations which appear to highlight the length of 'time', e.g. *at a time* (*when/of*), *for a long time*, *for some time*, *a long/short period of time* and *a short length of time*.

The second group of phraseological items associated with time$_3$ ('period') mainly involve the pattern 'ADJ *time*' (see Table 4. 5), and many of the adjectives which occur in the pattern seem to share an evaluative sense regarding the 'period of time', e.g. *good*, *hard*, *best*, *difficult*, *great* and *tough*. The association between the pattern 'ADJ *time*' and time$_3$ ('period') may be expected, because the concept of 'a period of time', apart from being discussed in terms of length (e.g. the group of phrases discussed above), can be evaluated or judged by human subjects. Some of these sequences which fit the pattern 'ADJ *time*' also tend to occur in the extended pattern 'have *a/an* ADJ *time*', such as *have a good time* and *have a great time*.

Table 4. 5 **The phraseological items associated with time$_3$ ('period') in the BoE**

Phraseological items	Freq	Freq per mil.	Example
1) phrases which associate with 'a period of time'			
at a time (*when/of*)	14,145	31. 43	*The clashes take place at a time when the government is trying to decide...*
for a long time	7,179	15. 95	*fundamentalism has been an important part of American life for a long time.*

Table4. 5(continued)

Phraseological items	Freq	Freq per mil.	Example
for some time	7,065	15. 70	*It has been known for some time that children also tend to learn more from...*
a long/short period of time	4,644	10. 32	*Researchers have analyzed data from a long period of time to show the...*
for a time	2,687	5. 97	*We set off in a southerly direction and for a time made good progress.*
(*long/short*) *length of time*	1,942	4. 32	... *societies have had full democracy for only a surprisingly short length of time.*
2) $\mathrm{ADJ}_{(\mathrm{evaluative})}$ + *time*			
(have *a*) *good time*	4,549	10. 11	... *and we all laughed and had a good time*;
(have *a*) *hard time*	1,883	4. 18	*People have a hard time understanding how important...*
(*the*) *best time*	1,320	2. 93	*A boy described the best time of his week as listening to a Led Zeppelin album...*
(have *a*) *difficult time*	1,174	2. 61	*American parties have had a difficult time fulfilling their democratic promise*
(have *a*) *great time*	1,099	2. 44	*It's a great meal and a great time*
(have *a*) *tough time*	614	1. 36	*the programme might have a tough time convincing the public that...*
(*a*) *bad time*	589	1. 31	... *this happens at a very bad time of the year*
(have *a*) *wonderful time*	399	0. 89	*She looked absolutely stunning and was clearly having a wonderful time*

4. 2. 5 Time$_4$: 'occasion' and phraseological features of time

For time$_4$ ('occasion'), the phraseological items which are associated with this sense are mainly adverbial phrases such as *for the first time*, *this time*, *every time* and *the last time*, as can be seen from Table 4. 6 below.

Among this group of phrases, it seems that the left collocates of *time* (or −1 collocates of *time*) are determiners which are associated strongly with a sense of 'countability' which could be a characteristic of the 'occasion' usage. For instance, many of these collocates of *time* are numerals: *first*, *second*, *one*, *third* and *fourth* (Table 4. 6). The remaining collocates, *this*, *last* and *next*, are associated with the concept of 'sequence' which may similarly indicate that an occasion or opportunity is 'countable'.

Table 4. 6 The phraseological items associated with time$_4$ ('occasion') in the BoE

Phraseological items	Freq	Freq per mil.	Example
(*for*) *the first time*	49,651	110. 34	*I remember seeing it for the first time in the Soviet Union, going around and ...*
this time	37,985	84. 41	*But this time chaos did not last long, for traditions of centralized rule were too...*
every time	10,739	23. 86	*Every time I go to the hairdresser's they threaten not to bleach it because...*
(*the*) *last time*	6,229	13. 84	*The last time I saw him was when I was six and I had to buy his book, stand in a line...*
(*the*) *next time*	5,180	11. 51	*This provides a useful guide for how much to purchase the next time she goes shopping*
each time	4,308	9. 57	*You rinse away skin cells by the hundreds each time you wash your hands*
(*for*) *the second time*	3,854	8. 56	*... cargo ship has been stopped and is being boarded for the second time in two days*
(*at*) *one time*	3,257	7. 24	*I remember one time Jackie was photographed at a party wearing...*
(*for*) *the third time*	2,431	5. 40	*Just last month it was honored for the third time in five years – with the prestigious...*
(*for*) *the fourth time*	753	1. 67	*... launch for the fourth time since May*

4. 3 Polysemy and phraseology: phrases

Using the example*time*, Section 4. 2 has illustrated that different senses of a polysemous word can be associated with unique phraseological features. This section further explores this relation between polysemy and phraseology with two phrases: *at the same time* and *big time*. It will be suggested that different senses of a phrase can also be closely connected with its phraseological or patterning features.

4.3.1 'at the same time'

The analysis of the phrase*at the same time* shows that it can exhibit multiple senses. In different contexts or with different co-texts, it can convey the sense of 'parallel time' (henceforth *at the same time*$_1$), 'in addition' (*at the same time*$_2$) and 'contrast' (*at the same time*$_3$) (cf. Nesi and Basturkmen 2009: 35; Walker 2014). More importantly, each use is associated with particular phraseological or patterning features of this phrase.

To illustrate the usage of *at the same time*, a random sample of 100 concordance lines are chosen from the BoE. The results show that in 33 instances, this phrase exhibits the sense of 'parallel time', i.e. when two events happen in parallel to each other. Figure 4.1 presents 15 concordance lines selected from the 33 instances.

11 different battery types can be charged **at the same time**. Each bank has its
12 my brothers went through the same thing **at the same time**, it helped us both
13 It would be like trying to drive two cars **at the same time**." He is happy to
14 us all to lead a routine life, go to bed **at the same time**, that sort of thing
15 chips together they will pick up a chip **at the same time**, and when out shop
16 Bruce raced towards it. They both arrived **at the same time**, and as they lunged
17 is taken by all kids at some point, even **at the same time**. Well, same day, not
18 for food; she simply ate the same food **at the same time** every day. So too
19 the first golfer to hold all four majors **at the same time**. Rosaforte records
20 do you think you can have more than one idea **at the same time**? Do you know what I
21 can happen when all 11 players play well **at the same time**," Thompson said
22 were they entertained under the same roof **at the same time**. As Motography de-
23 they both happened to be in the same place **at the same time** and liked each other
24 declaration from EC governments made **at the same time** as Article called for
25 down. The servants get their breakfast **at the same time** as we do, as we

Figure 4.1 Fifteen concordance lines of *at the same time*$_1$ selected from the BoE

As can be seen from the examples in Figure4.1, *at the same time* with this sense occurs more often at the end of a clause or utterance (see lines 11 to 22). The results also show that this phrase tends to follow verb phrases, e.g. *go through the same thing at the same time* in line 12, *drive two cars at the same time* in line 13 and *pick up a chip at the same time* in line 15. This tendency for *at the same time* to co-occur with verb phrases may be expected because the sense of 'parallel time' is associated with simultaneous occurrence of multiple events, i.e. actions. Thus the co-occurrence of this phrase with verb phrases could be considered to be the characteristic collocational behaviour of *at the same time*$_1$ (see Walker 2011: 298). In a few cases, the phrase *at the same time* also seems to co-occur with adverbial clauses of time which are conducted by conjunctions like *as*, *while* or *when* (especially *as*), e.g. lines 24-25.

To further explore the use of *at the same time*$_1$, the structure 'VP + *at the same time*' was searched using the whole BoE corpus. Verbs or verb phrases which precede *at the same time* within the span of 3 are shown in Table 4.7 below. Those verb phrases which occur outside this span are not focused on, taking account of the feasibility of the analysis.

It is interesting to note that the verbs or verb phrases in Table 4.7 seem to be more likely to be associated with actions or events (e.g. *do things*, *get up*, *set up* and *come out*) than other verbs which are associated with 'a state' (e.g. *is*, *are* and *have*) or 'cognition' (e.g. *think*, *understand* and *remember*). In other words, the verb phrases which co-occur with *at the same time*$_1$ are largely 'dynamic' rather than 'stative' (see Miller 2002: 144 and Declerck 2006: 68 for the definition of "dynamic verbs" and "stative verbs").

Table 4.7 **The pattern 'VP *at the same time*' in the BoE**

Verb /Verb phrase + *at the same time*		Freq	Freq per mil.	t-score
(do *them*) *all*	*at the same time*	308	0.68	13.91
(get/set/wake) *up*		119	0.26	5.64
(carry/come) *out*		95	0.21	4.39
(go/be) *on*		90	0.20	9.42
take *place*		88	0.20	8.14
do *both*		81	0.18	7.39
come		67	0.15	4.57
do *things*		62	0.14	6.45
happen		57	0.13	4.93
occur		54	0.12	4.41
(kick/go/take) *off*		47	0.10	3.68
be *taken*		44	0.10	5.55
be *made*		43	0.10	3.36
work		39	0.09	5.02

In another 35 instances in the 100-line sample from the BoE, this phrase isrelated to the usage of 'in addition' (*at the same time*$_2$). The analysis of these instances suggests that the contexts have less or little relation to 'time' or 'the sequence of occurred events'. Instead, the phrase appears to be associated more with a logical or argumentative relation. As can be seen from the following three examples, the phrase *at the same time* serves more as a discourse marker, similar to 'also' or 'furthermore'.

26 "This is an exceptional editorial product that meets the specific needs of one of the fastest growing business segments in the country, and **at the same time** is practical and inexpensive."

27 Moncur pushed the free-kick to Cottee, who held the ball long enough to give it back to him and **at the same time** take Dixon out of the picture.

28 First, they should show you what the software is capable of, using all of its bells and whistles. **At the same time** , they must make the process exciting–a rare talent.

It would appear that if the phrase *at the same time* is replaced with the word *also* or *in addition*, the meaning of these examples remains similar. This feature is particularly clear in example 28 where *at the same time* is grammatically parallel to the word "first" in the beginning of the text. It can be argued that the sentence with *at the same time* (*making the process exciting*) is regarded as an additional or second condition to what is described in the preceding text (*showing the software*).

In theremaining 32 instances in the 100-line sample, this phrase is associated with the 'contrast' use (*at the same time*$_3$), as shown in the following five examples (lines 29-33).

29 I don't fear death, illness or being maimed. **At the same time** I rather enjoy life and being fit and healthy.

30 the concept of chunk is a rather technical, and**at the same time** imprecise, term (Anderson, 1980).

31 This is a film which brings tears to your eyes <u>but</u> **at the same time** you are full of hope.

32 We increase our investment in businesses and markets with high growth potential. <u>But</u> **at the same time** , we don't hesitate to exit from areas that we view as unattractive.

33 So villagers seeking a stamp, a teabag or a packet of pills are increasingly forced out on to the road to locate them further afield. Yet, at the same time, public transport in the countryside is also declining.

It can be observed from these instances that *at the same time* mainly connects two clauses or sentences which express opposite or very different meanings, e.g. *don't fear death* and *rather enjoy life* in example 29, and *rather technical* and *imprecise* in example 30. In some of these examples (examples 31, 32 and 33), *at the same time* also co-occurs with words such as *but* and *yet* which further reflect this opposite meaning.

When the collocational behaviour of *at the same time*$_3$ is analysed using the whole BoE corpus, the above-mentioned feature turns out to be relatively frequent. As shown in Table 4.8, the four words, *but*, *yet*, *however* and *though*, can co-occur adjacently with *at the same time*. Among these collocates, *but* occurs most frequently with this phrase. The co-occurrence of *at the same time*$_3$ with words such as *but*, *yet*, *however* and *though* is also discussed under the term "lexical congruency" (Walker 2014), where the collocates or co-texts of a lexical item may reflect or "duplicate" the meaning of this item.

Table 4.8 The co-occurrence of *at the same time*$_3$ with the words with the contrastive meanings in the BoE

-1 collocate	Node	+1 collocate	Freq	Freq per mil.	t-score
but	*at the same time*	\	2,241	4.98	44.79
yet		\	382	0.85	19.08
however		\	33	0.07	3.86
\	*at the same time*	*however*	216	0.48	13.96
\		*though*	98	0.22	8.94

Therefore, the analysis of the phrase *at the same time* suggests that the sense or use of this phrase is associated with its phraseological behaviour. The results show that *at the same time*$_1$ ('parallel time') is used more or less as a time adverbial phrase which often follows verbs or verb phrases (e.g. *do things*, *get up* and *come out*). The other two uses, *at the same time*$_2$ ('in addition') and *at the same time*$_3$ ('contrast'), are related more to discourse use, and *at the same time*$_3$ also tends to co-occur with words such as *but*, *yet*, *however* and *though*.

4.3.2 'big time'

The analysis of thefrequent phrase *big time* (2,563 occurrences in the BoE) also suggests that it can exhibit multiple uses. The first use of this phrase involves sequences such as 'hit *the big time*' and 'make *the big time*' (1,178 occurrences in total in the BoE). These two sequences are also the most frequent phraseological items associated with *big time*. Examples of these two sequences are shown below.

34 by Frank Sinatra. Clooney, who **hit the big time** in the telly hospital drama ER
35 Hollywood, as she struggles to **hit the big time**. Amanda Davies, from Cardi
36 TheGlasgow four-piece **hit the big time** when their album The Man Who
37 sister Kim. Mick has never **hit the big time** as a musician and runs a CD
38 The 28-year-old, who first **hit the big time** when she was runner-up in the
39 up. Convinced the band could **make the big time**, he persuaded the lads how
40 West alight and she hopes to **make the big time** in the world of fashion and
41 mind Kevin Keegan would never **make the big time** in football. With two years to
42 the Australian players would **make the big time**. 'When I went there they were
43 along with the ambition to **make the big time** in popular music. Both drew

As can be seen, the two phraseological items *hit the big time* and *make the big time* in these lines involve the sense of 'becoming successful' or 'reaching the top or highest level of a certain field'. Based on the contexts of these two items (lines 34 to 43), it seems that the field most often related to these two sequences is the entertainment industry, e.g. film industry (lines 34 and 35), music business (lines 36, 37, 39 and 43) and sports (line 41).

The second use of*big time* involves the pattern '*a big time* N' (169 occurrences in the BoE). The nouns which follow *a big time* are usually words which refer to a person, e.g. *winner*, *player* and *rock star*, as shown in the following examples (lines 44 to 47). In these cases, '*a big time* N' is normally associated with the sense that the person being talked about in the context is rather famous.

44 countryman Jose Coceros became **a big-time** winner in April when he beat
45 fightback from cancer by becoming **a big-time** winner again. American golfer
46 He has proved over the years he is **a big time** player who rises to the big
47 he's really proven himself to be **a big-time** Hollywood star and director.

In a few concordance lines, the nouns which follow*a big time* can also be related to a negative sense such as *gangster*, *drug dealer* and *crime* (see lines 48 to 50), but cases of this feature are somewhat rare as there are only 9 instances in the BoE which include the use of negative nouns in the pattern '*a big time* N'. However, this rare feature is discussed here because it will be contrasted with the analysis of the use of *big time* in the pedagogic corpus.

48	crime one time doesn't mean you're	a big-time	gangster	or you're a child-
49	Police who suspected Ashley of being	a big-time	drug dealer	expected to find a
50	He was a petty thief roped into	a big-time	crime	. I don't believe an

The third use of*big time* is associated with the pattern 'VP *big time*' (112 occurrences in the BoE). In other words, this use is often exhibited when the phrase *big time* is used as an adverbial phrase, as shown in lines 51 to 58. It was also found that this pattern seems to occur frequently at the end of a clause or an utterance.

51	knew that he was going to make it	big-time.	Faith. His second season was
52	We are all hoping he will make it	big-time.	Perhaps Kildare will soon
53	that they know they've really blown it	big time.	Hansen: So when you accept
54	part of the Honda family but blew it	big time,	" a senior Honda executive told
55	means if I'm bad, I'll have blown it	big-time.	" Still, on balance, I reckon
56	the beginning of the end. He lost it	big time.	The more crack he took the
57	United Nations to tell me I messed up	big-time.	What is done is done but I
58	and we've really, really screwed up	big time.	Sorry, we'll try and do better

As can be seen from these examples, the use of *big time* serves to exaggerate the effect of the actions in the context, e.g. *make it big time*, *blow it big time* or *mess up big time*, similar to words like 'extremely' or 'very much'. Additionally, the verb phrases which precede *big time* in these cases appear to be mainly negative, e.g. *blew it*, *lost it*, *messed up* and *screwed up*.

The above discussion, therefore, again confirms the relation between meaning and phraseology. More importantly, the above results suggest that the disambiguating role of phraseology in meaning not only applies to a polysemous word, but also a 'polysemous' phrase.

4.4 Conclusion

In this chapter, I have discussed the relation between polysemy and phraseology using the examples of*time* and two phrases *at the same time* and *big time*. The results show that each sense or usage exhibited by a polysemous word or phrase is associated with unique phraseological features of this word or phrase. For instance, the uses of *at the same time* are differentiated by its phraseological behaviour (Section 4.3.1). Thus it is concluded that phraseology plays an important role in the phenomenon of polysemy. More specifically, it can be argued that the phraseological features or behaviour of a lexical item tend to disambiguate the multiple senses/uses associated with this item, and this further supports the point made by previous studies that context has a disambiguating role in meaning (see Moon 1987; Sinclair 1991; Deignan 2005; Hoey 2005; Hanks 2013).

Chapter 5 Metaphor and phraseology

This chapter further explores the role of phraseology in the construction of meaning in discourse (Research Question 1) by focusing on the relation between phraseology and metaphor (as well as that between phraseology and metonymy). It is organised into three parts. In Section 5.1, I will present the conceptual metaphors (or metaphorical mappings) associated with TIME which have often been listed in previous studies. Then in Sections 5.2 to 5.4, these conceptual metaphors, e.g. TIME IS MONEY and TIME IS MOTION, will be analysed using the BoE data in terms of their associated linguistic metaphors. The relation between the use of these linguistic metaphors and the phraseological behaviour of *time* will be explored. More complex phraseological features related to the linguistic metaphors of *time* will also be shown in order to illustrate how the patterning feature of language is equally important to the study of metaphor. In Section 5.5, I will discuss the use of several multi-word sequences, e.g. *the girl thing* and *the money thing*, and suggest that there is also a connection between metonymy and phraseology.

5.1 Conceptual metaphors associated with TIME

Many previous studies (e.g. Lakoff and Johnson1980a, 2003; Lakoff 1993; Gibbs 2008; Kövecses 2010) have suggested that 'time' as an abstract concept is usually 'talked about' in terms of more concrete concepts. In other words, the concept of 'time' is very likely to be associated with a metaphorical use. This section thus discusses the conceptual metaphors associated with TIME which have often been listed in previous studies. These metaphors will be investigated in the subsequent sections of this chapter to explore the relationship between metaphor and phraseology.

The conceptual metaphor associated with TIME which has been discussed most frequently in previous studies is probably TIME IS MONEY (cf. Lakoff and Johnson 1980a, 1980b, 2003; Achard and Niemeyer 2004; Steen 2007; Semino 2008; Kövecses 2010). This metaphor has often been used as an example to illustrate the existence of conceptual metaphors and the systematicity of metaphors in our language. It was first introduced by Lakoff and Johnson (1980a/2003: 7-8) who provided many linguistic examples (e.g. *you're wasting your time* and *how do you spend your time these days*) to show that the concept of 'time' can be associated with that of 'money'. They explained the connection between 'time' and 'money' from the cultural perspective. For example, they claimed that "work is typically associated with the time it takes" and since "time is precisely quantified, it has become customary to pay people by the hour, week, or year" (Lakoff and Johnson 1980a/2003: 8). The linguistic examples provided by Lakoff and Johnson (1980a/2003) are presented in Table 5. 1.

There are several reasons why this study uses examples from Lakoff and Johnson to introduce the metaphor TIME IS MONEY. One major reason lies in their relatively comprehensive list of language examples which is more detailed than many other cognitive studies (cf. Lakoff 1993; Kövecses 2010). Secondly, even though their studies were published many years ago, they are considered as amongst the seminal works on conceptual metaphor

Table 5. 1 The conceptual metaphor TIME IS MONEY and its associated linguistic metaphors of *time* discussed by Lakoff and Johnson (1980a/2003: 7-8)

Conceptual Metaphor	TIME IS MONEY
Linguistic Metaphor	I don't *have the time* to give you.
	I don't *have enough time* to spare for that.
	Do you *have much time* left?
	How do you *spend your time* these days?
	You're *wasting my time*.
	I' ve *invested a* lot *of time* in her.
	You're *running out of time*.
	You need to *budget your time*.
	You don't *use your time* profitably.
	He's living on *borrowed time*.
	I *lost a lot of time* when I got sick.
	Put aside some time for ping pong.

and their examplesof the metaphor TIME IS MONEY are still frequently cited among researchers who investigate metaphor (cf. Haser 2005; Knowles and Moon 2006; Gibbs 2008; Kövecses 2010). The third reason for presenting Lakoff and Johnson's examples here is to provide the opportunity to compare the results from a well-established metaphor analysis with the results from the corpus-based analysis (see Section 5.2). The comparison will reveal whether a more empirical approach generates more valid or comprehensive research results (cf. Deignan 2005, 2008a, 2008b).

In Lakoff and Johnson's (1980a/2003) study of the metaphor TIME IS MONEY, they also mention two other related conceptual metaphors: TIME IS A RESOURCE (e.g. the linguistic metaphor *I don't have the time to give you* in Table 5.1) and TIME IS A COMMODITY (e.g. the linguistic metaphor *you're running out of time* in Table 5.1). According to Lakoff and Johnson, the close relation between these three metaphors is the result of the interconnection between the concepts of 'money', 'resource' and 'commodity' in our society: "money is a limited resource and limited resources are valuable commodities" (2003: 9). For the sake of completeness, this study will explore the common metaphor TIME IS MONEY as well as its two related metaphors (see Section 5.2).

Another metaphor of TIME that is often cited is TIME IS MOTION (or TIME IS A MOVING OBJECT) which reflects the connection between 'time' with its movement (see Lakoff and Johnson 1980b, 1999; Lakoff 1993; Kövecses 2010; Boroditsky 2011). For instance, the following examples of *time* in Table 5.2 are often provided in previous studies (e.g. Lakoff and Johnson 1980b: 468; Lakoff 1993: 217; Kövecses 2010: 38). To some extent, they illustrate how the concept of 'time' is perceived in our daily life in relation to movement, more specifically, how the use of *time* in our language can be grounded in our understandings of motion through space (cf. Boroditsky 2011 for the factor of culture as an influence on the use of this metaphor).

Table5.2The conceptual metaphor TIME IS MOTION and its associated linguistic metaphors of *time* discussed in previous studies (e.g. Lakoff and Johnson 1980b: 468; Lakoff 1993: 217; Kövecses 2010: 38)

Table 5.2 The conceptual metaphor TIME IS MOTION and its associated linguistic metorphors of time discussed in previous studies

Conceptual Metaphor	TIME IS MOTION
Linguistic Metaphor	The *time will come* when...
	The *time has* long since *gone* when...
	The *time* for action *has arrived.*
	The *time has passed* when...
	Time flies.
	Time is flying by.
	Time goes by fast.

Lakoff and Johnson (1980b: 468) have suggested that time is often perceived as a moving object where either it is the future moving toward us, e.g. *the time will come* in Table 5.2, or it is us who are facing toward the future, e.g. *let's meet the future head-on* (Lakoff and Johnson 1980b: 469). This suggestion is also consistent with Kövecses (2010) which proposes that two special cases exist for the metaphor TIME IS MOTION: a) TIME as objects (future in particular) moving with respect to the observer; and b) TIME as fixed locations and the observer is moving with respect to TIME (ibid.: 37-38; also cf. Evans 2003: 57). These two movements or images of movements are illustrated in Figures 5.1 and 5.2.

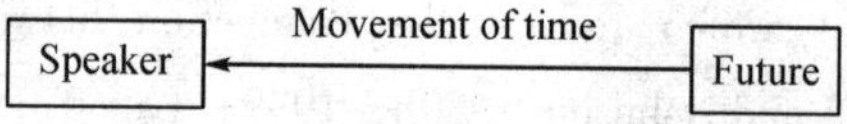

Figure 5.1 The conceptual image of 'future or time is moving toward us' reflected in the examples *the time will come when...* and *the time for action has arrived* in Lakoff and Johnson's (1980b) study

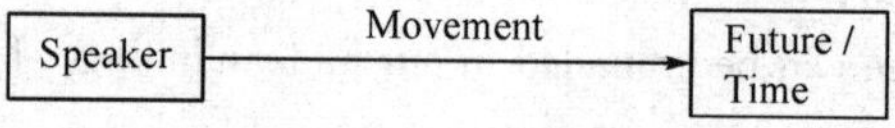

Figure 5.2 The conceptual image of 'us moving toward the future' reflected in the example *let's meet the future head-on* in Lakoff and Johnson's (1980b) study

Apart from the above-mentioned metaphors of TIME which have frequently been discussed in the previous literature, some studies have also shown that 'time' can be conceptualised in terms of other concrete concepts. For instance, Pérez Hernández

(2001) has proposed a model that includes four generic metaphors of TIME: TIME IS SPACE, TIME IS AN OBJECT, TIME IS A CONTAINER and TIME IS A FORCE, with each generic metaphor of TIME comprising several subtypes of metaphors (see Table 5.3).

As can be seen from Table 5.3, the two common conceptual metaphors of TIME, TIME IS MONEY and TIME IS MOTION, are only two subtypes of the high-level metaphor TIME IS AN OBJECT. The other metaphorical mappings such as TIME IS SPACE (in particular TIME IS A LOCATION) and TIME IS A FORCE can also be realised by linguistic metaphors of the word *time*, e.g. *by the time of the investigation* as an example of TIME IS A LOCATION and *time heals all wounds* as an example of TIME IS A FORCE.

Generally, Pérez Hernández's model of TIME shows that the conceptual mappings of TIME can be systematic, or in other words, the conceptual metaphors of TIME can be organised hierarchically. Additionally, her study reveals that conceptual metaphors can interact with each other or interact with other metaphorical and metonymic structures in order to provide an understanding of the concept of 'time'. However, the limitation of Pérez Hernández's (2001) study is that it is only a small-scale study in that the analysis is mainly based on 200 instances. To some extent, it could be argued that her study (and also Lakoff and Johnson's study) should call for a comparatively large scale investigation of metaphor.

To summarise the metaphors of TIME discussed in this section, the concept of 'time' has often been used metaphorically in terms of 'money', 'motion', 'location' and 'force' (or 'person'). Despite the fact that there are many studies which focus on the conceptualisation of TIME or the building of conceptual models of TIME, the nature of the majority of them appears to be more 'intuitive' than empirical and they seem to be largely based on a small amount of data. Thus it is argued that there is a need to conduct further studies of metaphor using a large corpus of real data.

Table 5.3　**The cluster model of metaphors of TIME adapted from Pérez Hernández** (2001: 68-69)

1. TIME IS SPACE	1.1 TIME IS A LOCATION
	at the time of the investigation
	by the time of the election
	1.2 TIME IS A PATH
	It's been a long day.
	I can't do it any longer.
	1.3 TIME IS AN AREA
	to be on time
	We should look ahead to the future.
2. TIME IS AN OBJECT	2.1 TIME IS A POSSESSION
	2.1.1 TIME IS A RESOURCE
	He had not much time left.
	He's running out of time.
	2.1.2 TIME IS MONEY
	Don't waste your time.
	He spends his spare time fishing.
	2.1.3 TIME IS A COMMODITY
	Buy me some time.
	My time will cost you $300.
	2.2 TIME IS A MOVING OBJECT
	when the time comes
	Time flies away.
3. TIME IS A CONTAINER	3. TIME IS A CONTAINER
	in 1977
	a family in times of difficulty
4. TIME IS A FORCE	4.1 TIME IS A CHANGER
	Time had made her look bad.
	Time will make you forget.
	4.2 TIME IS A HEALER
	Time heals all wounds.
	Time will take away the pain.

5.2 TIME IS MONEY and the phraseological behaviour of time

Lakoff and Johnson (1980a/2003) have provided their own language examples to demonstrate the existence of the metaphor TIME IS MONEY (see Section 5.1); however, their method of illustration has often been criticised because the conclusions they draw are mainly based on the analysis of 'invented' language examples rather than naturally-occurring data (see Knowles and Moon 2006; Deignan 2008a, 2008b; Littlemore 2009; McEnery and Hardie 2012; Li 2014). The following sections will thus use a corpus-based approach to examine the linguistic metaphors of *time* which are associated with the metaphor TIME IS MONEY and the other two related metaphors, TIME IS A RESOURCE and TIME IS A COMMODITY.

5.2.1 Phraseological features associated with TIME IS MONEY

Table 5.4 presents frequently occurring linguistic metaphors of *time* in the BoE which are associated with the metaphor TIME IS MONEY. The corpus searches for linguistic expressions which contain verbs take into account two aspects of the verb-noun collocations, namely the lemma form of these verbs and the varied positions of these verbs when co-occurring with *time*: allowing up to two slots between the verb and *time*, e.g. *spend time*, *spend more time*, and *spend too much time*. This principle also applies to other corpus searches for verb-noun collocations referred to in the following discussions in this chapter.

As can be seen from Table 5.4, those frequently occurring linguistic expressions which are associated with the metaphor TIME IS MONEY can be considered as fixed lexical items or multi-word sequences. In other words, the expressions which realise the metaphor TIME IS MONEY are not isolated individual words but phrases, collocations and patterns.

Table 5.4 The frequently occurring linguistic expressions of time which are associated with the metaphor TIME IS MONEY in the BoE. (The list of patterns for each verb-noun collocation is ranked according to frequency, e.g. '*spend time* v-ing' occurs more frequently than '*spend time with* n.' and the pattern '*spend time with* n.' occurs more frequently than '*spend time on* n.'.)

Linguistic expression			Freq	Freq per mil.	Example
1) verb phrase	*spend time*	v-ing *with* n. *on* n.	12,589	27.98	*spend time talking about this*; *spend time with his family*; *spend time on research*
	waste time	*on* n. *in* n.	3,259	7.24	*waste time on paperwork*; *waste time in a lawsuit*;
	make time	*for* n. *to*-inf.	2,251	5.00	*make time for your family*; *make time to see friends*
	save time	*and* n. *by*v-ing	1,274	2.83	*save time and money*; *save time by doing better*
	lose time		1,218	2.71	*lose time and effort*
2) noun phrase	*a waste of time*		1,460	3.24	*this is a waste of time*

This observation confirms the relation between metaphor and phraseology. As Deignan (2005: 218) argues, "there are relatively few figurative expressions that appear in isolation, and [...] the majority form part of a lexical string". To be more specific, the majority of the phraseological items associated with the metaphor TIME IS MONEY are verb phrases. This finding is also consistent with the results discussed in Section 4.2.1 which show that the phraseological items associated with the 'money' sense ($time_5$) in the BoE sample are mainly verb phrases. Similarly, Littlemore (2009: 45) asserts that "figurative use is often signalled by particular phraseology". The only exception to this particular association between TIME IS MONEY and verb phrases in Table 5.4 is perhaps the noun phrase *a waste of time*. However, it may still be possible to argue that this phrase is a type of grammatical variation of the verb phrase '*waste time on/in* n.' and therefore related to verb phrases.

Compared with the examples provided by Lakoff and Johnson (1980a/2003) as shown in Table 5.1, it can be argued that the list of frequently occurring linguistic metaphors generated with a corpus-based approach (see Table 5.4) may be more comprehensive. The corpus-based method can provide all the linguistic expressions which have been considered with their approach. In addition, it can reveal the syntagmatic or patterning features of these linguistic expressions. For example, *spend time* tends to precede 'v-ing', '*with* n' or '*on* n.'; and *waste time* tends to precede '*on* n.' or '*in* n.'. Lakoff and Johnson's list of linguistic metaphors of *time*, on the other hand, seems to be more of a random collection of language examples (see Section 5.1).

Another advantage in using the corpus-based method to analyse metaphor is that the frequency data of the linguistic expressions (as shown in Table 5.4) also indicate some features which may not be found with the approach used by Lakoff and Johnson. For instance, the current analysis shows that the verb phrase '*spend time* v-ing / *with* n. / *on* n.' is the most frequent expression associated with the metaphor TIME IS MONEY. It occurs at least four times more frequently in the BoE than the other expressions (see Table 5.4). The frequent occurrences of this verb phrase suggest that the concept of 'spending' may be most typically associated with the mapping of MONEY onto TIME. This association is also partially supported by the frequent co-occurrence of *spend* with the word *money*. As shown in Table 5.5, among the top 10 verb collocates of *money* in the BoE, *spend* is the second most frequent verb to co-occur with the word *money*. This frequent co-occurrence indicates that the verb *spend* can be considered as one of the most common lexical items in the MONEY domain, and therefore it may be natural or expected for the concept of 'spending' to be semantically mapped onto the TIME domain.

Table 5.5 **The top** 10 **verb collocates of *money* in the BoE. The search term for each combination in the BoE is 'verb@ +2money'.**

Verb		Freq	Freq per mil.
make	*money*	7,785	17.30
spend	*money*	5,041	11.20
raise	*money*	3,903	8.67
save	*money*	3,207	7.13
lose	*money*	2,270	5.04

Verb		Freq	Freq per mil.
earn	*money*	2,017	4.48
pay	*money*	1,904	4.23
borrow	*money*	1,196	2.66
invest	*money*	886	1.97
waste	*money*	678	1.51

Furthermore, the results from the corpus-based analysis also seem to challenge the validity of the metaphor analysis adopted by Lakoff and Johnson, as some of their examples turn out to be infrequent in the corpus. For instance, the example *invest time* (Lakoff and Johnson 1980a/2003: 7-8) (see Section 5.1) occurs 235 times in the BoE, which is only 0.52 times per million words. Another of their examples, *borrowed time* (Section 5.1), occurs 166 times in the BoE (0.37 times per million words), and their example *budget your time* (Section 5.1), in particular, occurs only once in the BoE (and also only once in the BNC). These examples arguably raise questions with regard to the traditional approach of 'intuitive' metaphor analysis (cf. McEnery and Hardie 2012: 186; Li 2014). This result thus suggests that it is clearly beneficial to incorporate a corpus-based method in the analysis of metaphor (see Deignan 2005, 2008b; Stefanowitsch and Gries 2006; Semino *et al.* 2013).

5.2.2 Phraseological features associated with TIME IS A RESOURCE

The list of frequently occurring linguistic metaphors of*time* which are associated with the metaphor TIME IS A RESOURCE similarly contains largely verb phrases, as shown in Table 5.6. The set of verb collocates of *time* associated with this metaphor, e.g. *take*, *have*, *give*, *find* and *get* in Table 5.6, is different from that associated with the metaphor TIME IS MONEY (e.g. *spend*, *waste* and *make*). These verbs (e.g. *take*, *have* and *give*) are related more to the concept of 'resource' than the concept of 'money'.

Additionally, the patterning features associated with these verbs seem to be different from those associated with the metaphor TIME IS MONEY. As can be seen from Table 5.6, these verb phrases tend to involve the *to*-infinitive clause (e.g. '*take time to*-inf.', '*have time to*-inf.' and '*give time to*-inf.'), whereas the verb phrases which are associated with the metaphor TIME IS MONEY, e.g. '*spend time* v-ing / *with* n. / *on* n.', '*waste time on/in* n.' and '*make time for* n. / *to*-inf.', do not seem to share a similar patterning feature. This result is considered interesting because it suggests that different patterning features may accompany different metaphors (even two related metaphors such as TIME IS MONEY and TIME IS A RESOURCE), i.e. the patterning features of language may reveal the use of different metaphors.

Apart from verb phrases, the other linguistic metaphors associated with TIME IS A RESOURCE also include a noun phrase*spare time* and two other sequences '*there's/is no time to*-inf. / *for* n.' and '*time is/'s/was up*'. It can be considered that the noun phrase *spare time* reflects the attribute of 'quantity' which is mapped from the

RESOURCE domain to the TIME domain, and that the other two sequences seem to possess the characteristic of resource in that it can be 'used up'.

Table 5.6 The frequently occurring linguistic expressions of *time* which are associated with TIME IS A RESOURCE in the BoE. ('poss.' in the sequence '[*in*] poss. *spare time*' stands for possessive pronouns such as *his*, *their* and *my*.)

Linguistic expression			Freq	Freq per mil.	Example
1) verb phrase	*take time*	*to*-inf.	11,879	26.40	*take time to settle down*;
	have time	*to*-inf. *for* n.	10,577	23.50	*have time to read it*; *have time for sports*;
	give time	*to*-inf.	3,443	7.65	*give time to set up*;
	find time	*to*-inf. *for* n.	1,746	3.88	*find time to meet up*; *find time for a debate*;
	get time	*to*-inf. *for* n.	1,493	3.32	*get time to practice*; *get time for sight-seeing*;
2) noun phrase	(*in*) poss. *spare time*		1,389	3.09	*in his spare time*; *writing in my spare time*;
3) other sequence	*there's/is no time*	*to*-inf. *for* n.	795	1.77	*there's no time to shop*; *there's no time for fear*;
	time	*is/'s/ was up*	403	0.90	*now time is up*;

5.2.3 Phraseological features associated with TIME IS A COMMODITY

There are fewer linguistic expressions which are associated with the metaphor TIME IS A COMMODITY compared to those associated with the previous two metaphors, as shown in Table 5.7 below.

Table 5.7 The frequently occurring linguistic expressions of *time* which are associated with TIME IS A COMMODITY in the BoE

Linguistic expression		Freq	Freq per mil.	Example
1) verb phrase	*buy time*	745	1.66	*he was trying to buy time*; *that should buy some time*

Table5. 7(continued)

Linguistic expression		Freq	Freq per mil.	Example
2) other sequence	*time consuming*	1,647	3. 66	*it is both time consuming and expensive*
	time is/'s/was running out	878	1. 95	*time is running out for him*
	running out of time	178	0. 40	*we're running out of time*

The main verb phrase which is associated with this metaphor is *buy time*, although it is possible to argue that this phrase may also exhibit the mapping of TIME IS MONEY since the verb *buy* is closely related to the concept of money. This could suggest that the relation between conceptual metaphor and linguistic metaphors may not be neatly represented by one conceptual metaphor accounting for many linguistic metaphors (cf. Lakoff and Johnson 1980a/2003). In the case of *buy time*, it realises multiple metaphorical mappings. In other words, the overlap between conceptual metaphors, such as the three metaphors of TIME, may also be reflected in the use of certain linguistic metaphors.

The other sequences associated with the metaphor TIME IS A COMMODITY include the adjectival phrase *time consuming* and two sequences which involve the phrasal verb *run out*, as in *time is running out* and *running out of time*. These sequences all seem to reflect the characteristic of ' consumption ' which is associated with the concept of commodity. These sequences could also be considered to realise the metaphor TIME IS A RESOURCE. Thus the latter two sequences, in particular, can be related to the use of resources, e.g. *the water was running out* or *running out of water* (data from the BoE).

5. 2. 4 More complex phraseological features related to metaphor

In the above three sections, it has been shown that each metaphor of TIME is associated with a particular list of linguistic expressions, which reveals that there is a strong association between metaphor and phraseology and in addition that phraseology may play a disambiguating role in metaphorical use. This section further discusses the role that phraseology plays in metaphor, in particular the phraseological features of *time* which are associated with a metaphorical use but cannot be fully explained from the perspective of conceptual mapping.

Spend time and *make time*. In section 5. 2. 1, I have categorised the two verb phrases *spend time* and *make time* under the list of linguistic metaphors which realise the metaphor TIME IS MONEY. The reasons for this categorisation are mainly: 1) Lakoff and Johnson (1980a/2003) and other cognitive linguists (e.g. Pérez Hernández 2001; Kövecses 2010) have used these two linguistic expressions as examples to illustrate the metaphor TIME IS MONEY; and 2) as suggested by Conceptual Metaphor Theory, metaphor at the linguistic level can be understood as a mapping of lexical items from the source domain to the target domain (see Lakoff and Johnson 1980b, 2003; Lakoff 1993; Kövecses 2010). For instance, when Lakoff and Johnson (2003: 7) illustrated the ARGUMENT IS WAR metaphor, they asserted that lexical items such as *indefensible*, *attack* and *won* which are associated with the WAR domain are systematically employed in connection with the ARGUMENT domain. Thus based on their suggestions, it can be argued that the lexical items *spend* and *make* which are perceived as items from the MONEY domain realise a metaphorical mapping when they are 'transferred' and used in connection with the TIME domain.

However, what this mapping theory cannot fully account for is the linguistic usage of *spend* and *make* with the word *time*, or more broadly with the TIME domain. As can be seen from Tables 5. 8 and 5. 9, *spend* and *make* exhibit different tendencies in the BoE with regard to co-occurring with nouns that are related to the concept of 'time'.

The verb *spend* occurs more frequently with nouns which are associated with the TIME domain, e.g. *time*, *years*, *hours* and *days*, than with other nouns which are associated with the MONEY domain, e.g. *money* and *pounds* (see Table 5. 8). The verb *make*, on the other hand, tends to co-occur with nouns which are associated with the MONEY domain, e.g. *money*, *profit* and *fortune*, more often than the word *time* (see Table 5. 9). Additionally, it seems that *make* co-occurs even more frequently with other types of nouns which are not categorised under either the TIME or MONEY domain (e.g. *difference*, *decision* and *mistake* in Table 5. 9).

Table 5.8 The frequent nominal collocates of the lemma spend in the BoE. The frequency data has taken into consideration the syntagmatic variations of these verb-noun collocations.

	TIME	Freq
SPEND	time	12,589
	years	5,852
	hours	3,819
	days	2,701
	months	2,273

TIME	Freq
weeks	1,354
minutes	916
weekend	887
Christmas	547
morning	475

MONEY	Freq
money	5,041
pounds	1,879
millions	788
dollars	525
fortune	495

Table 5.9 The frequent nominal collocates of the lemma make in the BoE

	TIME	Freq
MAKE	time	2,251

MONEY	Freq
money	7,785
profit	2,563
fortune	1,328
pounds	954
millions	620
dollars	202

Other	Freq
difference	9,569
decision	8,071
mistake	5,639
debut	5,213
point	4,627
progress	4,457

As initially argued, this different tendency for *spend* and *make* to co-occur with *time* cannot be accounted for by the simple 'one-to-one' conceptual mapping suggested by Conceptual Metaphor Theory, although admittedly, a cognitive perspective may partially explain why *make money* is more commonly used than *make time*. For instance, money is normally considered by previous cognitive studies (e.g. Lakoff and Johnson 1980a; Kövecses 2010) as being more 'concrete' (physically existing and touchable) than time, and therefore with the verb *make* which is also perceived to be largely associated with physical actions, *make money* may correspondingly be regarded as a more acceptable expression than *make time*. Nonetheless, the cognitive explanation cannot cover the other linguistic phenomena: for example, why *spend time* occurs more than *spend money*, and why *make* co-occurs even more frequently with *difference* and *decision* than with *time* or *money*.

From a corpus-linguistic point of view, these features of *spend* and *make* simply reflect their unique collocational behaviour: the tendency of a lexical item to co-occur with certain collocates or certain groups of collocates (see Sinclair 1991, 2004a;

Walker 2008, 2011; McEnery and Hardie 2012). McCarthy (1990) and Lewis (2000) on the other hand assert that this kind of linguistic phenomena indicates that some collocations can show a certain level of arbitrariness due to the language process of "lexicalisation" or "institutionalisation" (cf. Fernández-Domínguez (2009: 92) or Pavii Taka (2008: 6)).

The usage of *have* with *time*. Similarly, based on the suggestion from the Conceptual Metaphor Theory, when the verb *have* is used with the word *time*, the lexical item *have* is seen to have been semantically 'mapped' or 'transferred' from the RESOURCE domain to the TIME domain, and thus realise the mapping of TIME IS A RESOURCE (cf. Lakoff and Johnson 2003; Deignan 1997, 2005; Kövecses 2010). However, the current corpus-based analysis also shows that the co-occurrence of *have* with the word *time* can exhibit a pragmatic use in addition to realising a metaphorical mapping.

For instance, the use of expressions like *have a good time*, *have a hard time* and *have a great time* may be different from that of the verb phrase *have time*. Each expression is used more as one "unit of meaning" (Sinclair 2004a) or as a fixed phrase of discourse functions (e.g. "discoursal expression" (Carter 1998: 67) or "communicative phrase" (Piirainen 2008: 214)) than as a metaphorical expression which reflects the conceptual mapping of MONEY to TIME (cf. the metonymic explanation for *had a great time* in Pérez Hernández 2001: 78). In other words, the discoursal or pragmatic use may be particularly highlighted regarding these expressions.

Table 5.10 **The pattern 'have *a* ADJ *time*' in the BoE. (have is the lemma form of the verb *have*.)**

have + *a* + ADJ + *time*					Freq
have	*a*	*good*	*time*	/	1,524
		hard		v-ing	988
		great		/	758
		tough		v-ing	306
		difficult		v-ing	273
		wonderful		/	253

As shown in Table 5.10, the above-mentioned expressions fit the pattern 'have *a* ADJ *time*' and the words which appear in the adjectival position, e.g. *good*, *hard*, *great* and *tough*, mainly exhibit an evaluative sense. Thus the sequences which fit this pattern usually refer to an experience being evaluated as good, bad or difficult in text, as can be seen from concordance lines 1 to 5 below. Those sequences which contain the adjectives associated with negative senses, e.g. *hard*, *tough* and *difficult*, are also found to frequently precede the gerund, as in *have a hard time understanding* ... (line 2) and *have a tough time figuring out* ... (line 4).

1 just basically want them to have a good time , and we're teaching our
2 together, "says Hill. People have a hard time understanding how important a
3 a small party, and everyone had a great time . In fact, since Wednesday,
4 can handle it, but they will have a tough time figuring out the process in
5 agreement, one would have a difficult time coming up with a good

In another expression, *have the time of* one's *life* as shown in Table 5.11, the verb *have* simply cannot be treated as a lexical item being conceptually mapped or metaphorically extended from the RESOURCE domain to the TIME domain (cf. Lakoff and John 1980a, 2003; Kövecses 2010), because the metaphorical use associated with this expression is perhaps far less obvious than its pragmatic use.

Table 5.11 The pattern 'have *the time of* poss. *life/lives*' in the BoE. ('poss.' in the pattern stands for possessive pronouns.)

Pattern have + *the* + *time* + *of* + poss. + life						Freq
have	*the*	*time*	*of*	*their* *his* *my*	*life/lives*	295

As shown in examples 6 and 7, it can be argued that the entire sequence *have the time of their lives* is used as a fixed phrase or a unit to exhibit its meaning of 'having or enjoying a great experience'.

6 It was one of her last shows and she took them into the studio. Theyhad the time of their lives .

7 Besides, John and Carolyn were nowhaving the time of their lives . Their faces were on the covers of every top U. S. magazine.

The analysis of these phraseological items, e.g. *have a good time* and *have the time of my life*, therefore indicates that their pragmatic use may be easier to observe than their metaphorical use. More importantly, this means that the pragmatic use of these phraseological items has a significant role in their metaphorical use. As argued in an earlier section, the selection and use of linguistic metaphors may depend largely on the co-texts of the metaphorical expression so that the pragmatic meaning of the whole discourse is not interrupted (cf. Littlemore and Low 2006: 14-15; Kövecses 2010: 292-293).

The use of *take* with *time*. The co-occurrence of the verb *take* with *time* is also found to be associated with unique phraseological features or pragmatic use which are more complex than can be fully accounted for by the theory of conceptual mapping.

Taking the semi-fixed phrase *it takes time* for example, it seems that it is mainly its phraseological use that is being highlighted rather than its metaphorical use of 'TIME as A RESOURCE' (Section 5.2.2). As a semantic unit, it often exhibits a sense that a specific type of work which is to be completed is time-consuming. It was also found using the BoE data that this phrase co-occurs frequently with other items which further contribute to this sense (cf. "lexical congruency" in Walker 2014), as shown in Table 5.12. For example, its co-texts may involve adjectives related to length such as *long* and *some*, and modal verbs which can imply a long process such as *will* and *would*. Additionally, the verbs which appear in the to-infinitive clause in the sequence '*it takes time* to-inf.', such as *get used to*, *learn*, *build up* and *adjust*, seem to be associated more often with actions that require a longer time than actions that can be achieved instantly such as *run* or *jump*, as can be seen from examples 8 and 9.

8 Henry was used as a winger for some of the time with Juve andit **takes time to get used to** reverting back.

9 But such work is necessarily delicate and it **takes time to build up** trust, according to Rennie Johnston, senior outreach worker of long experience.

Table 5.12 The uses of the semi-fixed phrase '*it takes time ...*' in the BoE. (The total occurrence of this phrase is 2,770 times in the BoE.)

Theusage of *it takes time...*	Freq
1) co-occurrence with adjectives	

Table5. 12(continued)

Theusage of *it takes time...*					Freq
it	*took/takes*	*a long* *some* *a lot of* *too much*	*time*	…	1,148
2) co-occurrence with modal verbs					
it	*will* *would* *may*	*take*	*time*	…	656
3) co-occurrence with *to*-inf. clause					
it	*takes*	*time*	*to get used to* *to get over* *to get through* *to learn* *to build up* *to recover* *to adjust*		463

Another phrase*take your time* is considered to be even more formulaic (or lexicalised), and consequently its pragmatic use is more easily observed than its metaphorical use. As shown in lines 10 to 12 below, *take your time* can be regarded as a lexical unit which is usually used in a polite way to reassure the listener that (s) he can do things slowly without hurrying.

10	nobody will be quizzing you, take yourtime."	Gradually thing
11	reply, "answer shortly." You take your time,	Geo. There's no hurry
12	don't have to call anybody yet. Just take your time."	She propped her head

The phrase*time is money*. It may be natural to assume that the phrase *time is money* realises the metaphorical mapping of TIME IS MONEY because the phrase is identical to the literal form of the metaphor. Yet the uses of this phrase are more complex than can be entirely accounted for by the conceptual mapping.

In examples 13 to 15 below, the phrase *time is money* seems to exhibit a metaphorical use or realise the mapping of TIME IS MONEY. However, in examples 16 to 18, a pragmatic sense can also be detected from its contexts.

13 To Americans, time is money . We live by schedules, deadlines, and agen-

das;

14 Time is money in any business–and that is particularly true in the film industry.

15 you can't be a slouch in the studio because time is money and they won't ask you back if you aren't fast.

16 But why take a chance and leave it for a few days? Play safe and get your reply back to us TODAY! Time is money ! Take a look overleaf at our past lucky winners. They didn't waste time posting their replies back to us and are they glad they did!

17 Officials say they're feeling pressure from local investors to move more quickly despite the orders from Beijing to go slow. After all, says general manager En Kud, "Time is money , and if we move too slowly, opportunities will pass us by."

18 Time is money , and wasted time in court means higher charges for litigants and for the taxpayer. It also means that everyone else in the queue has to wait longer for justice.

For example, in example 16 which comes from an advertisement, the speaker is urging the reader to act very quickly. In addition, the highlighted word "today" in capitals and the three exclamation marks in the speech emphasise the tone of the speaker and reveal his/her purpose to urge the reader to take immediate action. In example 17, the co–text of the phrase, "if we move too slowly, opportunities will pass us by", similarly implies the importance of acting and moving fast. In example 18, the text that follows the phrase *time is money* also indicates the need to take immediate action so that the litigants and taxpayers can avoid higher charges and justice can be served. This pragmatic use exhibited by the phrase *time is money* in these contexts thus suggests that the conceptual metaphor cannot entirely account for or predict the use of its associated linguistic metaphors.

To summarise, the analysis suggests that there is a close association between metaphor and phraseology, and some phraseological features of *time* which are related to metaphor may not be fully accounted for by the Conceptual Metaphor Theory. These phraseological or patterning features of *time* reveal that there is a more complex aspect to metaphorical use at the linguistic level.

5.3 TIME IS MOTION and the phraseological behaviour of time

The TIME IS MOTION metaphor also appears to be associated with a particular list of linguistic metaphors. As shown in Table 5.13 below, the frequently occurring linguistic expressions associated with this metaphor are mainly sequences which involve motion verbs, as in *time passed*, *the time has come* and *time went on*. For each expression, the corpus search takes into account syntactic variations, e.g. the frequency data for *time passed* in Table 5.13 consider the occurrences of *time passed*, *time passes*, *time has passed* and *time is/was passing*.

Table 5.13 **The frequently occurring linguistic expressions of time which are associated with TIME IS MOTION in the BoE**

Conceptual metaphor	TIME IS MOTION	Freq	Freq per mil.
Linguisticmetaphor	*time passed*	985	2.19
	the time has come	949	2.11
	when the time comes	807	1.79
	time went on	563	1.25
	time goes by	354	0.79
	time flies	122	0.27

One similarity between this group of linguistic metaphors and the group oflinguistic metaphors associated with the three metaphors discussed above, e.g. TIME IS MONEY, is that they both largely involve verbs or verb phrases. However, what is different between these two groups is the grammatical role of the word *time*. For instance, with regard to the verb phrases which are associated with the metaphor TIME IS MONEY, such as '*spend time* v-ing / *with* n. / *on* n.', '*waste time on/in* n.' and '*make time for* n. / *to*-inf.', the word *time* appears to be the object of these verbs. In other words, the concept of time in these cases appears to be the 'object' of the actions (the object being acted upon) with largely human beings as the subject of the actions, e.g. *we need to spend time with the material* and *we will no longer waste time on useless negotiations*.

On the other hand, the word *time* in the linguistic metaphors associated with TIME IS MOTION in Table 5. 13 acts as the subject of the clause, e.g. *time passes*, *the time has come* and *time flies*; and thus the concept of time is normally the ' subject' of the actions, i.e. time does the action of 'passing', 'coming', and 'flying'. The reason for this difference could lie in the inherent nature of the source domain. For instance, the concept of 'money' or 'resource' may be generally regarded as passive or as passive 'objects' of any actions, and so when time is perceived as 'money' or 'a resource' it is likely to be seen as a passive object as well; whereas, the concept of 'motion' normally involves an active process which means that this 'active' nature may also be mapped onto the concept of 'time'.

Another difference between the linguistic metaphors of *time* in Table 5. 13 and those associated with the previous three metaphors relates to the frequency data. It seems that the metaphor TIME IS MOTION is far less frequently realised than the other metaphors (e.g. TIME IS MONEY and TIME IS A RESOURCE). This result suggests that time is more commonly conceptualised as money or as a resource than as a moving object. Yet surprisingly, this cognitive phenomenon has not been addressed (or even identified) by previous studies which used the traditional metaphor approach.

The phraseological items associated with the metaphor TIME IS MOTION also reveal a difference from Lakoff and Johnson's (1980b) suggestion about the direction of movement for 'time'. As discussed in Section 5. 1, Lakoff and Johnson (1980b: 468-469) have proposed two directions for this movement: it can either be the future moving toward us or us moving toward the future (cf. Kövecses 2010: 37-38). However, if time can be conceptualised as a kind of movement as they have suggested, based on the linguistic metaphors of *time* in Table 5. 13, it would be more likely that time is moving away from us in various directions or just moving randomly in no particular direction. For instance, linguistic expressions such as *time passed* and *time goes by* may indicate that the concept of time is moving away from us and then disappearing 'behind' us (see Figure 5. 3); the sequence *time went on* could suggest that time is probably moving away from us and disappearing 'ahead of' us (see Figure 5. 4).

The expression*time flies* in Table 5. 13, on the other hand, does not explicitly indicate that time is moving in any particular direction rather that it is moving randomly (cf. Pérez Hernández's (2001) discussion of different types of time movement). Only

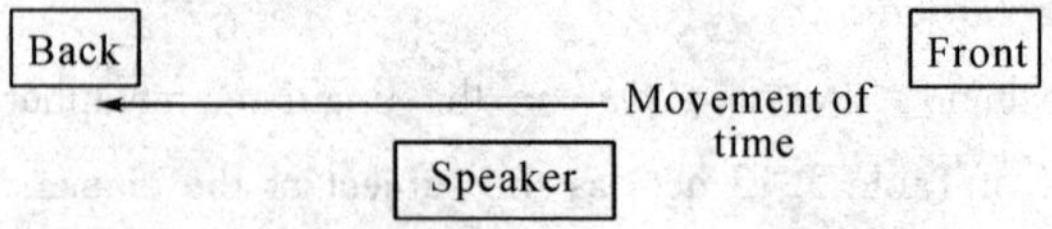

Figure 5. 3 **The image of time movement reflected from the examples *time passed* and *time goes by***

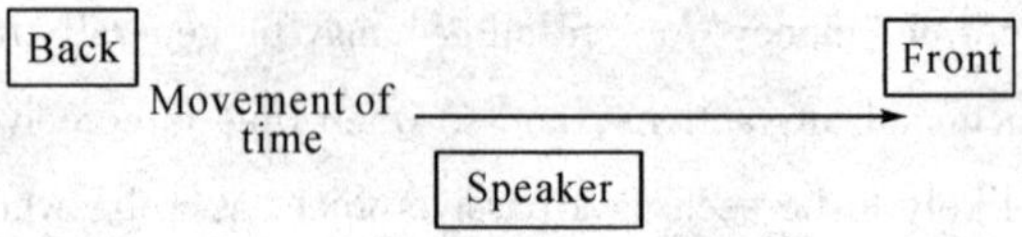

Figure 5. 4 **The image of time movement reflected from the example *time went on***

the two sequences *the time has come* and *when the time comes* seem to realise Lakoff and Johnson's (1980b) 'time direction' that the future is moving towards us (see Section 5. 1).

5. 4 Other metaphors associated with TIME

Apart from the metaphors of TIME which have been discussed so far, e.g. TIME IS MONEY and TIME IS MOTION, 'time' can also be conceptualised in terms of 'space', 'container' and 'force' (see Pérez Hernández 2001). This section will focus on two metaphors, TIME IS A LOCATION and TIME IS A FORCE (PERSON) which involve linguistic metaphors of the word *time*, to further investigate the relation between metaphor and phraseology.

In Pérez Hernández's (2001: 68) discussion of the metaphor TIME IS A LOCATION, she lists examples such as *at the time of the investigation* and *by the time of the election* (see Table 5. 3). As Pérez Hernández has suggested, in those cases *time* can be metaphorically referred to as 'a point in space' (hence 'location'). Her suggestion would mean that prepositional phrases such as *at the time* (*of/when*), *by the time*, *at that time* and *by that time* which resemble her two examples of *time* can be associated with the metaphor TIME IS A LOCATION. In other words, this metaphor is more likely to be associated with prepositional phrases.

It is important to note that the above suggestion from Pérez Hernández is to some extent different from one of the results presented in Section 4. 2. 3. These prepositional phrases, e.g. *at the time of* and *by the time*, have been categorised into the group related to the sense of 'a particular time point' which is regarded as being more literal than metaphorical. One of the major reasons for considering these prepositional phrases (or the sense of 'a particular time point') as being more literal is that they are considered as fixed or idiomatic lexical units and their phraseological nature is more likely to be highlighted than their metaphorical use. In other words, their phraseological features or pragmatic use are given more focus than their metaphorical use. Furthermore, the metaphorical mapping of LOCATION to TIME is not as apparent as the mapping of MONEY to TIME (or the mapping of MOTION to TIME).

If it is considered that these prepositional phrases such as *at the time of* and *by the time* are associated with the metaphor TIME IS A LOCATION (as Pérez Hernández has suggested), it means that metaphor is present in language more widely than originally expected and that metaphor is indeed ubiquitous in language (cf. Paprotté and Dirven 1985; Lakoff and Johnson 2003; Gibbs 2008; Kövecses 2010; Steen *et al.* 2010). Considering that these prepositional phrases are generally frequently occurring sequences in the BoE (see Section 4. 2. 3), the metaphor TIME IS A LOCATION can thus be regarded as a rather common, yet less 'obvious', metaphor of TIME.

The other mapping TIME IS A FORCE, as a generic metaphor in Pérez Hernández's (2001: 69) study, is comprised of two metaphors: TIME IS A CHANGER, e.g. *time will make you forget*, and TIME IS A HEALER, e.g. *time will heal your wounds*, (see Table 5. 3). These metaphorical mappings are similar to the form of personification of 'time' which according to Kövecses (2010: 39) can be regarded as a type of "ontological metaphor". In other words, these metaphors could also be labelled more broadly as TIME IS A PERSON (cf. Kövecses 2010: 55–56).

As discussedearlier, four sequences in the BoE sample exhibit the metaphorical mapping of TIME as A PERSON: *time waits for no man*, *time stood still*, *the scars of time* and *the long march of time*. The first linguistic metaphor *time waits for no man* seems to portray the 'strict' characteristic of time in that it will always be punctual and show no 'mercy' to anyone who is not on schedule, as shown in examples 19 and 20 below. This expression, however, does not occur very frequently in the BoE. There are only 15 occurrences in total for this expression and other similar sequences (e.g.

time waits for no one and *time waits no longer*) in the BoE.

19 Time waits for no man and there is no exception even if your name is Seaman or Peter Schmeichel.

20 Canterbury, so competitive under Blackadder, have found that time waits for no man , not even Andrew Mehrtens, whose play at fly half made him the world's best during the second half of the 1990s.

The second linguistic metaphor associated with the metaphor TIME IS A PERSON is *time stood still* which is slightly more frequent than the previous expression (*time waits for no man*). The search for *time stood still* and the other relevant sequences such as *time stands still* and *time standing still* returns 82 hits in the BoE. Three concordances of this linguistic metaphor are selected and shown below.

34 "It is not just the cattle. There is a whole different ecosystem out there that is unique. It is like time stood still , and it is worth preserving."

35 Everyone spoke of time standing still once the tornado was upon them. "I don't know whether you go into some kind of shock, but when it comes, time seems to stop."

36 When the offstage trumpet's forlorn calls rang over hushed strings, time stood still , no one breathed: we were at one with the composer, mourning the death and devastation of the First World War.

In example 34, the expression *time stood still* seems to exhibit the expected metaphorical use of 'time as a person': it stops moving on so that everything in the "ecosystem" remains unchanged. In examples 35 and 36, on the other hand, this expression also appears to be associated with an outside impact and a sense of strong emotions. For instance, in example 35, the incidence of "tornado" causes people to go into some kind of shock which 'causes' time to 'stand still'; in example 36, the "death and devastation of the First World War" invokes the emotion of sadness and grief which is why 'time stood still'.

The third linguistic metaphor *the scars of time* occurs rarely in the BoE with just three occurrences, as shown below. It seems that this expression reflects the opposite mapping of the metaphor TIME IS A HEALER by Pérez Hernández (2001). Time in this expression is portrayed more as the 'scarrer', i.e. it is time that has caused the mental or physical scars. To some extent, this expression can be related to the metaphor TIME IS A CHANGER in Pérez Hernández's model.

37 She invokes the scars of time on her own body, "neither young now nor fertile".

38 He had nearly reached the state of permanency too, but he carried about with himthe scars of time —the damaged shoes implied a different past, the lines of his face suggested hopes and fears of the future.

39 Picture restorers on the other hand are generally regarded as the good guys, patiently healing the scars of time and abuse like doctors tending to the seriously infirm.

The fourthexpression *the march of time* which is associated with the metaphor TIME IS A PERSON can also be argued to exhibit the mapping of TIME IS MOTION because of the association between the lexical item *march* and the concept of motion. One of its variations, *time marches on*, seems to be particularly related to the metaphor TIME IS MOTION. Both of these two linguistic metaphors are not frequent sequences in the BoE: the noun phrase *the march of time* occurs 52 times and *time marches on* occurs 19 times in the corpus. Examples of these two expressions are given below.

40 TheBell, where money is still stored in a drawer, not a till, and the bar is no more than a hatch in the wall, is a shrine to those who would resist the march of time .

41 It isthe march of time, of course, and time is catching up with Alain Prost.

42 Time marches on, conflict passes, taking with it 'half the seed of Europe' in the dying moments of symphony.

43 Well, time marches on and that wished-for help isn't arriving very quickly.

To recapitulate, even though the two conceptual metaphors, TIME IS A LOCATION and TIME IS A PERSON, are discussed relatively less frequently in previous studies, the analysis of thelinguistic metaphors of *time* associated with these two metaphors reveals that there may be a relation between metaphorical use and phraseology, i.e. each metaphor is associated with particular phraseological items.

5.5 Metonymic use of the word *thing*

Metonymy is defined asconceptual mappings within the boundary of a single domain or domain matrix. In this section, I will illustrate that metonymy, as another mechanism for the construction of meaning, can also be associated with phraseology. More specifically, the sequences which fit the pattern 'N/NP *thing*', e.g. *the girl thing*, *the money thing* and *the family thing*, are used as examples in order to demonstrate this association (see subsequent chapters for further discussion of the pattern 'N/NP *thing*' in terms of vague use).

The first phraseological item to be discussed is the sequence *girl thing* which fits the pattern 'N/NP *thing*' (or '*it* v-link *a* N *thing*'). As shown in examples 44 to 46 below, the sequence *girl thing* does not just refer literally to a single object owned by a girl; instead, it refers more broadly to a number of entities.

44 "I didn't know what it was that the boys did during recess, but I wanted to jump rope," he recalls. "So I brought a jump rope to school, only to discover that it was a '**girl thing**'."

45 we wondered if perhaps they weren't telling the truth. But then we concluded that lying is a BOY thing and telling the truth is a **GIRL thing** and if they said they were lesbians they must have been telling the truth because, er, lesbians always tell the truth.

46 To a lot of women it probably sounds as though I'm off my rocker, but I want to bond with my house. I want to become a home person. It's a **girl thing**, but that's how I feel.

In example 44, *the girl thing* refers to a kind of sport favoured by girls ("jump rope" in this case). In example 45, the speaker describes human behaviour in terms of "telling the truth" as *a girl thing* while "lying" is "a boy thing"; and in example 46, the desire to "bond with the house and become a home person" is perceived as *a girl thing*. This kind of broader or generalised reference exhibited by *the girl thing* to some extent reflects the metonymic reference PART FOR WHOLE (cf. Barcelona 2003; Kövecses 2010) where 'a physical possession by a girl' (literal understanding of *a girl thing*) as the PART accounts for 'any female-related event or business' (the WHOLE) such as the above broader referents of *girl thing* in examples 44 to 46 (i.e. "jump rope", "telling the truth" and "being a home person"). Similarly, as indicated by Mihatsch (2009: 87), generalised reference is most likely to be motivated by metonymy since it involves the high-level metonymy "MEMBER FOR CATEGORY" (see Radden 2002: 425).

Another item *the money thing* which fits the pattern 'N *thing*' is similarly associated with the metonymy PART FOR WHOLE. As can be seen from example 47 below, *the money thing* does not refer literally to paper currency but more broadly to the financial situation of the speaker; and in example 48, *the money thing* is used to describe more metonymically the state of ' getting rich'.

47 At the moment in your life, though, when you are finally trying to get the **money thing** together, you don't need to be told that love is at the root of everything and that money can't buy it. You already know all that. Well, don't you?

48 That's what I' ve got out of the game. People think I should be a millionaire but **the money thing** has only happened in the last few years. I still need to do something else.

The other phraseological items associated with the metonymy PART FOR WHOLE can also be*the family thing*, *the age thing* and *the fame thing*, etc. Examples of these three sequences are given below (examples 49 to 51).

49 It's kind of like **a family thing**: brothers and sisters pulling each other's hair out.

50 she co-stars with Sean Connery. She hit out at Australian actor Mel Gibson for his outspoken criticism of pairing younger women with much older men. She said: "I don't know quite what **the age thing** is all about but I think the charisma that Sean has is so fantastic, you kind of forget the age thing. Let's wait unit until Mel Gibson gets to his age and see if he has that staying power."

51 Unlike the guys in Jocks Wa Hey, Simone is not interested in fame and the glam life. "**The whole fame thing** really scares me - fame equates to a lack of freedom for me", she says.

These sequences all seem to have a broader metonymic reference than just their ' literal' reference. For instance, *the family thing* in example 49 refers to the ' tendency or habit to fight between siblings'; *the age thing* in example 50 refers to the ' age difference when younger women are paired with much older men in films'; *the whole fame thing* in example 51 refers to the state of ' being famous and having a glamorous life style'. Additionally, these sequences can also be associated with a vague use, in which case, it is reasonable to argue that metonymy may also be connected with the function of vagueness.

The above discussion is also supported by Littlemore and Tagg's (2014) study. For instance, in their corpus-based analysis of text messages, it has been shown that the example *the coffee thing* can exhibit the metonymic mapping of PART FOR WHOLE. The expression *the coffee thing*, as in the message "*Ok I'll go along with the coffee thing if you insist...*" (Littlemore and Tagg 2014: 21), refers more widely to various types of drinks or beverages than a cup of coffee, e.g. tea and water. It could also involve having different kinds of food, e.g. biscuits or cakes, or even simply imply a conversation between the speaker and the hearer. As a consequence, based on this example in their study and the above discussion of other similar sequences, it is reasonable to argue that there is an association between a metonymic use and this group of phraseological items.

5.6 Conclusion

In this chapter, I have discussed conceptual metaphors of TIME, e.g. TIME IS MONEY, TIME IS MOTION, TIME IS A LOCATION and TIME IS A PERSON, and a frequent metonymy PART FOR WHOLE, and I have reached the following conclusions:

1) Thelinguistic expressions which are associated with a metaphorical or metonymic use are largely more fixed phrases or multi-word sequences. In other words, the metaphorical or metonymic use is realised mainly by phraseological items rather than by single words, which confirms the association between metaphor (metonymy) and phraseology.

2) Each of themetaphors discussed, e.g. TIME IS MONEY, TIME IS A RESOURCE or TIME IS MOTION, is associated with a particular list of linguistic metaphors of *time* and unique patterning features of language, suggesting that phraseology can serve a disambiguating role in the metaphorical use of *time* (cf. Deignan 2005; Littlemore 2009).

3) Some of the phraseological features which are associated with a metaphorical use turn out to be very complex and cannot be fully explained by Conceptual Metaphor Theory. For instance, the collocational behaviour of*spend* and *make* and the pragmatic use of sequences such as *have a good time* and *take your time* do not seem to be ac-

counted for by the 'one to one' conceptual mapping of MONEY to TIME or RESOURCE to TIME (Section 5.2.4). Thus it is argued that the phraseological or patterning features of language found using a corpus-based approach can greatly complement conceptual metaphor studies (see Deignan 2005, 2008b).

Chapter 6 Evaluation and phraseology

This chapter focuses on another phenomenon which is important to the construction of meaning in discourse, evaluation, and investigates the relationship between evaluation and phraseology, or more specifically between evaluation and language patterns containing the word*thing* or *time*. In Sections 6.1 to 6.3, I will discuss four frequent language patterns: '*the* ADJ *thing* (*about* n. / *that*-cl.) *is/was*', '<topic> v-link ADJ *thing*', 'do *the* ADJ *thing*' and '(*the*) ADJ *thing to do*', and illustrate how the use of these patterns or their phraseological features are related to evaluation. These patterns are analysed because they were found to be frequently associated with the word *thing* in both the BoE sample and BNC sample, and the fact that they all contain adjectives also suggests that it is very likely that they will be associated with an evaluative use (see Hunston and Francis 2000; Hunston and Thompson 2000; Hunston 2011; Mindt 2011). In Section 6.4, I will focus on the patterns associated with the word *time*, e.g. '*at the time of the* N' and '*it* v-link *time to*-inf.', and further explore the role these patterns can play in evaluative use.

6.1 'the ADJ thing (about n. / that-cl.) is/was'

Of the four patterns associated with the word*thing*, '*the* ADJ *thing* (*about* n. / *that*-cl.) *is/was*' occurs most frequently in both the BoE sample and the BNC sample. For example, 100 out of the 500 concordance lines in the BoE sample contain the use of the pattern '*the* ADJ *thing* (*about* n. / *that*-cl.) *is/was*'. The adjectives which are associated with this pattern in the BoE sample are the following.

ADJ_1: *important* (11), *best* (5), *great* (3), *amazing* (2), *interesting* (2), *worst* (2), *astonishing* (1), *depressing* (1), *distinctive* (1), *funny*

(1), *greatest* (1), *hardest* (1), *impressive* (1), *perverse* (1), *saddest* (1), sensible (1), *unfortunate* (1)

ADJ_2: *first* (15), *one* (12), *last* (6), *other* (5), *third* (2)

ADJ_3: *only* (20), *whole* (4)

The number in the bracket after each adjective indicates the occurrences of the sequence with this adjective in the BoE sample. For instance, '*important* (11)' means that the sequence '*the important thing* (*that*-cl.) *is/was*' occurs 11 times in the BoE sample.

These adjectives can be broadly categorised into three groups. The first group (ADJ_1) involves the majority of the adjectives which appear to be associated with an explicitly evaluative meaning, e.g. *important*, *best*, *great* and *amazing*. These adjectives have often been considered as 'typical' evaluative words in previous studies (see Hunston and Thompson 2000; Hunston 2011). The second group (ADJ_2) contains the adjectives which seem to exhibit relatively neutral senses and are related to 'numbers' or 'sequences', e.g. *first*, *one*, *last*, *other* and *third*. The third group (ADJ_3) consists of the remaining two adjectives, *only* and *whole*, which do not seem to belong to the previous two groups. In Sections 6.1.1 to 6.1.3, the sequences which involve the above three groups of adjectives will be examined using the whole BoE corpus.

6.1.1 Sequences associated with the ADJ_1 group

Table6.1 below lists the sequences for the pattern '*the* ADJ *thing* (*about* n. / *that*-cl.) *is/was*' which involve the adjectives that are explicitly evaluative (the ADJ_1 group) using the BoE data. As can be seen, the most frequent sequences in this group include '*the* (*most*) *important thing* (*that*-cl.) *is/was*', '*the best thing* (*that*-cl. / *about* n.) *is/was*' and '*the worst thing* (*that*-cl. / *about* n.) *is/was*'.

Table 6.1 The sequences in the ADJ_1 group for the pattern '*the* ADJ *thing* (*about* n. / *that*-cl.) *is/was*' in the BoE

Sequence of the pattern (ADJ_1 group)	Freq (BoE)	Freq per mil.
the (*most*) *important* *thing* (*that*-cl.) *is/was*	2,430	5.40
the *best* *thing* (*that*-cl. / *about* n.) *is/was*	1,321	2.94
the *worst* *thing* (*that*-cl. / *about* n.) *is/was*	1,185	2.63

Table6. 1 (continued)

Sequence of the pattern (ADJ$_1$ group)				Freq (BoE)	Freq per mil.
the		*good*	*thing* (*about* n. / *that*-cl.) *is/was*	929	2. 06
the		*great*	*thing* (*about* n.) *is/was*	574	1. 28
the		*funny*	*thing* (*that*-cl. / *about* n.) *is/was*	387	0. 86
the	(*most*)	*interesting*	*thing* (*that*-cl. / *about* n.) *is/was*	374	0. 83
the	(*most*)	*amazing*	*thing* (*that*-cl. / *about* n.) *is/was*	162	0. 36
the		*hardest*	*thing* (*that*-cl. / *about* n.) *is/was*	161	0. 36
the		*sensible*	*thing* (*that*-cl. / *about* n.) *is/was*	50	0. 11
the		*saddest*	*thing* (*about* n. / *that*-cl.) *is/was*	49	0. 11
the		*greatest*	*thing* (*that*-cl. / *about* n.) *is/was*	37	0. 08
the		*unfortunate*	*thing* (*that*-cl. / *about* n.) *is/was*	35	0. 08
the		*astonishing*	*thing* (*about* n. / *that*-cl.) *is/was*	29	0. 06
the	(*most*)	*depressing*	*thing* (*about* n. / *that*-cl.) *is/was*	26	0. 06
the	(*most*)	*impressive*	*thing* (*about* n.) *is/was*	24	0. 05

Some of these sequences have a lower frequency, in particular those at the bottom of the list which occur less than 100 times in the BoE. All the sequences in Table 6. 1, regardless of their frequency, seem to be associated with "cataphoric reference" where the referents are largely found in the subsequent text of these sequences (see Halliday and Hasan 1976: 33; Francis 1986), as can be seen from examples 1 to 5 below. In other words, it can be argued that the use of the pattern '*the* ADJ *thing* (*about* n. / *that*-cl.) *is/was*' in text fulfils the role of introducing new information (see Schmid 2000: 332-334; Aijmer and Stenström 2004: 48).

1 The important thing is for everyone to try and get behind Trevor and help us up the table.

2 Hansen: It sounds like the best thing we can do for our children essentially is keep all line of communication open.

3 The worst thing about rap is its fascination with death, with evil.

4 The most depressing thing is the number of women who have reached powerful positions who boast of returning to work a week after their baby was born.

5 But the impressive thing was the way he worked so hard for the whole 90 minutes.

It is significant that most of the adjectives involved in these sequences exhibit an evaluative meaning which is more 'positive' than 'negative', as shown in Table 6.1. For instance, among the top 7 most frequent sequences in the BoE (i.e. those which occur more than 300 times), only one sequence, '*the worst thing* (*that*-cl. / *about* n.) *is/was*', contains an adjective which is associated with a 'negative' evaluative meaning. The other more frequent sequences contain adjectives which exhibit a 'positive' sense, e.g. *important*, *best*, *good*, *great*, *funny* and *interesting*. If all the sequences in this table are taken into account, it is still the case that the majority are associated with a 'positive' sense (11 out of the 16 sequences).

One reason for this result could be that the speaker or writer uses this pattern '*the* ADJ *thing* (*that*-cl.) *is/was*' to talk about positive things more often than negative things (contrast the use of the pattern '<topic> v-link ADJ *thing*' in Section 6.2). Further, since the sequences associated with the pattern '*the* ADJ *thing* (*that*-cl.) *is/was*' can serve the function of introducing new information in discourse as discussed above (also see Schmid 2000: 332-334; Aijmer and Stenström 2004: 48), it could also be concluded that when this pattern is used to start a new topic (which is often the case), it is likely that the speaker or writer is trying to begin on a positive note or maintain a positive tone.

A further examination using the BNC sample supports the above result. It was found that the adjectives which are involved in the ADJ_1 group in the BNC sample are also largely associated with a positive evaluative meaning: at least 10 out of the 14 adjectives exhibit a positive rather than a negative sense (as shown below).

important (8), *great* (2), *best* (1), *interesting* (1), *worst* (1), *astonishing* (1), *funny* (1), *sensible* (1), *good* (1), *logical* (1), *mad* (1), *noticeable* (1), *remarkable* (1), *vital* (1)

Another feature that is observed from the sequences associated with the ADJ_1 group (Table 6.1) is that many adjectives involved in these sequences occur frequently in the superlative form. For instance, the five adjectives, *important*, *interesting*, *amazing*, *depressing* and *impressive*, usually follow the modifier *most* in these sequences, as in '*the* (*most*) *important thing* (*that*-cl.) *is/was*' and '*the* (*most*) *interesting thing* (*that*-cl.) *is/was*'; while the other adjectives occur in their superlative forms, e.g. *best*, *worst*, *hardest*, *saddest* and *greatest*. The reason for this could be that a speaker tends to focus on 'extreme' cases in a conversation, e.g. *the most important thing* or *the most interesting thing* (contrast the 'gradedness' of adjectives in Hunston and Sinclair 2000: 92). It is possible that by using these sequences which involve adjectives in the superlative form, the speaker can highlight or even exaggerate the situation so that he/she will receive greater attention from his/her audience(s) (cf. Kreuz and Caucci 2009: 336 for a discussion of exaggeration or hyperbole exhibited by *the best meal I ever had*). This association between the ADJ_1 group and adjectives in the superlative form is further supported by the analysis using the BNC sample. For example, the sequences which occur most frequently in the BNC sample are '*the most important thing* (*that*-cl.) *is/was*', '*the best thing* (*that*-cl.) *is/was*', '*the worst thing* (*that*-cl.) *is/was*' and '*the most sensible thing* (*that*-cl.) *is/was*'.

One last point that should be noted about the sequences associated with the ADJ_1 group is that even though the adjective in each sequence may determine the evaluative nature (or the potential evaluative meaning) associated with the sequence, it is the entire sequence that exhibits an evaluative use. In other words, the evaluative nature lies not just in each adjective in the sequence, but in each entire multi-word sequence. For instance, when Hunston and Francis (2000: 134) discuss the association between the lexical item *the most difficult thing is to score a goal* and evaluation, they suggest that each part of this sequence serves a different evaluative role, as shown in Table 6. 2.

Table 6. 2 **The example given by Hunston and Francis (**2000: 134**) to illustrate the association between the sequence of *thing* and evaluation**

Evaluative category	Evaluative carrier		Evaluative entity
ADJ	general noun	v-link	*to*-inf.
The most difficult	*thing*	*is*	*to score a goal...*

As can be seen from Table 6. 2, the adjective *difficult* (or *most difficult*) is defined as the evaluative category; the word *thing* is described as the evaluative carrier; and the *to*-infinitive clause is regarded as the evaluative entity (also see Hunston and Sinclair 2000: 91). Therefore, it should be considered that it is the entire sequence that is associated with evaluation rather than just the adjective.

6.1.2 Sequences associated with the ADJ_2 group

The phraseological items in the ADJ_2 group contain adjectives which are related to 'numbers' or 'sequence', e.g. '*the one thing* (*that*-cl.) *is/was*' and '*the first thing* (*that*-cl. / *to do*) *is/was*', as shown in Table 6.3.

Admittedly, these phraseological items in the ADJ_2 group appear to be less 'evaluative' than those in the ADJ_1 group as the adjectives in this group do not normally exhibit an explicitly evaluative meaning. Two items from Table 6.3, however, are associated with an evaluative use through their phraseological behaviour.

Table 6.3 The ADJ_2 group of sequences for the pattern '*the* ADJ *thing* (*about* n. / *that*-cl.) *is/was*' in the BoE

Sequence of the pattern (ADJ_2 group)				Freq (BoE)	Freq per mil.
the	*one*	*thing*	(*that*-cl.) *is/was*	3,755	8.34
the	*first*	*thing*	(*that*-cl. / *to do*) *is/was*	2,349	5.22
the	*last*	*thing*	(*that*-cl.) *is/was*	1,712	3.80
the	*other*	*thing*	(*that*-cl.) *is/was*	1,193	2.65
the	*second*	*thing*	(*that*-cl. / *to do*) *is/was*	271	0.60

Table 6.4 The frequent forms for the sequence '*the one thing* (*that*-cl.) *is/was*' in the BoE and the association with 'certainty'

Association betweenone thing and 'certainty'			Freq (BoE)	Freq per mil.
one	*thing*	*is/'s certain*	483	1.07
one	*thing*	*is/'s for sure*	342	0.76
one	*thing*	*is* (*very/absolutely/crystal*) *clear*	317	0.70
one	*thing*	*is/'s for certain*	152	0.34
one	*thing*	*is sure*	114	0.25

The first item which was found to be associated with evaluation is '*the one thing* (*that*–cl.) *is/was*'. The analysis suggests that this phraseological item is often followed by words or phrases which are related to 'certainty', e.g. '*one thing is certain*', '*one thing is for sure*' and '*one thing is* (*very/absolutely/crystal*) *clear*', as shown in Table 6.4.

Examples of these frequent sequences from the BoE are also presented below.

6 But one thing is certain: If we do not have a good general theory of the past, then we have absolutely no hope of speculating intelligently about what is ahead.

7 One thing is for sure, life is so short and we really, really must make the best of it.

8 One thing is absolutely clear: there is no room for people with extremist views in the Conservative Party.

9 One thing is for certain, we don't need anybody who's less than 100 per cent committed in body and soul to Wales.

10 One thing is sure, you' ll have a memorable holiday in the sun in Puerto Rico.

The occurrences of the above sequences, e.g. *one thing is certain* and *one thing is for sure*, indicate that there is an association between the phraseological item '*the one thing* (*that*–cl.) *is/was*' and an evaluative sense of 'certainty' (see Hunston and Thompson 2000: 23–25).

Another phraseological item associated with an evaluative use is '*the last thing* (*that*–cl.) *is/was*'. The analysis shows that the sequence '*the last thing*' is often followed by the verb *want* or *need*, as in '*the last thing I want is*', '*the last thing we need is*' or '*the last thing they would want to do is*' (see Table 6.5). Examples of these three sequences are also provided below.

11 We are both professional footballers andthe last thing I want is to see another player get into trouble.

12 The last thing we need is another summer of unrest.

13 Their respect for the game is absolute andthe last thing they would want to do is to force a change upon its essentially male nature.

Table 6.5 The association between the sequence *the last thing* and a sense of 'undesirability' in the BoE

Sequence of the pattern (ADJ_2 group)					Freq (BoE)	Freq per mil.
the	*last*	*thing*	*I/you/we*	*want (to do) is*	539	1.20
the	*last*	*thing*	*I/he/she*	*wanted was*	275	0.61
the	*last*	*thing*	*we/you*	*need is*	218	0.48
the	*last*	*thing*	*I/they*	*would/will want (to do) is*	124	0.28
the	*last*	*thing*	*he/we*	*needed was*	119	0.26
the	*last*	*thing*	*he*	*needs is*	101	0.22
the	*last*	*thing*	*he*	*wants is*	90	0.20
the	*last*	*thing*	*I*	*expected was*	55	0.12

This frequent co-occurrence of '*the last thing*' with verbs like *want*, *need* or *expect* (see Table 6.5) indicates that the phraseological item '*the last thing* (*that*-cl.) *is/was*' is often associated with people's desires; and from these sequences in Table 6.5 (e.g. '*the last thing I want is*' and '*the last thing we need is*'), it would seem that it is usually an 'unwanted' desire or stance shown from the speaker (cf. Lemke 1998 for the evaluative dimension of "desirability").

6.1.3 Sequences associated with the ADJ_3 group

The ADJ_3 group contains the remaining two sequences which have not been included in the previous two groups, as can be seen from Table 6.6.

Table 6.6 The ADJ_3 group of sequences for the pattern '*the* ADJ *thing* (*that*-cl.) *is/was*' in the BoE

Sequence of the pattern (ADJ_3 group)				Freq (BoE)	Freq per mil.
the	*only*	*thing*	(*that*-cl.) *is/was*	3,138	6.97
the	*whole*	*thing*	(*that*-cl.) *is/was*	1,648	3.66

Even though the adjective*only* in the sequence '*the only thing* (*that*-cl.) *is/was*' (Table 6.6) is not as explicitly 'evaluative' as the adjectives in the ADJ_1 group (e.g. *important* and *best*), it is possible to identify an evaluative sense from the use of the entire sequence '*the only thing* (*that*-cl.) *is/was*' in context. For instance, the two most frequent forms of this phraseological item are '*the only thing I can do/say is*' (occurs 477 times in the BoE) and '*the only thing I/he could do/think of* was' (occurs 268 times in the BoE), and they appear to be related to a sense of 'passiveness' and 'restriction', where the speaker seems to express a limited ability to do something. As shown in examples 14 to 17, the stance of the speakers is that 'it is not possible for them to be in complete control' and that they could only do what they can do and 'accept' the situation they find themselves in.

14 **The only thing I can do is** feed them and give them some water and medical care, and let the politicians get involved here.

15 If the Latin community feels that they have been targeted, **the only thing I can say is** that that is not the case.

16 **The only thing I could think of doing was** taking a more detailed look at it, which involved running the chart paper faster to spread it all out - a bit like doing a photographic enlargement.

17 And **the only thing he could do was** to resort to his war powers. Then he had to be very careful.

The other sequence in the ADJ_3 group, '*the whole thing* (*that*-cl.) *is/was*', appears to be more 'descriptive' than evaluative. The analysis of this sequence suggests that it can be associated with a negative semantic prosody which is considered as a type of implicit evaluation (see Hunston 2011: 55-65) where the evaluative meaning is associated with the co-texts of a lexical item (cf. Louw 1993; Sinclair 2004a; Hoey 2005; Stubbs 2007a; Stewart 2010). For instance, by analysing a random sample of 100 lines of the pattern '*the whole thing is* ADJ', it was found that in 77 out of the 100 concordance lines, the adjectives in this pattern are related to a negative sense, e. g. *dirty*, *nonsense*, *hopeless*, *stupid* and *rubbish*. In other words, the adjectives which are frequently used to describe *the whole thing* are often negative. As can be seen from Figure 6.1, 20 concordance lines are selected from the 100-line sample and they reflect the association between this sequence and a negative sense. Thus it is reasonable to argue that *the whole thing* occurs frequently in a negative semantic environment.

18	bore going all the way through.	The whole thing is	dirty and greasy. But what
19	of the Royal Society, says	the whole thing is	nonsense. Gender
20	election because they figured	the whole thing is	hopeless anyway?
21	for the wrong amount. She said:	"The whole thing is	stupid." An Agency
22	Kate are involved. She said:	"The whole thing is	rubbish. My son and his
23	could not be chucked out.	The whole thing is	insane. A family of
24	surface. It was enormous. I think	the whole thing is	scary. It was 100 yards
25	or even the black kid? I think	the whole thing is	immoral. It is like they
26	That's an understatement. You know,	the whole thing is	crazy. I was eighteen when
27	was something in the house. And	the whole thing is	uncanny," Helena
28	would oppose such exclusivity.	"The whole thing is	absurd," said the
29	a naked woman. As Noel says:	"The whole thing is	ludicrous. One of my mates
30	the savings have been made.	The whole thing is	nonsensical. Moreover, the
31	director was quoted saying:	"The whole thing is	mad. It's the biggest can
32	whenever golfers were playing.	"The whole thing is	impractical. It's very
33	the reasoning behind it.	The whole thing is	silly," said Tom, but I
34	and this happens," he said.	The whole thing is	horrifying and extremely
35	who declined to be named, said:	"The whole thing is	appalling. It goes
36	offence, "Mr Guy said.	The whole thing is	unwise at a time when
37	theLondon department store.	The whole thing is	ridiculous," Christine

Figure 6.1 **Twenty concordance lines of '*the whole thing is* ADJ' which are associated with a negative evaluation (data from the BoE)**

Similarly, when the related pattern '*the whole thing was* ADJ' is examined in 100 randomly selected concordance lines, the results show that in the majority of the concordance lines (63 out of the 100), the adjectives which are used to describe *the whole thing* are associated with a negative sense, at least. Again 20 concordance lines of '*the whole thing was* ADJ' which reflect the association between this item and a negative sense are presented in Figure 6.2. These concordance lines confirm the tendency for *the whole thing* to occur in a negative semantic environment.

The analysis of the pattern '*the* ADJ *thing* (*that*-cl.) *is/was*' thus far shows that this pattern is closely connected with evaluation. It is fair to say that the sequences in the ADJ_1 group are related to evaluation because the adjectives involved in them are associated with an explicitly evaluative sense (Section 6. 1. 1). The results also suggest that the majority of the adjectives involved in the sequences in the ADJ_1 group are associated with a 'positive' evaluative sense. In addition, the sequences in the ADJ_2 group and ADJ_3 group which contain adjectives with a more 'descriptive' sense can also be associated with an evaluative use. It has been illustrated, for instance, that the sequence '*the one thing* (*that*-cl.) *is/was*' can be related to a sense of 'certainty'; the sequence '*the last thing* (*that*-cl.) *is/was*' may exhibit a sense of 'undesirability'; and the sequence *the whole thing* can be associated with a negative semantic prosody (cf. Hoey 2005 for the discussion of "pragmatic association" as a related term to semantic prosody).

38 to work. In fact, I decided the whole thing was crazy and couldn't work.
39 in a state of detached agitation: the whole thingwas surreal, bizarre. I wrote
40 downstairs. Security throughout the whole thingwas appalling," Guasch
41 Saturdays, but she wouldn't stop. The whole thingwas baffling. Either mccall
42 his body arched against the sky. The whole thingwas absurd: the boy was
43 checked with the woman involved. The whole thingwas outrageous. The most
44 Jowan Jermyn decided that the whole thingwas ridiculous and they
45 -maticallydump the Dome. We know the whole thingwas useless. Why hang on?
46 absolute nonsense, you know the whole thingwas nonsense. Mrs. Thatcher can
47 and then left. Very glad, for the whole thingwas futile really, and he was
48 then to theBell at Walberswick. The whole thingwas ludicrous' cos birdsong
49 said from the very beginning that the whole thing was illegal. REP: But the US
50 And got no coherent answers. The whole thingwas hopeless. Angrily the
51 -lities) following their inquiry. The whole thingwas scandalous." They remain
52 and it was all going on at once. The whole thingwas preposterous. For some
53 the funds in my war chest. The whole thingwas painful. People actually
54 Of course I had a feeling. The whole thingwas impossible. My mind was
55 would drive him insane soon. The whole thingwas sickening, the reality so
56 understood all the jokes. The whole thingwas disruptive in the
57 rude, and largely unsuccessful. The whole thingwas unsatisfactory and pure

Figure 6. 2 Twenty concordance lines of '*the whole thing was* ADJ' which are associated with a negative evaluation (data from the BoE)

6.2 '<topic> v-link ADJ *thing*'

The pattern '<topic> v-link ADJ *thing*' is the second most frequent pattern associated with the word *thing* in both the BoE sample and BNC sample (cf. the discussion of the pattern 'v-link ADJ n' in Hunston and Francis 2000: 131). The 'v-link' in the pattern refers mainly to link verbs (also called the copula) like *is*, *was* and the combination of modal verbs and *be* such as *may be* and *can be*. The '<topic>' slot in this pattern refers to the grammatical subject of the sequence, which can be a proper noun, a pronoun, a nominalised phrase or clause, etc. For instance, in this example, '*the NHS is still a good thing*', the proper noun '*NHS*' is regarded as the '<topic>'; and in the sequence '*buying your own home is unequivocally a good thing*', the nominalised phrase '*buying your own home*' is considered as the '<topic>'.

The adjectives which occur in this pattern in the BoE sample are shown as follows.

good (13), *bad* (6), *best* (3), *big* (3), *important* (3), *terrible* (3), *dangerous* (2), *active* (1), *amazing* (1), *awkward* (1), *dictatorial* (1), *difficult* (1), *easy* (1), *embarrassing* (1), *emotional* (1), *great* (1), *hardest* (1), *healthy* (1), *horrible* (1), *instinctive* (1), *local* (1), *meaningful* (1), *mental* (1), *nearest* (1), *new* (1), *nice* (1), *noisiest* (1), *practical* (1), *precious* (1), *private* (1), *regular* (1), *single* (1)

Compared with the list of adjectives which occur in the pattern '*the* ADJ *thing* (*that*-cl.) *is/was*' (Section 6.1), this list contains more types of adjectives; 32 adjectives occur in the pattern '<topic> v-link ADJ *thing*' in the BoE sample while 24 adjectives occur in the pattern '*the* ADJ *thing* (*that*-cl.) *is/was*'. In other words, there are probably more types of sequences associated with the pattern '<topic> v-link ADJ *thing*' than those associated with the pattern '*the* ADJ *thing* (*that*-cl.) *is/was*'.

From the comparison between the two lists of adjectives for the two patterns, what can also be observed is that although some adjectives are common to both lists, a few adjectives tend to be associated with either the pattern '*the* ADJ *thing* (*that*-cl.) *is/was*' or the pattern '<topic> v-link ADJ *thing*'. For instance, the adjectives which are related to the sense of 'sequence' (e.g. *first*, *one*, *last* and *second*) and those which are less 'evaluative' (e.g. *only* and *whole*) appear to occur more frequently in the sequences which fit the pattern '*the* ADJ *thing* (*that*-cl.) *is/was*' (see Section 6.1). Adjectives like *good*, *bad*, *big*, *terrible* and *dangerous*, however, seem to largely occur in the sequences which fit the pattern '<topic> v-link ADJ *thing*'. This difference regarding the adjectives reflects the different usages of the two patterns. The pattern '*the* ADJ *thing* (*that*-cl.) *is/was*', as discussed in Section 6.1, mainly serves the function of introducing new information in text and the list of adjectives for this pattern indicates that it can exhibit both evaluative and 'descriptive' uses. The pattern '<topic> v-link ADJ *thing*', on the other hand, strongly exhibits an evaluative use. For instance, the '<topic>' in the pattern can be considered as the "evaluated entity", the adjective as the "evaluative category" and the word *thing* as the "evaluative carrier" (see Hunston and Francis 2000: 132-136; Mahlberg 2005: 152-154).

Additionally, the comparison shows that the list of adjectives which occur in the pattern '<topic> v-link ADJ *thing*' contains more 'negative' adjectives (e.g. *bad*, *terrible*, *dangerous*, *awkward*, *dictatorial*, *difficult*, *embarrassing*, *hardest*, *horrible* and *noisiest*) than the list of adjectives associated with the pattern '*the* ADJ *thing* (*that*-cl.) *is/was*'. One of the reasons why the pattern '*the* ADJ *thing* (*that*-cl.) *is/was*' involves more 'positive' adjectives has already been provided in Section 6.1.1. To reiterate, the pattern '*the* ADJ *thing* (*that*-cl.) *is/was*' mainly serves to introduce new information and it is argued that this information may often be positive rather than negative. The reason why the pattern '<topic> v-link ADJ *thing*' involves relatively more 'negative' adjectives can similarly be related to the usage of this pattern in discourse. Since the pattern '<topic> v-link ADJ *thing*' is largely associated with the evaluation of a situation or '<topic>', it is reasonable to assume that this evaluation could be either positive or negative (as in *the NHS is still a good thing* or *it is a bad thing*).

The above result that the pattern '<topic> v-link ADJ *thing*' involves both positive and negative evaluation in the BoE sample is also confirmed by the analysis of this pattern using the whole BoE corpus. As shown in Table 6.7, the frequently occurring sequences for this pattern involve both the sequences which are relatively positive (e.g. '<topic> v-link *a good thing*' and '<topic> v-link *the best thing*') and the sequences which appear to be negative (e.g. '<topic> v-link *a bad thing*' and '<topic> v-link *a terrible thing*').

Table 6.7 **The frequent sequences for the pattern '<topic> v-link ADJ *thing*' in the BoE**

Sequence of the pattern	Freq (BoE)	Freq per mil.
<topic> *is/ 's* *a* *good* *thing*	2,079	4.62
<topic> *is/ be* *a* *bad* *thing*	1,102	2.45
<topic> *is/ 's* *the* (*most*) *important* *thing*	1,100	2.44
<topic> *was/ is* *the* *best* *thing*	1,093	2.43
<topic> *'s/ is* *a* *big* *thing*	504	1.12
<topic> *is/ 's* *a* *terrible* *thing*	342	0.76
<topic> *'s/ is* *a* *great* *thing*	293	0.65
<topic> *is/ 's* *the* (*most*) *difficult* *thing*	221	0.49
<topic> *is/ was* *the* *hardest* *thing*	182	0.40
<topic> *is/ 's* *a* *dangerous* *thing*	167	0.37
<topic> *'s/ is* *a* *nice* *thing*	135	0.30
<topic> *is/ 's* *an* *easy* *thing*	130	0.29

It was also found that some sequences for the pattern '<topic> v-link ADJ *thing*' (Table 6.7) can occur in longer and more fixed lexical units. The sequence '<topic> v-link *the best thing*' for example, occurs frequently in the form such as '*it was the best thing that could have happened to me*' (see lines 58 to 60) and '*this is the best thing that could have happened (to us)*' (lines 61 to 63); and these two longer sequences seem to be relatively fixed (cf. the concept of "syntagmatic fixedness").

58 off my pedestal, but it was the best thing that could have happened to me . Up

59 hour of the day but it was the best thing that could have happened to me to

60 helped Vegas. 'It was the best thing that could have happened to me . I

61 who think this is- this is the best thing that could have happened to the ANC
62 young kids-I think this is the best thing that could have happened. Unident-
63 won't be complaining. This is the best thing that could have happened to us. If

Similarly, the results show that the sequence '<topic> v-link *the important thing*' tends to be followed by postmodifiers like *in the world* or *in my life*, as in the longer and relatively fixed unit '<topic> *is the most important thing in the world / in my life*' (see lines 64 to 69).

64 the tale is that love is the most important thing in the world and that one
65 communists: Freedom is the most important thing in the world." PHOTOS. To
66 To me, being myself is the most important thing in the world. For so long

67 Paul: "My family is the most important thing in my life. Before we had
68 ago. Our relationship is the most important thing in my life and although he
69 agrees -sort of. Music is the most important thing in my life, but it isn't

6.3 'do the ADJ thing' and '(the) ADJ thing to do'

In addition to the two frequentlanguage patterns discussed above, another two patterns which occur relatively less frequently in the BoE, 'do *the* ADJ *thing*' and '(*the*) ADJ *thing to do*', can also be associated with an evaluative use.

Table 6.8 lists the sequences which are associated with the pattern 'do *the* ADJ *thing*' in the BoE. Since some of the sequences (e.g. 'do *the smart thing*') have a relatively lower frequency, only those sequences with a t-score which is higher than 2.4 are listed in this table. It has been suggested that the combinations with a t-score above 2.4, or sometimes even 40, may be regarded with confidence as strong collocations (cf. Barnbrook 1996: 97; Hunston 2002a: 72; Hoover *et al.* 2014: 154)

Table 6.8 The pattern 'do *the* ADJ *thing*' in the BoE. (The lemma do represents all word forms: *do*, *does*, *doing*, *did* and *done*.)

ADJ$_1$ group			Freq	t-score
DO the	right	thing	1,634	40.34
	decent		153	12.36
	wrong		149	12.16
	honourable		61	7.81
	sensible		47	6.84
	best		35	5.57
	correct		9	2.93
	responsible		9	2.90
	smart		7	2.60
	honest		7	2.59
	proper		7	2.58
	worst		7	2.53
	logical		6	2.43

ADJ$_2$ group			Freq	t-score
DO the	same	thing	1,463	38.19
	whole		90	9.39
	only		77	8.15
	real		19	4.09
	obvious		15	3.81

It can be seen from Table 6.8 that the majority of the adjectives (the ADJ$_1$ group) involved in this pattern seem to be associated with 'morality', e.g. *right*, *decent*, *honourable* and *responsible*, or 'rationality', e.g. *sensible*, *correct*, *smart* and *logical*, while the other adjectives (the ADJ$_2$ group) vary in meaning and appear to be more 'descriptive', e.g. *same*, *whole* and *only*. This result could indicate that the pattern 'do *the* ADJ *thing*' is often used to convey the evaluative sense that people need to do things based on morality or rationality (see three examples of the pattern below).

70 On the ethical issues surrounding the deployment and operation of technology, I think it's fair to say that professional engineers want to do the right thing. They do not want bridges to fall, airplanes to crash, the environment to become polluted, or rockets to explode.

71 Sir John Birt should do the decent thing and voluntarily decide to go early in the interests of the BBC.

72 I think Mr Murray has realised it is time to do the honourable thing. He came out last week, 13 months after he acquired these shares, to try and justify his position.

Additionally, the adjectives involved in the sequences in the ADJ$_1$ group are mainly positive words, e.g. *right*, *decent*, *honourable*, *responsible*, *sensible* and *correct*; only two adjectives in this group, *wrong* and *worst*, exhibit a 'negative' meaning. Thus the above-mentioned evaluative usage associated with the pattern 'do *the ADJ thing*' can be further described as judging the 'thing' to be done as morally correct or logically sound.

The other pattern '(*the*) ADJ *thing to do*', as shown in Table 6.9, is also strongly associated with morality and rationality.

Table 6.9 **The pattern '(*the*) ADJ *thing to do*' in the BoE**

ADJ_1 group			Freq	t-score
the	right	thing to do	537	23.12
	best		303	17.36
	wrong		59	7.65
	sensible		36	5.99
	smart		24	4.89
	natural		22	4.65
	wisest		16	4.00
	proper		16	3.98
	normal		16	3.97
	safest		14	3.74
	logical		14	3.74
	correct		12	3.44
	responsible		11	3.28
	worst		9	2.96
	appropriate		8	2.80
	kindest		7	2.65
	prudent		7	2.64
	important		7	2.49

ADJ_2 group			Freq	t-score
the	only	thing to do	101	9.85
	obvious		27	5.18
	fashionable		7	2.64

ADJ3 group			Freq	t-score
the	simplest	thing to do	34	5.83
	hardest		24	4.90
	easiest		21	4.58

It can be seen from Table 6.9 that the list of sequences associated with the pattern '(*the*) ADJ *thing to do*' in the ADJ_1 group resembles the list of sequences in the ADJ_1 group associated with the pattern 'do *the* ADJ *thing*' (Table 6.8). However, the pattern '(*the*) ADJ *thing to do*' involves a longer list of adjectives which are associated with an evaluative sense that the 'thing' is usually morally correct or more rational.

The sequences in the ADJ_2 group in Table 6.9 may be regarded as the more 'descriptive' group of this pattern, and are similar to the sequences in the ADJ_2 group of the pattern 'do *the* ADJ *thing*' (see Table 6.8). The sequences in the ADJ_3 group which fit the pattern '(*the*) ADJ *thing to do*', however, involve another evaluative sense: 'difficulty', e.g. *the simplest thing to do*, *the hardest thing to do* and *the easiest thing to do* (see Table 6.9).

Therefore, the analysis so far suggests that several types of evaluative uses can be associated with language patterns containing the word *thing*. In previous sections, the results have shown at least three types of evaluative use that are associated with language patterns: a) the evaluative use that highlights the sense of 'positive' or 'negative'; b) the evaluative use that highlights a sense of 'certainty' (which is exhibited in the sequence '*the one thing* (*that*-cl.) *is/was*'); and c) semantic prosody (associated with the sequence '*the whole thing* (*that*-cl.) *is/was*'). In this section, the results for these two patterns, 'do *the* ADJ *thing*' and '(*the*) ADJ *thing to do*', further reveal that they can exhibit evaluative senses which are related to 'morality', 'rationality' and 'difficulty'.

6.4 Phraseological items associated with time

This section analyses two phraseological items associated with *time*, '*at the time of the* N' and '*it* v-link *time to*-inf. /*that*-cl.', and further illustrates how they are related to an evaluative use. The first pattern, '*at the time of the* N', seems to largely involve nouns which are associated with a negative meaning. Table 6.10 lists the sequences associated with the pattern '*at the time of the* N' in the BoE (the t-scores for these sequences are also shown).

As can be seen, themajority of the nouns which occur in this pattern (the $NOUN_1$ group) appear to be associated with a negative sense, e.g. *attack*, *murder*, *accident*, *incident* and *crash* (cf. "disaster vocabulary" in Ungerer 1997: 315). The other nouns which occur in this pattern (the $NOUN_2$ group) seem to exhibit a 'neutral' sense, e.g. *exchange*, *contract* and *sale*. This result is also confirmed by the BNC data, as many nouns with a negative sense tend to occur in this pattern in the BNC, e.g. *accident*, *murder*, *incident*, *offence*, *attack*, *crash*, *trial* and *loss*.

Furthermore, the above result is supported by Hunston's (2011) study which shows that a negative evaluation can be associated with a similar pattern with *time*, '*a time of* N'. Hunston (2011: 161) suggests that it is very likely for *a time of* to occur with negative words like "*crisis*, *war*, *change* and *tension*".

However, it should be borne in mind that the negative evaluation associated with the pattern '*at the time of the* N' may be related to the construction of the corpus because of the journalistic content in the two corpora, in particular the BoE. In other words, the evaluative use exhibited by this pattern could be related to the factor of discourse or genre (see Stubbs 2001 for the relation between register and evaluative meanings of a lexical item such as undergo; also cf. Hoey 2005: 23 for the discussion of the discourse-specific feature of primings).

Table 6.10　　The pattern '*at the time of the* N' in the BoE

	NOUN$_1$	Freq	t-score
at the time of the attack	murder	107	10.30
	accident	95	9.72
	incident	91	9.52
	crash	84	9.15
	invasion	55	7.40
	trial	31	5.56
	offence	28	5.24
	explosion	28	5.28
	murders	27	5.18
	killing	25	4.99
	shooting	24	4.87
	offences	24	4.88
	fire	24	4.89
	killings	20	4.39
	blast	20	4.46
	crime	19	4.35
	raid	16	3.94
	disaster	16	3.99
		15	3.84

NOUN$_2$	Freq	t-score
exchange	90	9.45
contract	46	6.74
sale	36	5.95
transaction	36	5.99
purchase	32	5.62
merger	31	5.55
revolution	26	5.07
gulf	25	4.95
election	22	4.60
investment	20	4.34

The second item '*it* v-link *time* ...', involves four related patterns: '*it* v-link *time to*-inf.', '*it* v-link *time that*-cl.', '*it* v-link *time for* n. *to*-inf.' and '*it* v-link *time for* n.', as shown in Table 6.11. Examples for each pattern are also provided.

Table 6.11　　The four patterns associated with '*it* v-link *time*...' in the BoE

Pattern	Freq	Freq per mil.	Example
it v-link *time to*-inf.	3,768	8.37	*it is time to act*; *it was time to write the essay*
it v-link *time that*-cl.	1,131	2.51	*itis time that something is done about it*; *it is time that this was sorted out*
it v-link *time for* n. *to*-inf.	1,038	2.31	*it is time for the nation to move forward*; *it was time for me to send out the letter*
it v-link *time for* n.	941	2.09	*it was time for a change*; *it is time for a new challenge*

It is argued that these four patterns with *time* are related to evaluation because their use can be associated with an evaluative sense of 'importance'. To illustrate this point, the pattern '*it* v-link *time to*-inf.' will be used.

As shown in the examples below, this pattern is used to convey the sense that the 'things' which appear in the *to*-infinitive clause, e.g. 'take seriously the beliefs and practices' in example 73, 'show Congress that the majority of Americans don't make exceptions' in example 74 and 'address the problem of hunger in America' in example 75, are so important that action needs to be taken immediately. It can be seen from these examples that the speaker intends to persuade his/her audience (s) about the significance of the actions. The use of these sequences such as '*it is time to*-inf.' and '*it was time to*-inf.' also reflects the determination of the speaker and his/her resolution to take action.

73 After decades of development disasters, many caused by 'development from above', it is time to take seriously the beliefs and practices of those most directly affected by aid efforts.

74 It is time to show Congress that the majority of Americans don't make 'exceptions' about LIFE!

75 in both thoseplaces, he said in speeches it was time to address the problem of hunger in America.

Another reason for arguing that the four patterns are associated with evaluation lies in their resemblance to adjective patterns such as '*it* v-link ADJ *to*-inf.', '*it* v-link ADJ *that*-cl.' and '*it* v-link ADJ *for* n. *to*-inf.' which are largely associated with an evaluative use (see Hunston and Francis 2000; Hunston and Sinclair 2000; Hunston 2011). For instance, as shown in the following examples, the sequences for '*it* v-link *time to*-inf.' seem to be similar to the sequences for '*it* v-link ADJ *to*-inf.' with regard to both their form and use.

76	Zodiac, Saturn, simply means	it is	time	to remember that the most important
77	and directed byMoscow.	It is	important	to remember that this inner core
78	been crying out for peace.	It is	time	to make it work. Lawrie mcmenemy,
79	family isn't easy, she says	it is	possible	to make it work and get through it
80	but football is changing and	it is	time	to move on. I have taken bags of

81	may be right when you say	it is	best	to move on and give her a chance to
82	Messrs Gingrich and Dole –	It is	time	to believe that the states and
83	work. She will argue that	it is	wrong	to believe employees do best when
84	Security state on the other.	It is	time	to take a closer look at the organiza
85	Decree, which indicates why	it is	necessary	to take a closer look at the pastoral

To briefly recapitulate, the analysis ofthe patterns such as '*at the time of the* N' and '*it* v-link *time to*-inf.' supports the relation between pattern and evaluation. More specifically, the pattern '*at the time of the* N' seems to be associated with a negative evaluation and the pattern '*it* v-link *time to*-inf.' can exhibit an evaluative sense of 'importance' (cf. Miller and Johnson 2014 for the analysis of this pattern in parliamentary debates).

6.5 Conclusion

In this chapter, I have analysed four patterns associated with*thing* ('*the* ADJ *thing* (*that*-cl.) *is/was*', '<topic> v-link ADJ *thing*', 'do *the* ADJ *thing*' and '(*the*) ADJ *thing to do*') and two patterns associated with *time* ('*the time of the* N' and '*it* v-link *time to*-inf.'). Three main findings emerge from this part of the analysis.

1) The results show that the patterns under investigation are all associated with anevaluative use, which confirms the relation between phraseology and evaluation (see Hunston and Thompson 2000; Hunston 2011). This also suggests that it is of great significance for further studies to focus on the patterning feature of language or use patterns as a starting point to explore evaluative use.

2) The analysis reveals that each pattern may be related to slightly different evaluative uses. For instance, the pattern '*the* ADJ *thing* (*that*-cl.) *is/was*' is associated more frequently with a positive evaluation (Section 6.1) while the pattern '<topic> v-link ADJ *thing*' involves both positive and negative evaluative uses (Section 6.2). It was also found that some adjectives occur either in the pattern '*the* ADJ *thing* (*that*-cl.) *is/was*' or in the pattern '<topic> v-link ADJ *thing*', i.e. it is

rarely the case that the group of adjectives which occur in one pattern would be the same with that for another pattern. Thus it can be argued that different patterns (even two related patterns) may differentiate the evaluative uses exhibited by these patterns.

3) Therelation between pattern (or phraseology) and evaluation is reflected in at least eight types of evaluative uses exhibited by patterns or phraseological items, as summarised in Table 6. 12.

Table 6. 12 **The association between phraseological items and evaluative use**

Phraseological item	Feature
one thing is for sure *one thing iscertain*	associated with an evaluative sense of 'certainty' (Section 6. 1. 2)
'*the last thing* (*that*-cl.) *is/was*'	associated with an evaluative sense of 'undesirability' (Section 6. 1. 2)
the whole thing	associated with a negativesemantic prosody (Section 6. 1. 3)
'<topic> v-link *a good thing*' '<topic> v-link *a bad thing*'	associated with an evaluative sense of 'positive' or 'negative' (Section 6. 2)
do the right thing *do thehonourable thing*	associated with an evaluative sense of 'morality' (Section 6. 3)
thesensible thing to do *thesmart thing to do*	associated with an evaluative sense of 'rationality' (Section 6. 3)
the hardestthing to do *thesimplest thing to do*	associated with an evaluative sense of 'difficulty' (Section 6. 3)
'*it* v-link *time to*-inf.' *the most important thing is*	associated with an evaluative sense of 'importance' (Section 6. 4)

Chapter 7　Vague use and phraseology

In this chapter, I will explore the relation between phraseology and vague use. This investigation will mainly focus on the analysis of *thing* because this word, or the phraseology associated with this word, is often considered to be related to vague use, as suggested by many researchers (e. g. Crystal and Davy 1975; Channell 1994; Carter and McCarthy 1997; Aijmer 2002; Cutting 2007; Ädel and Reppen 2008; Anderson 2013). The word *time* or phraseology containing the word *time* will also be discussed in order to show that vague use covers a much broader range than previously expected and further reveal the relationship between vague use and phraseology.

In Section 7. 1, I will present an overview of the frequent sequences that are associated with the vague use of *thing* and reveal the connection between the vague use of *thing* and phraseology. Sections 7. 2 and 7. 3 will analyse in detail two vague expressions, *that sort of thing* and *the vision thing*, and attempt to illustrate that there is a close relationship between vague use, phraseological behaviour and discourse use. In Section 7. 4, I will examine several phrases associated with *time*, e. g. *from time to time* and *once upon a time*, and show that a relation between vague use and phraseology can also be demonstrated in the case of phraseology associated with *time*.

7. 1　Frequent vague expressions associated with thing

The identification of the frequent sequences which are associated with a vague use is mainly based on the adapted definition of vague language by Channell (1994) and conducted making use of sample analysis. This section will present these identified vague expressions using the BoE data and compare these expressions with the categories of vague language which have been established in previous studies.

The current analysis shows that the main vague expressions associated with the word *thing* are largely fixed phrases or patterns, i.e. the vague use is exhibited mainly by phraseological items. These vague expressions can be generally categorised into two groups. The first main group contains vague sequences like *that sort of thing* and *that kind of thing*, as shown in Table 7.1. This group of sequences, compared to the second group (see Table 7.2), occurs very frequently in the BoE.

Table 7.1 The first group of vague expressions such as *that sort of thing* and *that kind of thing* in the BoE

Sequence				Freq (BoE)	Freq per mil.
that/ this / the	*sort*	*of*	*thing*	5,992	13.32
	kind			2,632	5.85
	type			323	0.72

The identification of this group of sequences as vague expressions is expected because many previous studies (e.g. Channell 1994; Carter and McCarthy 1997; Aijmer 2002; Ädel and Reppen 2008; Anderson 2013) have suggested that these sequences exhibit a vague use and also that they occur frequently in informal conversations. In other words, the sequences shown in Table 7.1 could be seen as the 'typical' vague expressions associated with the word *thing*. They have often been considered by previous studies to involve many interpersonal functions which contribute to the fluency or cohesion of human interaction, e.g. they are used to project shared knowledge (Ädel and Reppen 2008), emphasise or withhold certain information (Drave 2002), or serve as a politeness strategy (Fernandez and Yuldashev 2011). As a consequence, the most frequent sequence in this group *that sort of thing* will be chosen for a detailed analysis in Section 7.2 to further explore its vague use and other language functions exhibited by this phrase.

The second group largely involves combinations of nouns or noun phrases (e.g. *vision*, *family* and *long term*) and *thing*, as can be seen from Table 7.2. These combinations can be loosely referred to as the pattern 'N *thing*'. Many of these sequences also tend to occur in the extended pattern '*it* v-link *a* N *thing*', for instance, *it's a family thing*, *it was just a spur of the moment thing* and *it's a girl thing* (see Table 7.2). Although this group contains a large number of vague expressions, many of them occur with a relatively low frequency in the BoE. Thus only those sequences with a t-score above 3 are presented in Table 7. 2.

Some of the sequences in this group, e.g. *it's a family thing*, *a girl thing* and *the money thing*, have also been discussed in terms of their metonymic use (Section 5. 5). To reiterate, these sequences can realise a metonymic mapping of PART FOR WHOLE. For instance, the sequence *a girl thing* refers more broadly or metonymically to any female-related event, affair or business. The inclusion of these sequences in the category of vague language here suggests that to some extent there is an overlap between vague use and metonymic use. In other words, vague use can also be related to metonymic use. More importantly, this association between vagueness and metonymy is largely reflected in the use of phraseological items, which means that there is a close relationship between phraseology, vagueness and metonymy. By contrast, previous studies on vague language have rarely discussed the relationship between metonymy and vague use (cf. Littlemore 2009: 115; Littlemore and Tagg 2014: 21) or the role of phraseology in the interaction between these two phenomena. The above finding, therefore, could potentially broaden the scope of research on vague use or on metonymy or on the construction of meaning in discourse as a whole.

When the vague expressions discussed above are compared with previous systems of classification of vague language, it seems that the categories of vague language established in previous studies may not cover all the vague expressions associated with *thing*. For instance, it was suggested in an earlier section that Channell (1994), Wang (2005) and Cutting (2013) are regarded as three comprehensive studies which all involve an investigation of different categories of vague language (cf. Stenström *et al*. 2002; Cutting 2007; Koester 2007; Anderson 2013). To reiterate, Channell (1994) mainly divides vague language into three categories: vague approximators and quantifiers (e.g. *about*, *approximately*, *bags of*, *some* and *many*), vague category identifiers (e.g. *or something like that*, *and things* and *and things like that*), and placeholder words (e.g. *thingy* and *whatsitsname*). Wang (2005) proposes a system which classifies vague language into five categories according to pragmatic functions: 'impression' indicators (e.g. *a lot* and *approximately*), 'unspecificity' indicators (e.g. *at six-ish*), 'fuzziness' indicators (e.g. *sort of* and *kind of*), 'etcetera' indicators (e.g. *and things like that*) and 'uncertainty' indicators (e.g. *maybe*). Cutting's (2013) framework further adds more lexical items in the categorisation of vague language (e.g. general nouns like *thing* and *place*).

Table 7.2 The second group of vague expressions in the BoE: the pattern '*N thing*' or '*it* v-link *a* N *thing*'

Noun / Noun phrase			Freq (BoE)	t-score
the	*vision*	*thing*	114	10.65
(it's) a	*family*		54	7.06
(it's) a	*long/short term*		51	7.00
it was (just) a	*spur of the moment*		48	6.79
(it's) a	*girl*		41	6.29
<Topic> *is a*	*two-way*		40	5.57
(it's) a	*(working/middle) class*		39	6.03
the	*money*		35	5.52
the	*rock*		32	5.56
the	*sex*		31	5.41
(it's) a	*power*		23	4.45
the	*age*		23	4.56
(it's) a	*fashion*		23	4.71
(it's) a	*confidence*		22	4.59
(it's) a	*love*		19	3.99
<Topic>*is a*	*boy*		19	4.21
the	*pop*		18	4.28
(it's) a	*man*		18	3.45
the (whole)	*fame*		18	4.21
the	*swamp*		17	4.24
the	*woman*		17	3.79
the	*England*		17	3.59
(it's) a	*team*		17	3.62
this	*drug*		17	3.98
(it was) a	*last-minute*		17	3.95
(it's) a	*gender*		15	3.84
(it was) an	*image*		14	3.62
(it's) a	*material*		14	3.62
(it's) an	*ego*		14	3.73

When compared with these three frameworks, the first group of vague expressions associated with *thing* in this study, i.e. sequences like *that sort of thing* (see Table 7.1), are related to "vague category identifiers" in Channell's framework or "etcetera indicators" in Wang's system or "general extenders" in Cutting's study. The second group, the pattern 'N *thing*' (or '*it* v-link *a* N *thing*'), however, does not seem to match any of the categories provided by Channell (1994), Wang (2005) or Cutting (2013).

Therefore, the comparison between the main vague expressions associated with *thing* and the previous frameworks of categorisation of vague language reveals that there are more vague lexical items than those which have been analysed or noted in previous studies. More specifically, the second group of vague expressions ('N *thing*' or '*it* v-link *a* N *thing*') does not seem to have been given proper attention in categorisations of vague language in previous studies. Admittedly, it is possible to argue that the lack of attention to this group of expressions is due to the fact that they occur relatively less frequently and that it is more likely that a large corpus such as the BoE will reveal the use of phraseological items with lower frequencies. Nonetheless, this finding suggests that vague language is probably more 'common' in language than previously thought.

7.2 'that sort of thing'

As the mostfrequent sequence in the first group of vague expressions (see Table 7.1 in Section 7.1), *that sort of thing* can also exhibit multiple linguistic features which are significant to the use of this phrase. The following sections will discuss four features associated with this vague expression.

7.2.1 Positioning

One of the features exhibited by this vague expression is that it tends to occur in the final position of a clause or utterance in the BoE. For instance, among the total 3220 occurrences of *that sort of thing* in the BoE, 2012 instances (around 60%) are cases of this phrase appearing in the clause-final position. Figure 7.1 presents 15 randomly selected concordance lines of this sequence from the BoE, and it can be seen that the majority of these concordance lines show this feature.

The position where *that sort of thing* tends to occur could reflect part of its role in discourse. For instance, Hoey (2005) focuses on written discourse and shows that there is a close relation between the textual position of a lexical item and its uses in the text. He proposes the term "textual priming" (or "textual colligation") to suggest that the position where a lexical item is 'primed' (for many language users) to occur in the text or conversation is an important characteristic associated with this item and this feature of a lexical item can indicate its role in the construction of meaning in discourse or the organisation of the discourse (Hoey 2005: 129-151).

For example, the sequences which fit the pattern '*the* ADJ *thing* (*that*-cl.) *is*' normally occur in the initial position of a clause and it has been shown that they tend to introduce a new piece of information in discourse. In other words, the positioning of this pattern is closely related to its function in text or discourse. In the case of *that sort of thing*, the fact that it occurs frequently in the final position of a clause or utterance (or that it is 'primed' for most language users to occur in the final position of a clause) suggests that this phrase tends to conclude or characterise one piece of information.

1	of our shopping down... and	that sort of thing	. How many pairs of shoes
2	of some of the string sounds and	that sort of thing	to give us appropriate
3	the meetings and dialogues and	that sort of thing	. Q: Okay. Can you tell the
4	were there was no troubles about	that sort of thing	. I always remember one who
5	in the local press and all	that sort of thing	which you've just mentioned
6	you're actually doing? And	that sort of thing	? Well it' ll be in lots of
7	after. And also status and all	that sort of thing	but erm Right. like end of
8	dhal, London pea-souper,	that sort of thing	. But it's the design that
9	missile sites, radar sites,	that sort of thing	. The Turks like the F-lll,
10	seems to be no time any more for	that sort of thing	. They came straggling
11	with tubes and wind and-and	that sort of thing	? Why not just do it all
12	matters such as OECD, APEC and	that sort of thing	. But the thing that, as I
13	folding bombs and knives and	that sort of thing	. The writing style across
14	normal way to school and all	that sort of thing	. Yes. And you couldn't get
15	of mine, Howdy Doody, is good at	that sort of thing	. Finds tickets worth $300

Figure 7.1 Fifteen random concordance lines of *that sort of thing* from the BoE

7.2.2 'and that sort of thing'

Another significant feature which can be observed from the concordance lines of *that sort of thing* is that the word *and* tends to precede this phrase. As shown in Figure

7.1, 10 out of the 15 random concordance lines contain the co-occurrence of the word *and with the phrase that sort of thing* (see lines 1, 2, 3, 5, 6, 7, 11, 12, 13 and 14). This feature is confirmed by further examining the collocational behaviour of *that sort of thing* in the BoE. For example, Table 7.3 below lists the collocates of this phrase within a span of 3.

Table 7.3 **The picture function for *that sort of thing* in the BoE with the collocates in each column sorted by frequency**

the	and	and	that sort of thing	and	i	i
and	to	all	that sort of thing	<p>	yeah	the
to	t	do	that sort of thing	but	the	you
a	you	for	that sort of thing	i	mm	s
of	the	about	that sort of thing	you	you	to
you	that	of	that sort of thing	it	it	it
don	of	like	that sort of thing	so	yes	a

These collocates of the node (*that sort of thing*) in each column are ranked according to frequency in this table. As can be seen, the word *and* often precedes the phrase, constructing new extended phrases such as *and that sort of thing* (767 occurrences in the BoE) and *and all that sort of thing* (200 occurrences).

The extended phrase, *and that sort of thing*, is also referred to as a "referent-final tag" by Aijmer (2002: 212) since this phrase often follows the referent and serves to conclude or categorise what the speaker/writer intends to refer to, as in this example *to allow family visits and that sort of thing*. This point by Aijmer also coincides with the tendency for *that sort of thing* to occur in the final position of a clause or utterance (see Section 7.2.1). In comparison, Channell (1994: 131) uses the label "vague category identifier" to describe this kind of phrase (see Section 7.1.2). The words or phrases which precede the phrase *and that sort of thing* are defined by Channell as the "exemplar" (cf. "referents" in Aijmer's term) which is considered to serve the purpose of helping the listener to establish which category of entities the speaker is referring to (ibid.).

The "exemplar", according to Channell (1994), seems to consist mostly of noun phrases and verb phrases, but the current analysis of 100 randomly-selected concordance lines of this phrase in the BoE yields slightly different results. It was found that in 55 instances, the sequences which precede *and that sort of thing* are nouns or noun phrases (N/NP + *and that sort of thing*); in 24 instances, *and that sort of thing* is preceded by verb phrases (VP + *and that sort of thing*); and then in 19 instances, it is preceded by clauses and sentences (cl. + *and that sort of thing*). Examples for each type of the exemplar are provided respectively in Figure 7.2.

Noun / Noun Phrase + *and that sort of thing*

16	And mittens and scarves	and that sort of thing	? Miller: Yes. Simon: Wooly
17	image ofyourself – scars	and that sort of thing	– that count so much."
18	want autographs, pictures	and that sort of thing	. Kids always find out

Verb Phrase + *and that sort of thing*

19 They need to be sure they're catching up on their sleep and doing exercises and that sort of thing.

20 No more jogging in shorts and that sort of thing?

Clause / sentence + *and that sort of thing*

21 they like to knowwho' s serving them dinner at the local restaurant and that sort of thing.

22 that is to say what they were planning to do, what had been done, what needs to be done and that sort of thing.

Figure 7.2 **The three types of sequences which tend to precede *and that sort of thing* (data from the BoE)**

The analysis of the 100 concordance lines of this phrase also suggests that many concordance lines contain more than one referent preceding *and that sort of thing* (see Aijmer 2002: 212). In other words, a list of items can occur before this phrase in a piece of text (see examples 16, 18, 19 and 22). In these cases this phrase is also referred to as a "list completer" (Channell 1994; Aijmer 2002). The current study found that there are in total 29 instances out of the 100 concordance lines which involve the use of this phrase being a "list completer" (18 instances in the noun phrase category, 8 instances in the verb phrase category, and 3 instances in the clause category). In contrast, there appear to be "very few" examples of this 'list-completing' feature in Channell's data (see Channell 1994: 134–135; also cf. Murphy 2010: 87).

7.2.3 Negative reference

In Schmid's (2000) study of shell nouns, the phrase *that sort of thing* was briefly discussed in terms of its evaluative use. Schmid (2000: 93-94) analysed several examples of this phrase from an early version of the BoE (225 million tokens) and claimed that a negative evaluation or connotation can often be detected from the use of this phrase in context. However, a detailed analysis of the use of *that sort of thing* in the current study reveals that it is not always associated with a negative evaluation or connotation. For instance, it was shown in Section 7.2.2 that the sequence *and that sort of thing* mainly serves a pragmatic function of identifying or marking the vague category, and also that it is rare for this sequence to be associated with a negative evaluation, e.g. *to allow family visits and that sort of thing* and *they want autographs, pictures and that sort of thing*.

Table 7.4 The sequences associated with 'V/VP *that sort of thing*' in the BoE. The frequency data in the table account for the co-occurrence of the verbs or verb phrases and *that sort of thing* within a span of 3.

Verb or Verb Phrase	Node	Freq	t-score
do	*that sort of thing*	239	12.05
like		72	7.86
say		30	4.12
be *good at*		17	4.12
see		17	3.46
be *interested in*		12	3.40
expect		11	3.32
talk *about*		10	2.99
think *about*		8	2.63
want		8	2.18
get/be *used to*		7	2.45
put up with		6	2.41
get away with		6	2.44
worry *about*		5	2.23

Instead of a negative evaluation or connotation (cf. Schmid 2000: 93), the current analysis suggests that this phrase exhibits morefrequently a negative reference, i.

e. the vague category which *that sort of thing* refers to may be associated with a negative sense. Additionally, this negative sense associated with *that sort of thing* is not an inherent property of this phrase but rather a feature which depends greatly on its context. It was found that this feature is more often observed when the phrase *that sort of thing* co-occurs with verbs or verb phrases.

Table 7.4 shows the frequent verbs or verb phrases which co-occur with *that sort of thing* within a span of 3. As can be seen, the majority of the verbs or verb phrases seem to involve a neutral semantic sense, e.g. *do*, *say* and *see*, with some associated with a positive sense, e.g. *like*, *be good at* and *be interested in*. Only a few verb phrases appear to be associated with a negative sense, e.g. *worry about*, *put up with* and *get away with*. This result again challenges Schmid's (2000: 93-94) suggestion that *that sort of thing* often shows a negative evaluation or connotation.

In the very few cases where *that sort of thing* co-occurs with verbs or verb phrases which involve a negative sense (e.g. *put up with* and *get away with*), it is easy to see that this phrase is related to a negative reference. Taking the verb phrase *put up with* for example, it can hardly be argued that the things or situations people 'put up with' should be pleasant, as can be seen from examples 23 and 24.

23 Evelyn saw no reason why she should put up with that sort of thing from a girl who was not much older than herself ...

24 In the days when my daughter was competing, about 15 years ago, you could find yourself being held up on the course for 25 minutes while a fence was rebuilt. People just won't put up with that sort of thing any more. They are looking for good going and a high standard of fence construction, landings and take-offs.

To illustrate in more detail the association between 'V/VP *that sort of thing*' and a negative reference, the example 'do *that sort of thing*' is firstly used since the lemma do co-occurs most frequently with *that sort of thing* as shown in Table 7.4. The analysis of the co-texts of this sequence shows that 'do *that sort of thing*' is frequently associated with a negative form and the use of modal verbs. For instance, Figure 7.3 provides 15 randomly selected concordance lines of *do that sort of thing*, and it can be seen that the lexical items which frequently precede *do that sort of thing* are *don't*, *does not*, *can't*, *wouldn't* and *wasn't able to*. This establishes that *do that sort of thing* is frequently associated with negation (or a negative form), and thus it is quite possible that the entity *that sort of thing* refers to may be associated with a negative sense. However, more context is required in each of these concordance lines to be able to decide with certainty whether there is an association between *do that sort of thing* and a negative reference.

25 for them." He does not do that sort of thing any more, and we are now
26 I was fine because I don't do that sort of thing . But isn't that a rotten
27 don't know why these people do that sort of thing do you. Dear oh dear.
28 Your bedroom. We just can't do that sort of thing where you could with other
29 exploded, ‘Country folk don't do that sort of thing . People in The Archers
30 He simply replied: ‘We don't do that sort of thing up here". There is no doubt
31 he thinks that I wouldn't do that sort of thing erm I don't know what he'd
32 but it just came out. I don't do that sort of thing every day. But the match
33 gets destroyed. Youcan' t do that sort of thing inLondon. Not for very
34 and that I wasn't able to do that sort of thing I was much too lackadaisi-
35 Ididn't come to the BBC to do that sort of thing . Jerry Springer does it
36 and goin and erm they don't do that sort of thing . Mm. It's just care.
37 you thought what? You could do that sort of thing if you opened your own
38 and they said No we don't do that sort of thing any more but ... Pride do
39 embarrassing; you just don't do that sort of thing ." News 5. Teen publisher

Figure 7. 3 Fifteen random concordance lines of *do that sort of thing* from the BoE

A detailed examination of the concordance lines in Figure 7. 3 shows that in the majority of these cases the sequence *do that sort of thing* indeed refers to negative entities. For instance, lines 25 to 27 in Figure 7. 3 are provided with more contexts below.

25 "That was not my ex-husband's attitude," the girl revealed. Once, he kidnapped from me my son and my daughter." "That couldn't have been pleasant for them." "He does not do that sort of thing any more, and we are now quite civilized with each other and he has remarried."

26 Richard, 42, told viewers he was B-tested after a lunch. The result was negative. He said: "Somebody saw me in a restaurant and phoned police. I was fine because I don't do that sort of thing . But isn't that a rotten thing to do?

27 I mean if they were going to ram-raid or something or break in somewhere.

Mm. I don't know what Maybe they had something they wanted to transport. Isn't it a shame. You don't know why these people **do that sort of thing** do you. Dear or dear.

In example 25, the wife states that the thing that herex-husband does not do any more refers to ' kidnapping her children' , and hence it is reasonable in this case to argue that *do that sort of thing* involves a negative sense. In example 26, this sequence similarly refers to a concept which is associated with a negative sense: DWI - 'driving while intoxicated of alcohol'. In example 27 where *do that sort of thing* does not occur adjacently with lexical items in the negative form (such as examples 25 and 26), this sequence is still related to a negative sense because it refers to the criminal behaviour, i.e. 'raiding and breaking in'.

Generally, based on the randomly-selected examples in Figure7. 3, the analysis shows that the majority of these examples indicate that there is an association between *do that sort of thing* and a negative sense. This argument is also supported by the analysis of all the occurrences of *do that sort of thing* in the BoE. The results show that around 58% of the occurrences of this sequence are associated with a negative reference (35% of the occurrences are related to a neutral reference and 7% related to a positive reference).

However, since the association between 'V/VP *that sort of thing*' and a negative reference is considered a feature of probability, there are also exceptions where this sequence does not involve a negative reference. For example, concordance lines 28 and 33 in Figure 7. 3 are provided with more contexts below. As can be seen from these two examples, even though they both involve the form of *can't do that sort of thing*, the referents of *that sort of thing* are arguably related to a neutral sense.

28 Right you' ve done wrong you go in your bedroom. We just can't **do that sort of thing** where you could with other children. The other children we can. If they' ve been naughty they go to their rooms as a punishment that they can't go out they're grounded they stop in.

33 in one of those mock-comic movies glorifying unending cops-and-robbers car chases during which a fortune's worth of equipment gets destroyed. You can't **do that sort of thing** in London. Not for very far, anyway. The police driver, correctly trained, had his brakes on well before the Mini's.

In example 28, *do that sort of thing* refers to ' telling children to go to their rooms as a punishment' and the lexical item *can't* may be related to the speaker's inability to 'ground the children' or the inappropriateness for the speaker to do so. Similarly, in example 33, the sequence *can't do that sort of thing* is associated more with the impossibility of a "cops-and-robbers car chase" in crowded London streets rather than a negative sense.

The second most frequent sequence for 'V/VP *that sort of thing*', 'like *that sort of thing*' (Table 7.4), is also used as an example because the verb like appears to be positive. A detailed examination of this sequence also shows that this sequence exhibits very frequently a negative reference. For instance, many occurrences of this sequence is associated with items such as *don't*, *does not* or *didn't*, as shown in examples 40 and 41 below. In these two cases, the speakers both use *that sort of thing* to refer to negative things or things that they do not approve of.

40 A lot of them don't want permanent relationships anyway. They want a one-night stand and I don't **like that sort of thing**.

41 One of the misunderstandings is that we strive to make pop records about pop records. I don't think we do and, in fact, I really don't **like that sort of thing**. Most of what we do is meant totally sincerely.

Additionally, a sense of 'comparison' or 'distancing' can be detected from these two examples. The speaker seems to be distancing himself/herself from others in terms of their stance on what *that sort of thing* refers to. In example 40, using the phrase *that sort of thing*, the speaker separates himself/herself from the other people ("they" in the example) in terms of what a person would want in a relationship; similarly in example 41, the speaker uses this phrase to refer to "one of the misunderstandings" about what he/she does and emphasises that instead 'the job is actually done with total sincerity'.

In a few instances where *like that sort of thing* involves a neutral reference, it also seems that the use of this phrase can reflect the speaker's stance. In example 42, for instance, *that sort of thing* refers to "getting together with the family" which is usually regarded as neutral or perhaps positive; however, the speaker uses this phrase to distance himself/herself from other people, especially in terms of the stance on staying with the family. The underlined items in example 42 further indicate this attitude from the speaker that he/she does not enjoy family gatherings. Example 43 is a similar case: the use of *that sort of thing* does not involve a negative reference, but it appears to reflect the speaker's intention to separate himself/herself from others (or "kids") with regard to the stance on "staying at home and doing things".

42 I mean it was just a a case of getting together with the familyand whatever. Erm erm everybody enjoyed the day. Erm it's it's just whether you like that **sort of thing**. Yeah. Erm I, I don't.

43 I stay at home and do other things. But you see there's kids that don't like **that sort of thing**. I do. But kids don't.

Since it is not feasible to discuss each sequenceassociated with 'V/VP *that sort of thing*' in detail, a sample of 100 concordance lines was randomly selected from the BoE to further examine the association between 'V/VP *that sort of thing*' and a negative reference. The results suggest that 66% of the concordance lines in the sample involve a reference to negative entities; 29% of the concordance lines are related to a neutral reference; and the remaining 5% of the sample are related to a positive reference. In other words, it is indeed the case that the majority of the concordance lines for 'V/VP *that sort of thing*' are associated with a negative reference.

Therefore, the above discussion suggests that the phrase *that sort of thing* is associated with a negative reference, although this association depends greatly on the context in which the phrase occurs. The results show that not all occurrences of *that sort of thing* are related to a negative reference. For instance, the use of *and that sort of thing* discussed in Section 7.2.2 does not involve a negative reference (or negative evaluation/connotation as Schmid (2000) suggested). It was found that this feature of negative reference appears more frequently when the phrase *that sort of thing* co-occurs with verbs or verb phrases. Additionally, the results suggest that the negative reference of *that sort of thing* may reflect the speaker's stance or opinion on things: that is to say it is more often that the speaker disapproves of the entities which *that sort of thing* refers to. In the other cases where the speaker does not show a negative attitude to the referred entities, the use of *that sort of thing* may also serve a pragmatic or interpersonal role whereby the speaker can distance or separate himself/herself from other people in terms of their attitudes towards the referred entities (see examples 42 and 43).

7.2.4 Co-occurrence with discourse markers

The analysis of *that sort of thing* also shows that this phrase may co-occur with discourse markers. As listed in Table 7.5, the adjacent collocates of *that sort of thing* can be markers or hedges like *you know*, *erm*, *yeah*, *I think* and *I mean*. Three examples of the co-occurrence of the phrase with *you know* are also shown below.

44 but it's like, get a good night's sleep, eat a good breakfast, you know, that sort of thing .

45 We—we need generators, we need, you know, food, medical supplies and that sort of thing , you know?

46 Ford: Kaseki? Jose: Yeah, kaseki housewife. A housewife who doesn't know the heat in the kitchen, you know, because she has 20 maids working for her. You know, that sort of thing , you know.

Table 7.5 **The co-occurrence of *that sort of thing* with discourse markers in the BoE**

The use of*that sort of thing* with discourse markers			Freq (BoE)	t-score
you know	*that sort of thing*	(*you know*)	62	7.34
	that sort of thing	*erm*	46	6.60
yeah	*that sort of thing*		34	5.82
	that sort of thing	*er*	33	5.47
Mm	*that sort of thing*		25	4.76
	that sort of thing	*I think*	16	3.97
	that sort of thing	*I mean*	14	3.73

In both examples 44 and 45, the phrase *that sort of thing* is related to the use of "list-completers" (Channell 1994; Aijmer 2002) as discussed in Section 7.2.2. The use of the discourse marker *you know* in these two examples connects different parts of the list of items and the tag (*that sort of thing*), which could be considered as a discourse strategy used by the speaker to create more time to think about the list of items or the vague category he/she is referring to. Additionally, the use of *you know* in these two examples could serve to attract the listener's attention, establish a common ground between the interlocutors and create a friendly environment. In example 46, the phrase *that sort of thing* does not follow any list of items which may help the listener understand the vague reference of *that sort of thing*; hence the occurrence of *you know* in this example could be intended to check the understanding of the hearer and at the same time evoke a response from the hearer, which may achieve a shared understanding of the situation and also establish intimacy with the other interlocutor.

Although the frequency data of the co-occurrence of the phrase with some discourse markers are relatively low (see Table 7.5), the co-occurrence of *that sort of thing* with these discourse markers indicates the social significance of vague language (cf. Channell 1994; Aijmer 2002; McEnery *et al.* 2006; Cutting 2013). From examples 44 to 46 which show the co-occurrence of *you know* with *that sort of thing*, at least three interpersonal or discourse functions can be identified: hedging, establishing a common ground and maintaining a friendly tone (cf. Aijmer 2002: 217). These interpersonal functions can contribute greatly to the cohesion of human interaction, or in Cutting's (2007) term "social cohesion".

Furthermore, these hedges, e.g. *you know*, *erm*, *yeah*, *I think* and *I mean*, can mark the discourse type. In other words, the co-occurrence of *that sort of thing* with the above-mentioned discourse markers may be more characteristic of spoken discourse. The source data from the BoE also confirm this point. For instance, the co-occurrence of *that sort of thing* and *you know* originates mainly from the bespok subcorpus which contains largely spoken data.

7.3 'the vision thing'

The phrase *the vision thing* is selected to be analysed in detail in this section because it is the most frequent sequence in the second group of vague expressions (Section 7.1.1). What is unique about the use of this phrase is that it occurs largely in the texts in newspapers and magazines. In comparison, many previous studies on vague use have stated that vague language is normally used in informal conversations. Only a few researchers (e.g. Koester 2006, 2010; Cotterill 2007; Walsh *et al.* 2008; Handford 2010) have focused on the analysis of vague language in relatively more formal text-types. The use of this sequence in journalistic texts could indicate that vague use is associated with a broader range of genres some of which may be more formal.

One reason why *the vision thing* occurs frequently in journalistic texts could be that it is mainly used in a political context and that politics happens to be a common topic in the media. As shown in Figure 7.4, several names of politicians can be noted in the co-texts of this sequence, e.g. George Bush (lines 47, 49, 50, 56, 57, 58 and 59), Blair (line 48) and Clinton (line 47).

The analysis of*the vision thing* also suggests that it may realise a unique interpersonal use. For instance, as can be seen from the concordance lines in Figure 7.4, there are frequent uses of quotation marks on *the vision thing* and other collocates of this sequence such as *call*, *namely* and *his version of*. With these in the context, it can be inferred that the speakers probably intend to use this sequence to emphasise (e.g. *we call it 'the vision thing'* in line 52), express irony (e.g. *The Government is fond of the vision thing, but just what is its picture of secondary education?* in line 61), show disapproval (e.g. *accused Clinton of lacking 'the vision thing'* in line 47), or distance themselves from the content of their speech (e.g. *give the country his version of the vision thing* in line 55). The latter use in particular is frequently observed. This result is considered as being distinctive and interesting because it means that the use of this sequence may help the speaker to build a more secure environment for himself/herself by showing distance from the conversation.

47 everaccused Clinton of lacking ' the vision thing ', as Bush once described
48 Blair admits a problem with the vision thing . Tom Baldwin Deputy Polit-
49 Bush for not having, namely the vision thing . I think the parties in
50 starting to come up again and ' the vision thing ' - that George Bush said
51 hounded by what he oncecalled ' the vision thing '. It makes Daniel Murphy
52 Carl: Oh, thanks. We call it ' the vision thing '. Only way to see out real
53 uncomfortable with what hecalls the vision thing . Conservatives considered
54 a better future. Hemocks it as ' the vision thing '. Kathleen Hall Jamie
55 give the countryhis version of the vision thing . He stumbled at his state
56 Problem with Bush - Bush called the vision thing and... Fleming: Yes, yes,
57 what Bush dismissivelycalled ' the vision thing '. Kissinger, who had geo
58 Where is what George Bushcalled ' the vision thing '? What is going to be
59 what George Bush used tocall ' the vision thing ' has probably mastered one
60 bosses lack what might becalled the vision thing . Their own histories laud
61 areas. The Government is fond of the vision thing , but just what is its picture

Figure 7.4 Fifteen random concordance lines of *the vision thing* from the BoE

In addition, this interpersonal use is different from the other aforementioned interpersonal uses which have been commonly demonstrated by previous studies, e.g. establishing a common ground and maintaining a friendly environment (see Section 7.2.4). Instead of promoting the conversation in the 'normal' or expected way, such as by providing a positive environment or 'keeping the hearers or interlocutors close' (see Channell 1994; Aijmer 2002; Cutting 2007), the vague use of *the vision thing* as shown in Figure 7.4 seems to fulfil the role of protecting the speaker (or writer) by reducing potential doubts or criticisms, and thus to some extent also ensures the continuity of the conversation.

7.4 Vague use and phraseology associated with time

Few studies so far have investigated the word*time* or phraseology associated with it in terms of vague use, most probably because the vague use associated with the word *time* is much less obvious than that with the word *thing* (cf. Crystal and Davy 1975; Channell 1994; Cutting 2007; Ädel and Reppen 2008). The following sections will discuss the use of several phraseological items associated with *time* and show that these items can also be related to vague use.

7.4.1 'from time to time'

Channell (1994) has described single words such as *often*, *sometimes* and *occasionally* as vague words and refers to these words as vague quantifiers of frequency. The current investigation suggests that the phrase *from time to time* can also exhibit this vague quantification. As shown in examples 62 and 63 below, *from time to time* is used mainly as an adverbial phrase of time which does not seem to specify how often an event occurs. For instance, it is not made explicit in example 62 how often or exactly when the public service messages are broadcast or televised, or in example 63 how many times "the topic" has come up.

62 From time to time, the society also prepares public service messages for broadcasting or televising.

63 I would like to see BACDS own a dance hall in the East Bay. I know that from time to time this topic has come up, but nothing to my knowledge has

been done about it.

Thus it can be argued that to some extent the phrase *from time to time* is similar to the above-mentioned vague words like *sometimes* and *occasionally* which are associated with the use of vague quantification of frequency (see Channell 1994: 116-118).

The detailed analysis of *from time to time* also shows that this phrase occurs frequently in business-related texts, which again indicates the broad range of genres where vague language can be found. One of the reasons why *from time to time* occurs frequently in "business discourse" (Koester 2010: 5) could be that its unique use of vague quantification may serve the intended purpose in context. For instance, by being vague about how frequently an action occurs, potential conflicts or inconsistencies may be avoided, as shown in the following three examples of this phrase.

64 Foreign currency management. The Company enters into foreign exchange contracts **from time to time** as a hedge against accounts receivable and accounts payable denominated in foreign currencies.

65 Suitable interface standards will be published **from time to time** in the Official Journal of the European Communities under the ONP Reference List of Standards.

66 As is typical in the semiconductor industry, the Company has received notices **from time to time** from third parties alleging infringement claims. Although there are currently no pending claims or lawsuits against the Company regarding any possible infringement claims, ...

In example 64, since the file of "Foreign currency management" does not specify how often the company needs to enter into foreign exchange contracts, only "from time to time", this policy gives it the flexibility to fulfil this requirement. Similarly, as can be seen from example 65, by using *from time to time*, "suitable interface standards" will not need to be published soon or regularly such as once a week because the action of publication even once in a year will be considered within the scope of "from time to time". In addition, the use of vague quantification exhibited by *from time to time* also serves to mitigate any problems for the firm. For instance, in example 66, the use of the phrase *from time to time* enables the company to be non-specific about how often it has received notices from third parties alleging infringement claims which may damage its image or reputation.

In addition, this vague use of *from time to time* extends to the field of laws and policies which are usually considered as rather formal and 'precise' in terms of the choice of language. As can be seen from example 67, the vague expression *from time to time* is used as part of the Parliament of Canada Act. It was also found that this phrase appears in the US constitution (see example 68). In this example, the use of *from time to time* provides a level of flexibility for the president with regard to the frequency for giving information to the Congress (cf. Bessette and Tulis 2010: 158-160 for the interpretation of this example).

67 The privileges, immunities, and powers to be held, enjoyed, and exercised by the Senate and by the House of Commons, and by the Members thereof respectively, shall be such as are **from time to time** defined by Act of the Parliament of Canada, but so that any Act of the Parliament of Canada defining such privileges, immunities, and powers shall not confer any privileges, immunities ...

68 TheUS constitution requires that the president "shall **from time to time** give to Congress information on the state of the Union and recommend to their consideration such measures as he shall judge necessary and expedient".

Interestingly, these two examples where the vague use of *from time to time* provides flexibility for future actions or events involve certain duties or responsibilities: e.g. in example 67, the Act of the Parliament needs to provide particular definitions and in example 68 the president is required to give information to the Congress.

In other examples which concern both responsibility and authority, the vague use of *from time to time* not only provides flexibility with regard to fulfilling the obligations but also increases the authority's potential power or political influence.

69 The NASD may **from time to time** make such changes or adjustments in such fees, dues, assessments, and other charges as it deems necessary or appropriate to assure equitable allocation of dues among members.

70 ii) except as expressly provided in this Section 2. 26, each provision of this Agreement shall be subject to such reasonable changes of construction as the Administrative Agent may **from time to time** specify to be necessary or appropriate to reflect the introduction of or changeover to the euro in participating member states.

For instance, in example 69, the NASD has aresponsibility to make adjustments in fees, dues, etc.; and the vague quantifier, *from time to time*, allows flexibility of frequency with regard to the NASD taking actions. On the other hand, the power of NASD in terms of making changes when it deems necessary or appropriate appears to be extended with the use of *from time to time*. Similarly, in example 70, it seems that the administrative agent has flexibility with regard to both his/her duty and power.

To briefly summarise, the phrase *from time to time* can exhibit the use of vague quantification regarding the frequency of an event or action. This phrase is used particularly frequently in business-related discourse and legal documents. The results show that its use in business discourse may serve to avoid potential inconsistencies or conflicts and to mitigate existing problems for a company (see examples 64 to 66). It can also provide flexibility with regard to the frequency with which any obligation has to be fulfilled in legal documents (examples 67 to 70).

Similarly to *from time to time*, the adverbial phrases *time and time again* and *time after time* can also be perceived as vague quantifiers of frequency. The phrase *time and time again*, for instance, does not specify the frequency of the occurrence of an event. In example 71, this phrase can be interpreted as 'frequently' or 'regularly', i.e. the "theme of good vs. evil" in Ustinov's work appears rather frequently.

71 The theme of good vs. evil is one thatUstinov says he has returned to in his work time and time again.

The phrase *time after time*, as shown in example 72 below, similarly involves a vague reference with regard to the frequency of the occurrence of an event.

72 Time after time throughout history, stories have emerged of people who help others because of conscience and courage.

Regarding this set of vague expressions associated with *time*, it can be seen that all of them realise the vague quantification of frequency. Where they differ, however, is in the connection between their use and genre, i.e. each phrase is associated more often with a particular type of text (cf. Hoey 2005 for the 'discourse-specific' factor in the use of lexical items). For instance, Table 7.6 lists respectively the top three subcorpora of the BoE in which these items occur. As can be seen, the phrase *from time to time* occurs more frequently in business-related texts (39.4%) than spoken texts (e.g. the American spoken subcorpus, 9.1%), which is consistent with the results discussed earlier. The phrase *time after time* occurs more often in the subcorpora of written texts such as leaflets, letters and advertisements (e.g. British ephemera subcorpus and American ephemera subcorpus) while *time and time again* occurs in the subcorpora of both written texts (e.g. British ephemera subcorpus) and spoken texts (e.g. American spoken subcorpus).

Table 7.6 **The comparison between the set of vague expressions such as *from time to time* in terms of their occurrences in different subcorpora in the BoE**

Lexical item	Subcorpus of the BoE	Freq per mil.	%
from time to time	wbe (UK Business)	152.5	39.4
	brephem (British ephemera)	48.7	12.6
	usspok (American spoken)	35.1	9.1
time and time again	brephem (British ephemera)	3.7	13.2
	sunnow (Sun & News of the World, UK)	2.5	8.9
	usspok (American spoken)	2.5	8.9
time after time	brephem (British ephemera)	3.0	16.3
	usephem (American ephemera)	2.6	14.1
	brmags (British magazines)	1.3	7.1

7.4.2 Phrases with a vague reference

The phrases investigated in Section 7.4.1, e.g. *from time to time* and *time and time again*, are mainly related to vague quantification of frequency. This section will discuss some phrases, e.g. *once upon a time* and *in no time*, which involve a general vague reference to time.

The phrase *once upon a time* is considered to be rather lexicalised, i.e. the whole combination is used as a single unit with a specific meaning (because of a gradual historical process of formal or semantic changes and loss of motivation). As shown in examples 73 to 75, this phrase refers vaguely to a time period that may be far back in the past.

73 Once upon a time, there was a horse named Clever Hans. Indeed, Hans was very clever: He was able to count, spell, add, subtract, and even tell time.

74 It's called, "A Happy Thought". "Once upon a time there was a man who lied, so his most-prized possession turned black and fell off. ...

75 **Once upon a time**there was a millionaire who had a passion for horse racing. He decided to award a prize of 10,000 to anyone who could predict the outcome of any horse race.

Based on these examples, it seems that it is often the pattern '*there* v-link N' that tends to follow *once upon a time* in the text, e.g. *there was a horse* (example 73), *there was a man* (example 74) and *there was a millionaire* (example 75). In these cases, the link verbs and the verbs in the co-texts of *once upon a time* are normally in the past tense. This result is related to the 'typical' use of this phrase in text, i.e. the phrase *once upon a time* is usually used in narratives, in particular as a story-telling technique. The following example from the BoE, for instance, comments on the common features of stories and suggests that the traditional story usually starts with *once upon a time* and ends with *they lived happily ever after* (cf. Herman *et al*. 2005; Cadden 2010).

76 Langer's (e.g., Langer, 1986) studies could write simple reports and simple stories, narratives containing story grammar elements and other features common in stories (e.g., starting with, "**Once upon a time**" and ending with, "They lived happily ever after"...

A detailed analysis of *once upon a time* also shows that when this phrase is not used in stories or fairytales to refer vaguely to an ancient time in the past, it is possible that *once upon a time* is associated with a sense of contrast between different scenarios. For instance, in the following examples, it appears that the use of *once upon a time* does not necessarily emphasise that the event happened in ancient times; instead, the phrase seems to be related more to a discourse function of comparison between the past and present. In example 77, the writer/speaker uses *once upon a time* to compare the change in people's etiquette on trains and buses, e.g. the students used to stand up for their elders "once upon a time" but they may not do so nowadays.

In example 78, rather than emphasising the point that the event happened a long time ago, the phrase *once upon a time* is used to emphasise how the role of the media has shifted, from "watchdog" to "dogsled". The use of this phrase in example 79 is similarly related to a sense of contrast: showing a change in belief with regard to who or what created the earth and everything on it.

77 **Once upon a time** students stood up for their elders on the trains and buses. Some still do. **Once upon a time** men stood up for women on trains and bu-

ses. Few still do.

78 ... because the Redskins are so important here, that they won't ask any member of the Redskins a tough question. And **once upon a time** , the media was supposed to be the watchdog. Now the media's become a member of the dogsled.

79 **Once upon a time** it was God who created the earth and the species that dwell upon it. Now it is evolution which is the creative agent.

In a few cases, the above-mentioned use of *once upon a time* may also indicate exaggeration or irony. In example 80 below, for instance, the importance of lunch in people's lives in the past and present are compared; and the difference between people's viewpoints on lunch appears to be exaggerated by describing how lunch was sacred "once upon a time" and how it has "shrunk to the point of invisibility" today.

80 **Once upon a time** lunch was sacred. Lunch was a fixed point. No one questioned lunch. It was a meal when you sat down, ate three courses off plates with cutlery, drank with restraint and conversed with your fellows. What has become of lunch today? It has shrunk to the point of invisibility.

81 **Once upon a time**, universities had a mission which is probably why they did not need to devise statements about it. Their mission was to seek truth and disseminate whatever truths they found. There were rules for the search and for dissemination.

In example 81, from a first look, the writer seems to be just talking about a past event when universities had a mission and knew the rules for search and dissemination, and not mentioning what thesituation is like nowadays. However, the descriptions about universities' missions in the past as the ideal scenario and the repeated use of past tense signal possible sarcasm and suggest that universities nowadays are not fully aware of or familiar with their mission such that they need to devise statements about it.

In other words, the analysis of *once upon a time* suggests that this phrase can involve a vague reference to time, ranging broadly from an ancient time to any time point in the past. The results show that this phrase is frequently used as a narrative technique at the beginning of a fairytale. In the other cases when the phrase is not used to tell a story, it is possible that it is associated with a discourse use of comparison between the past and present, or between an idealised past and reality today.

The other phraseological items which can be associated with a vague reference to time include phrases like *in no time* and *at some time in the future*. These two phrases are both related to reference to a point on the timeline and neither specifies exactly when this time point or period is. The phrase *in no time*, as shown in example 82 below, exhibits the sense that the event will happen soon, which is similar to the adverb *immediately*.

82 you can enjoy shopping for your needlework and craft patterns and supplies while relaxing in yourfavourite easy chair. And your selections will be delivered to your door **in no time** at all - rain or shine!

83 I find it difficult to accept that**at some time in the future** we might be forced off the roads for good, in fact I fervently hope that such a scenario does not come to pass.

The phrase*at some time in the future* refers to an imprecise point in the future (see example 83). It can be argued that to some extent the sense of vagueness exhibited by this phrase is largely associated with the word *some* in this sequence which is considered as an approximator of quantity in both Channell's (1994) and Wang's (2005) categories of vague language. Other related fixed phrases such as *at some time in the past* and *at some time in their lives* also concern a vague reference to a time point.

The phrases discussed in this section and in Section 7. 4. 1, consequently, indicate that the word *time* (or more accurately phraseology associated with the word *time*) can exhibit a vague use. More specifically, phrases like *from time to time* and *time and time again* can be regarded as vague quantifiers of frequency, and phrases such as *once upon a time* and *in no time* involve a vague reference to time. Therefore, the current analysis of phraseology associated with *time* similarly shows that there are more lexical items with vague use than has been suggested in previous studies (cf. Section 7. 1).

7. 5 Conclusion

In this chapter, I have examined the vague use associated with*thing* and *time*, and the results suggest that, firstly, vague use is frequently exhibited by phraseological items rather than individual words, which establishes that phraseology is important to vague use, and more broadly to the construction of meaning in discourse.

Secondly, the analysis of phraseology with a vague use shows that there are aspects of vague language which await further exploration. For instance, the results reveal that there are more vague lexical items in language than previously expected, e.g. the pattern 'N/NP *thing*' or '*it* v-link *a* N *thing*' (Section 7.1) and phrases such as *from time to time* and *once upon a time* (Section 7.4). These phraseological items with a vague use do not appear to be fully reflected in the framework of vague language provided by previous studies. Additionally, the results show that vague use can be found in a broader range of genres, more specifically, in both informal conversations and relatively more formal texts, e.g. newspaper articles, business discourse and legal documents (Sections 7.3 and 7.4.1). These findings also suggest that it is beneficial to look at vague use from a corpus perspective, especially with large quantities of data, as it can reveal more complex features of language which may be 'hidden' to traditional analysis which uses 'created' examples.

Thirdly, the uses of these vague phraseological items are closely related to the organisation of discourse or the 'social' aspect of discourse (i.e. meaning beyond lexis). The phrase *that sort of thing*, for instance, tends to characterise or conclude one piece of information by appearing normally at the end of a clause or utterance (Section 7.2.1); when this phrase occurs in the sequence 'V/VP *that sort of thing*', it can be associated with a negative reference and sometimes shows the speaker's disapproval of the entities which *that sort of thing* refers to (Section 7.2.3). The phrase *the vision thing*, which is often used in 'political' discourse, may reflect an interpersonal use in context which protects the speaker and distances himself/herself from the words in the conversation (Section 7.3). Similarly, the phrase *once upon a time* can exhibit a sense of contrast (usually with exaggeration or irony) when it is not used as a narrative technique (Section 7.4.2). In other words, it is argued that the study of phraseology can contribute to a more profound understanding of vague use (or the construction of meaning in discourse in general).

PART THREE

Phraseology and English language teaching

Chapter 8 Phraseology represented in teaching and learning

8.1 Introduction: phraseology and pedagogy

Given the importance of phraseology in language use, in particular the construction of meaning in discourse, another objective of the current study is to examine the representation of phraseology in English teaching inChina, more specifically the representation of phraseology in English course-books used in Chinese universities and in English essays written by college learners in China. This section aims to show the importance of teaching phraseology and the challenges involved in teaching it.

8.1.1 Significance of teaching phraseology

One of the main reasons for teaching phraseology isthat "phraseological competence", i.e. knowing an appropriate number of phraseological items and knowing how to use these items effectively in context, is essential for learners (see Sinclair 1991; Howarth 1996; Lewis 2000; Biber 2006; Meunier and Gouverneur 2007; Ellis 2008; Meunier and Granger 2008; Siepmann 2008). Phraseological competence is a crucial part of linguistic competence or communicative competence, and more importantly the skill of using phraseological items properly in context is indispensable to achieving native-like competence (see Wray 2002; Schmitt 2005; Kennedy 2008; Meunier and Granger 2008; Herbst *et al*. 2011). Similarly, as argued by Meunier and Granger (2008: 247), "phraseology should occupy a central and uncontroversial position in instructed second language acquisition". In other words, teaching phraseology should be a core part of teaching the use of English language in the classroom (cf. Siepmann

2008: 185).

Secondly, teaching phraseology can benefit the learners' communicative competence in general. Since phraseology is pervasive in language use, the four major English skills—reading, listening, speaking and writing - involve the use of phraseology. That is to say, these skills which are important to learners' communicative competence can be greatly improved by learning phraseology (see Sinclair 1991, 2004a; Howarth 1996; Lewis 2000; Ellis 2008; Meunier and Granger 2008; Stubbs 2009b). In addition, a better command of phraseology may promote motivation to learn and use the language. For example, being able to use phraseological items provides an "efficient means to interact with other speakers" which will on the one hand "ease frustration" and on the other "engender social motivation for learning the language" (Nattinger and DeCarrico 1992: 114). Further, the use of phraseological items can contribute to the promotion of fluency. Many researchers (e.g. Wray 2002; Schmitt 2005; Coxhead 2008) have emphasised that learners find phraseological items (especially formulaic sequences) highly memorable and easy to pick up and thus learning phraseology helps develop their fluency. As Nattinger and DeCarrico (1992: 32) put it, "prefabricated speech has both the advantage of more efficient retrieval and of permitting speakers (and hearers) to direct their attention to the larger structure of the discourse, rather than keeping it focused narrowly on individual words as they are produced".

Another reason that phraseology needs to be taught in pedagogic materials or classrooms is that learners often have problems in using phraseological items effectively. As will be shown in the subsequent sections, the way phraseology is used by university learners in China in their essays is not entirely satisfactory, especially compared to the way it is used by 'native' speakers of English. For instance, the results from the current study suggest that the learners tend to use a limited variety of phraseological items repeatedly in their essays while appearing to use rarely many other phraseological items which occur frequently in the English language. In other words, it is likely that these university learners do not have a vast repertoire of phraseology in their writing. Additionally, the phraseological items that these learners use repeatedly in their essays tend to involve many grammatical errors or misused collocations. Similarly, Osborne (2008: 67-83) has illustrated that even in the written productions of university-level learners of English, errors (e.g. incorrect pluralised adjectives and inappropriate adverb placement) can occur due to phraseological effects. For instance, the lexical item *native speaker* should not be pluralised as *natives speakers* because this item as one individual unit can "share or transfer grammatical features" (Osborne 2008: 81); the co-occurrence of the components in a multi-word sequence, e.g. *follow blindly everything* (example from Osborne 2008: 81), *set aside time* and *have one thing in common*, can be rather institutionalised in the way that changing the order of the components in the multi-word sequence can be unnatural even though grammatically correct (e.g. *set time aside* and *have in common one thing*). Therefore, in order to achieve an advanced level of using phraseological items, the learners, regardless of their level of linguistic competence, need to be given assistance from teachers and pedagogic materials.

8.1.2 Challenges of teaching phraseology

Previous researchon the teaching of phraseology has revealed several challenges. One of these challenges relates to an awareness of the importance of teaching phraseology. For example, Biber *et al.* (2004) have examined the representation of phraseology in university classroom teaching and course-books by comparing the frequency of the use of lexical bundles, and the results indicate surprisingly that course-book authors do not incorporate more lexical bundles in the course-books despite a heavy reliance on bundles in classroom teaching. Similarly, Meunier and Gouverneur (2007) have investigated the treatment of phraseology in five general advanced EFL course-books and suggested that a number of aspects related to phraseology could still be improved in these course-books, e.g. the metalanguage used to refer to phraseology and the way phraseological exercises are integrated in the course-books. In Römer's (2006) survey on pedagogic materials, she also concludes that with regard to the phraseological nature of language, there are "considerable mismatches between naturally occurring English and the English that is put forward as a model in pedagogical descriptions" (Römer 2006: 126). Therefore, it is important that both teachers and course-book writers raise their awareness of the significance of phraseology in language teaching.

The second challenge is related to the methodology of teaching phraseology. As stated by Kennedy (2008: 38), "[t]here is no tried and true 'method' for teaching phraseology". Meunier and Gouverneur (2007: 121) have also indicated that "information on the selection of learning and teaching-prone formulaic sequences is nowhere to be found, and precise guidelines on how to teach formulaic sequences [are] just as scarce". In other words, not only is there no fixed and 'solid' methodology for teaching phraseology, but few useful methods have been suggested as to how it should be taught.

The current study, therefore, also attempts to provide a few insights in this area by investigating the representation of phraseology in both a pedagogic corpus and a learner corpus. For instance, it will be suggested that the learners should be taught phraseology through a method that combines explicit and implicit teaching. The use of some phraseological items in the learners' writing appears to be problematic even when they are exposed implicitly to the correct use of these phraseological items in English course-books. In other words, the implicit learning of phraseological items will not be enough to achieve a higher level of phraseological competence. The explicit teaching of phraseology in pedagogic materials or in classrooms is equally necessary. Additionally, it will be recommended that the teaching of phraseology or the design of future pedagogic materials refer to relevant corpus-based studies on phraseology (see Sinclair 2004b; Römer 2006; Aijmer 2009; Cheng 2010; Reppen 2010). These studies may provide some insights into what needs to be considered in the areas of teaching phraseology. For example, the current study reveals that there are problems of both 'over-representation' and 'under-representation' of phraseological items in the pedagogic corpus. This result could indicate the need for future pedagogic materials to pay more attention to the selection and presentation of phraseological items, e.g. the frequency and the range of phraseological items (cf. Meunier and Granger 2008; Aijmer 2009; Reppen 2010; Granger *et al.* 2013). Another recommendation is to teach phraseology to advanced learners using concordances (cf. Sinclair 1991, 2003, 2004b; O'Keeffe *et al.* 2007; Reppen 2010). This method can enable learners to notice the collocational or phraseological features of a lexical item by themselves. It may also be easier in this case for teachers to elicit the use of a lexical item from learners. For instance, with the language activities I have proposed for teaching phraseological items based on the current corpus-based analysis (see Section 8.5), teachers can act more as facilitators; and learners will be the main investigators of language use in order to develop their phraseological competence (cf. "Data-Driven Learning" in Johns and King 1991).

8. 1. 3 The aim of this chapter

In the previous chapters, I have investigated the relation between phraseology and fourphenomena (i. e. polysemy, metaphor, evaluation and vague use), and the findings indicate that phraseology has an important role in the construction of meaning in discourse. In this chapter, to achieve the second objective of the current study, I will examine the representation of phraseology in English teaching in China and see whether the significance of phraseology is well reflected in the pedagogic corpus compiled of English course-books used in Chinese universities (CEC) and in the learner corpus of university students' writing (CLEC).

In Section 8. 2, I will discuss the selection of phraseological items associated with the two words (*time* and *thing*) in the pedagogic corpus (CEC) by comparing the frequency data of phraseological items in the CEC and in the BoE. The 'frequency' approach, comparing frequency of phraseology between pedagogic English and 'native' English, can potentially reveal the 'over-representation' or 'under-representation' (or 'mis-representation') of certain phraseological items in the pedagogic corpus (see Biber *et al.* 2004; Römer 2006; Meunier and Gouverneur 2007). In Section 8. 3, I will further explore another aspect of the representation of phraseology in the pedagogic corpus: how the uses of phraseological items are presented, e.g. whether the frequent uses of a phraseological item (such as *at the same time* and *big time*) are presented to the learners. The investigation of these two aspects of phraseology will provide some valuable insights into the design of future pedagogic materials.

Section 8. 4 then focuses on examining phraseology in the learner corpus (CLEC). Similarly, I will first compare the frequency data of phraseology in the learners' writing with those in the reference corpus (BoE) in order to find whether the learners 'overuse' or 'underuse' certain phraseological items (see Renouf 1998; Meunier *et al.* 2011; Granger *et al.* 2013). Then I will also discuss how some phraseological items are used in the learner corpus, e.g. whether these phraseological items are used correctly in the learners' writing and whether the learners use them in the same way as 'native' users of English.

8.2 Phraseological items selected in the CEC

In previous chapters, it has been shown that the polysemous natureof *time* and the metaphorical use of this word are mainly reflected in frequently occurring phraseological items. Similarly in the case of *thing*, evaluative use and vague use are also largely associated with phraseological items. The examination of these phraseological items in the CEC, however, seems to suggest that the representation of these items is problematic, because many of them appear to be either 'over-represented' or 'under-represented' (Paquot 2008; Hasselgård 2009; Callies and Zaytseva 2013) in the English course-books selected in the CEC. In the following two sections, I will discuss in detail how these phraseological items are represented in the CEC with regard to the frequency data of these items.

8.2.1 Phraseological items associated with time

The examination of the selection of phraseological itemsassociated with *time* in the CEC will mainly focus on the frequently occurring phraseological items discussed in Chapters 4 and 5. In Chapter 4, the phraseological items related to the four main senses of *time* ($time_1$ to $time_4$) have been analysed; and in Chapter 5, I have explored the phraseological items associated with conceptual metaphors of TIME such as TIME IS MONEY and TIME IS A RESOURCE. The following discussion will compare the frequency data of these phraseological items in the BoE and in the CEC.

As suggested in Section 4.2.2, $time_1$ ('actual time on a clock') is mainly associated with phraseological items such as the frame '*the time is* + ? + *minutes past/before the hour*', the phrase *what time* and 'tell (*the*) *time*'. These phraseological items are compared in the BoE and in the CEC in terms of the frequency data, as shown in Table 8.1. As can be seen from this table, the normalised frequencies of these phraseological items in the two corpora appear to be rather different except for the sequence 'tell (*the*) *time*' which has similarly low frequencies in the two corpora (0.33 times per million in the BoE and 0.72 times per million in the CEC). The frame '*the time is* + ? + *minutes past/before the hour*' occurs rarely in the CEC (only once), but this result is not surprising because it has been shown that this frame occurs mainly in the texts of radio broadcasts from the 1990s which are unique to the construction of the BoE.

Table 8. 1 **The phraseological items which are associated with the sense of 'actual time on a clock' in the BoE and in the CEC**

Phraseological item with $time_1$ ('clock')	BoE		CEC	
	Freq	Freq per mil.	Freq	Freq per mil.
the time is + ? + minutes past/ before the hour	2,536	5. 64	1	0. 14
what time	1,862	4. 14	80	11. 59
tell (*the*) *time*	147	0. 33	5	0. 72

The normalised frequency of the phrase *what time* in the CEC is almost three times that of the phrase in the BoE (Table 8. 1), which means that this phrase appears far more frequently in the pedagogic corpus than in the BoE. Considering that this phrase is not among the most frequent phraseological items associated with *time* and additionally that $time_1$ is not the most frequent sense of *time*, the considerable attention paid to this phrase in English course-books thus raises a question of what criteria are used to determine which phraseological items are essential to learners and how often they should be presented in pedagogic materials. Since the course-books in the CEC are all designed for university - level learners of English, the repeated presentation of this phrase *what time* in the pedagogic corpus may be considered as a problem of 'over-representation' (see Paquot 2008; Hasselgård 2009; Callies and Zaytseva 2013).

Table 8. 2 shows the phraseological items which are related to the sense of 'a particular time point' ($time_2$). These are among the most frequent phraseological items and thus it is important to present them in pedagogic materials. However, as can be seen from this table, many of these phraseological items occur less frequently in the CEC than in the BoE.

For instance, the normalised frequency of the most frequent item in this table '*at the time* (*of* n.)' in the CEC is almost half of that in the BoE. Items such as *by the time* (*that*-cl.), *at any* (*other*) *time*, *at this time*, '*it* v-link *time to*-inf.', '*it* v-link *time that*-cl.' and '*it* v-link *time for* n.' in Table 8. 2 also occur less frequently in the CEC than in the BoE. A few items, as an exception, appear to have a higher normalised frequency in the CEC than in the BoE, e.g. *at that time* and *by that time*.

To better illustrate this difference, the normalised frequencies of these phraseological items in the two corpora are again presented in Figure 8. 1.

Table 8. 2 **The phraseological items which are associated with the sense of 'a particular time point' ($time_2$) in the BoE and in the CEC**

Phraseological item with $time_2$ ('point')	BoE		CEC	
	Freq	Freq per mil.	Freq	Freq per mil.
at the time (*of* n.)	32,862	73. 03	256	37. 10
by the time (*that*-cl.)	15,470	34. 38	226	32. 75
at that time	7,807	17. 35	164	23. 77
at any (*other*) *time*	6,580	14. 62	66	9. 57
at this time	5,487	12. 19	61	8. 84
*it*v-link *time to*-inf.	3,768	8. 37	46	6. 67
by this time	2,130	4. 73	34	4. 93
by that time	1,424	3. 16	36	5. 22
*it*v-link *time that*-cl.	1,131	2. 51	11	1. 59
*it*v-link *time for* n. *to*-inf.	1,038	2. 30	13	1. 88
*it*v-link *time for* n.	941	2. 09	7	1. 01

A similar conclusion can be reached from comparing the two lines (the 'CEC line' and the 'BoE line') in Figure 8. 1. A few phrases occur more frequently in the CEC than in the BoE, but the majority of the phrases associated with $time_2$ occur less frequently in the CEC, in particular the phrase '*at the time* (*of* n.)'.

Similarly, the frequency data of the phraseological items related to the sense of 'a period of time' ($time_3$) in the two corpora are provided in Table 8. 3 and the normalised frequencies of these items are represented in Figure 8. 2.

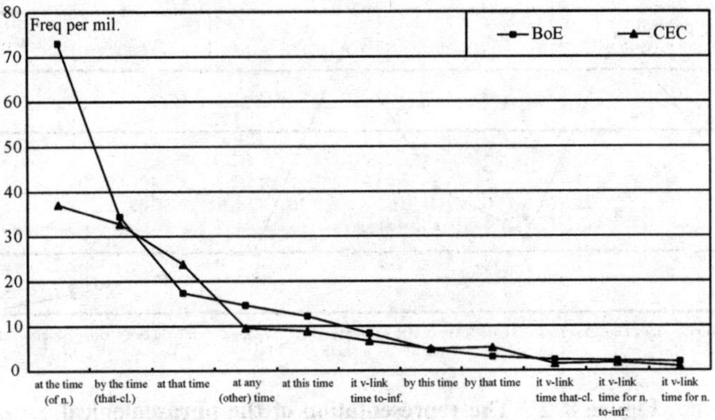

Figure 8. 1 The representation of the phraseological items associated with $time_2$ ('point') in the BoE and in the CEC

Table 8. 3 The phraseological items which are associated with the sense of 'a period of time' ($time_3$) in the BoE and in the CEC

Phraseological item with $time_3$ ('period')	BoE		CEC	
	Freq	Freq per mil.	Freq	Freq per mil.
at a time when-cl. / *of* n.	14,145	31.43	187	27.10
for a long time	7,179	15.95	317	45.94
for some time	7,065	15.70	87	12.61
have *a* ADJ *time*	6,345	14.10	145	21.01
a (long) period of time	4,644	10.32	304	44.06
for a time	2,687	5.97	71	10.29
this time of year	2,431	5.40	44	6.38
(long) length of time	1,942	4.32	22	3.19
this time (a) round	1,534	3.43	1	0.14

Table 8. 3 suggests that some phraseological items associated with $time_3$ ('period') occur a lot more frequently in the CEC than in the BoE, e.g. the items such as *for a long time*, 'have *a* ADJ *time*', *a (long) period of time* and *for a time*. On the other hand, the frequent phrase *this time (a) round* in Table 8. 3 occurs rarely in the CEC. In Figure 8. 2, this feature is shown in a simpler and more striking way. It appears that there is a significant variation between the 'CEC line' and the 'BoE line'.

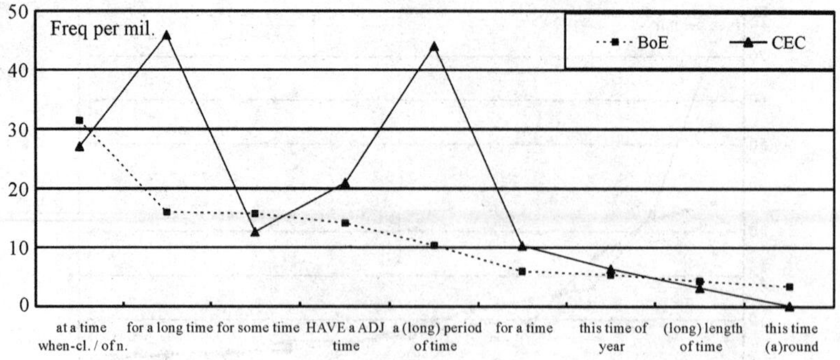

Figure 8.2 The representation of the phraseological items associated with $time_3$ ('period') in the BoE and in the CEC

Even though the reason for this variation with regard to the normalised frequencies of these items is not easily inferred, it is questionable that the CEC present some phrases far more frequently than the BoE whereas it rarely present others. Thus this 'over-' or 'under-representation' revealed in the current investigation indicates that more attention will be needed in the presentation of phraseology in future pedagogic materials (cf. Meunier and Granger 2008; Granger *et al.* 2013).

The comparison of the phraseological items related to the sense of 'occasion' ($time_4$) between the BoE and the CEC seems to suggest that they are more or less similar in terms of the normalised frequency, but their occurrence in the CEC is generally higher than in the BoE (see Table 8.4 and Figure 8.3).

Table 8.4 The phraseological items which are associated with the sense of 'occasion' ($time_4$) in the BoE and in the CEC

Phraseological item with $time_4$ ('occasion')	BoE		CEC	
	Freq	Freq per mil.	Freq	Freq per mil.
for the first time	30,799	68.44	526	76.23
every time (*that*-cl.)	10,739	23.86	160	23.19
(*the*) *next time* (*that*-cl.)	5,180	11.51	116	16.81
each time (*that*-cl.)	4,308	9.57	98	14.20
the last time (*that*-cl.)	4,018	8.93	31	4.49
at one time	3,257	7.24	95	13.77
for the second time	2,013	4.47	60	8.70

Table8. 4(continued)

Phraseological item with $time_4$ (‘occasion’)	BoE		CEC	
	Freq	Freq per mil.	Freq	Freq per mil.
for the third time	992	2. 20	50	7. 25
for the last time	970	2. 16	25	3. 62

It can be seen from Figure 8. 3 that apart from the phraseological items ‘*every time* (*that*-cl.) ’ and ‘*the last time* (*that*-cl.) ’, the other items related to the sense of ‘occasion’ occur more frequently in the CEC than in the BoE. This result could be interpreted as a positive aspect of the course-books which have been included in the pedagogic corpus since the result would mean that they have given adequate attention to these phraseological items. In addition, since there seems to be only a small variation between the ‘CEC line’ and the ‘BoE line’ in Figure 8. 3 (contrast the two lines in Figure 8. 2), it is reasonable to argue that the representation of these phraseological items is more or less well-balanced.

In addition to the phraseological items which are associated with the four main senses discussed above, some frequently occurring phraseological items can also be related to a metaphorical use, e. g. the linguistic metaphors associated with TIME IS MONEY and TIME IS A RESOURCE.

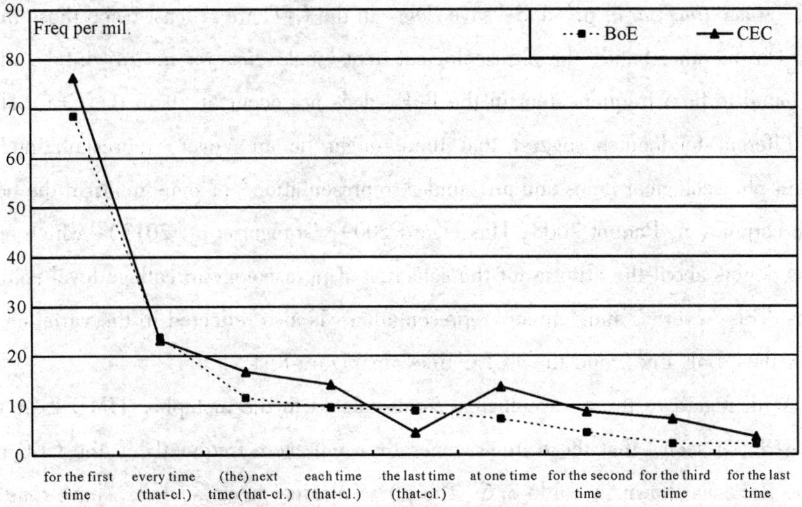

Figure 8. 3 The representation of the phraseological items associated with $time_4$ (‘occasion’) in the BoE and in the CEC

In Table 8.5, the phraseological items related to the metaphor TIME IS MONEY are compared between the BoE and the CEC with regard to the frequency data.

Table 8.5 The phraseological items which are associated with the conceptual metaphor TIME IS MONEY in the BoE and in the CEC

Phraseological itemassociated with TIME IS MONEY	BoE		CEC	
	Freq	Freq per mil.	Freq	Freq per mil.
spend *time* v-ing / *with* n.	12,589	27.98	398	57.68
waste *time on/in* n.	3,259	7.24	101	14.64
make *time for* n. / *to*-inf.	2,251	5.00	0	0.00
a waste of time	1,460	3.24	30	4.35
save *time*	1,274	2.83	55	7.97
lose *time*	1,218	2.71	12	1.74
invest *time in* n. / *to*-inf.	235	0.52	18	2.61

It can be seen from the comparison of the normalised frequencies of these items that some items occurconsiderably more frequently in the CEC than in the BoE. For instance, the occurrences of the phraseological items such as 'spend *time* v-ing / *with* n.', 'waste *time on/in* n.' and 'save *time*' in the CEC are at least twice those in the BoE. On the other hand, the phraseological item 'make *time for* n. / *to*-inf.', which was found to be a frequent item in the BoE, does not occur at all in the CEC. These two different tendencies suggest that there might be an 'over-representation' of certain phraseological items and an 'under-representation' of some items in the pedagogic corpus (cf. Paquot 2008; Hasselgard 2009; Granger *et al.* 2013), which again raises doubts about the criteria for the selection of phraseology in college level course-books. This 'over-' and 'under-representation' is also reflected in the variation between the 'BoE line' and the 'CEC line' in Figure 8.4.

With regard to the phraseological items related to the metaphor TIME IS A RESOURCE, it seems that these items generally occur more frequently in the CEC than in the BoE, as shown in Table 8.6. The phraseological items such as 'have *time to*-inf. / *for* n.', 'find *time to*-inf. / *for* n.', '(*in*) poss. *spare time*' and '*there is no time to*-inf. / *for* n.', in particular, occur at least twice as frequently in the CEC as

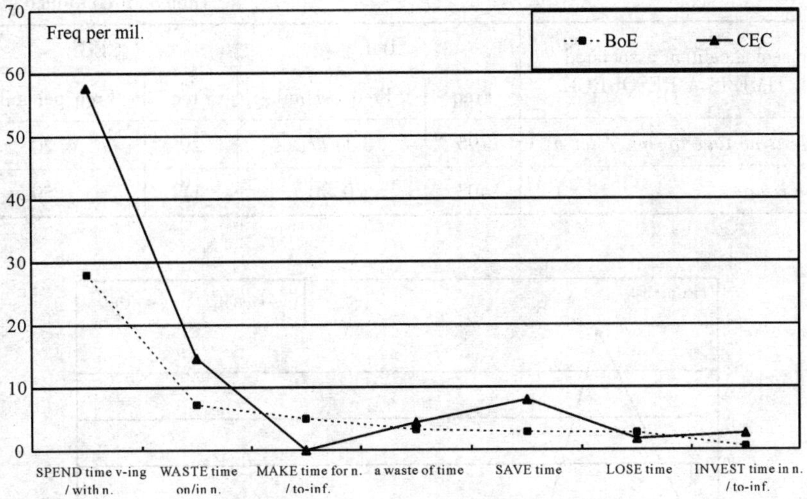

Figure 8. 4 **The representation of the phraseological items associated with TIME IS MONEY in the BoE and in the CEC**

in the BoE.

This observation could be interpreted as a positive feature of the course-books in the CEC since it shows these phraseological items more frequently; however, it could also be argued that some of these items, especially 'have *time to*-inf. / *for* n.', are 'over-represented' in the CEC (see Figure 8. 5).

Table 8. 6 **The phraseological items which are associated with the conceptual metaphor TIME IS A RESOURCE in the BoE and in the CEC**

Phraseologicalitem associated with TIME IS A RESOURCE	BoE		CEC	
	Freq	Freq per mil.	Freq	Freq per mil.
take *time to*-inf.	11,879	26. 40	222	32. 17
have *time to*-inf. / *for* n.	10,577	23. 50	472	68. 41
give *time to*-inf.	3,443	7. 65	59	8. 55
find *time to*-inf. / *for* n.	1,746	3. 88	62	8. 99
get *time to*-inf. / *for* n.	1,493	3. 32	16	2. 32
(*in*) poss. *spare time*	1,389	3. 09	77	11. 16

Table8. 6(continued)

Phraseologicalitem associated with TIME IS A RESOURCE	BoE		CEC	
	Freq	Freq per mil.	Freq	Freq per mil.
there is no time to-inf. / *for* n.	795	1. 77	29	4. 20
time is up	403	0. 90	11	1. 59

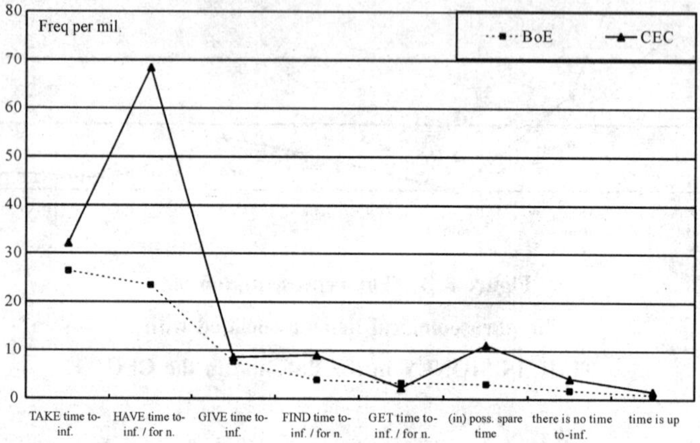

Figure 8. 5 The representation of the phraseological items associated with TIME IS A RESOURCE in the BoE and in the CEC

The discussion given above of the phraseological items associated with *time* in the CEC has thus provided a general picture of how they are represented in the pedagogic corpus, especially in terms of the frequency data of these items. The results show that the CEC 'over-represents' or 'under-represents' certain phraseological items. It is especially alarming that the phraseological items related to $time_1$ ('clock') like *what time is it* seem to be 'over-represented' in the CEC (see Table 8. 1). Additionally, the two particular phraseological items related to the metaphoric use of *time*, 'spend *time* v-ing / *with* n.' and 'have *time to*-inf. / *for* n.', occur significantly more frequently in the CEC than in the BoE (see Figures 8. 4 and 8. 5). Some frequently occurring items in the BoE, on the other hand, appear to occur rarely in the CEC, e.g. *this time (a) round* (see Table 8. 3) and 'make *time for* n. / *to*-inf.' (see Table 8. 5). This unbalanced picture could indicate that there is still a need to pay more attention to the selection of phraseological items in the pedagogic materials or the criteria used for such selection. It is argued in this study that if the pedagogical materials include a more 'balanced' selection of phraseological items, e.g. by making sure that the frequency of phraseological items in the pedagogic materials is more or less similar to that in the reference corpus, it is possible that the pedagogic materials could reflect the way language is used in a more representative manner (see Römer 2006; Meunier and Gouverneur 2007; Meunier and Granger 2008; Callies and Zaytseva 2013).

To further illustrate how the phraseological items associated with *time* are presented in the CEC, all the phraseological items observed with the BoE are examined (including the above-mentioned phraseological items), as shown in Figure 8.6. The normalised frequency is again used to compare the occurrences of these 79 phraseological items in the two corpora because it may to some extent compensate for the difference in size between the two corpora.

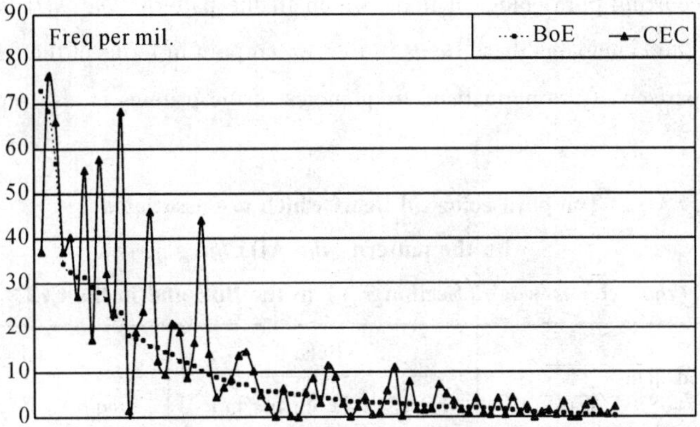

Figure 8.6 The overall representation of the phraseological items associated with *time* in the BoE and in the CEC

The results show that there is a considerable variation between the 'BoE line' and the 'CEC line' (Figure 8.6). The 'CEC line', especially the left side of the line, appears to 'move' dramatically up and down (in the form of a 'zigzag'). This variation between the two lines is consistent with the above argument that some phraseological items occur significantly more frequently in the CEC than in the BoE while some items occur much less frequently or even rarely in the CEC. Therefore, the overall picture of the phraseological items represented in the CEC also suggests that the presentation of phraseology in the pedagogic materials is somewhat 'unbalanced' in terms of its selection.

8.2.2 Phraseological items associated with thing

The examination of phraseological items associated with *thing* in the CEC similarly shows that the presentation of phraseology may be problematic. For instance, the phraseological items which are associated with an evaluative use (see Sections 6.1 and 6.2) and the items associated with a vague use (see Section 7.1) seem to be represented in an 'unbalanced' way in the CEC. The following paragraphs will discuss this finding in detail.

In Chapter 6, it was shown that the evaluative use is mainly associated with language patterns with *thing*, e.g. the pattern '*the* ADJ *thing* (*that*-cl.) *is/was*' (Section 6.1) and '<topic> v-link ADJ *thing*' (Section 6.2). Table 8.7 below lists the frequently occurring phraseological items which fit the pattern '*the* ADJ *thing* (*that*-cl.) *is/was*' and compares these items in the two corpora in terms of the frequency data. The comparison of the normalised frequencies of these items is also represented in Figure 8.7.

Table 8.7 The phraseological items which are associated with the pattern '*the* ADJ *thing* (*that*-cl.) *is/was*' (Section 7.1) in the BoE and in the CEC

Phraseological item	BoE		CEC	
	Freq	Freq per mil.	Freq	Freq per mil.
the thing (*that*-cl.) *is*	5,435	12.08	69	10.00
(*the*) *one thing* (*that*-cl.) *is*	3,755	8.34	83	12.03
the last thing (*that* cl.) *is*	3,143	6.98	24	3.48
the only thing (*that*-cl.) *is*	3,138	6.97	87	12.61
the (*most*) *important thing* (*that*-cl.) *is*	2,430	5.40	45	6.52
the first thing (*that*-cl.) *is*	2,349	5.22	74	10.72
the whole thing (*that*-cl.) *is*	1,648	3.66	84	12.17
the best thing (*that*-cl.) *is*	1,321	2.94	33	4.78

Table8. 7(continued)

Phraseological item	BoE		CEC	
	Freq	Freq per mil.	Freq	Freq per mil.
the other thing (*that*-cl.) *is*	1,193	2. 65	13	1. 88
the worst thing (*that*-cl.) *is*	1,185	2. 63	8	1. 16
the next thing (*that* cl.) *is*	1,164	2. 59	21	3. 04
the good thing (*about* n.) *is*	929	2. 06	4	0. 58
the great thing (*about* n.) *is*	574	1. 28	6	0. 87
the funny thing (*that* cl.) *is*	387	0. 86	9	1. 30
the (*most*) *interesting thing* (*that*-cl.) *is*	374	0. 83	4	0. 58

From Figure 8. 7, it is easy to note that there is a large variation between the 'BoE line' and the 'CEC line'. This variation suggests that certain phraseological items in this group are either 'over-represented' or 'under-represented', which is similar to the results from the examination of phraseological items associated with *time* (see Figure 8. 6). Table 8. 7 shows a detailed picture of this result. It can be seen that some phraseological items such as '*the only thing* (*that*-cl.) *is*', '*the whole thing* (*that*-cl.) *is*', '(*the*) *one thing* (*that*-cl.) *is*' and '*the first thing* (*that*-cl.) *is*' occur a lot more frequently in the CEC than in the BoE, whereas the normalised frequencies of the sequences such as '*the last thing* (*that* cl.) *is*', '*the worst thing* (*that*-cl.) *is*' and '*the good thing* (*about* n.) *is*' in the CEC are only (or less than) half of those in the BoE.

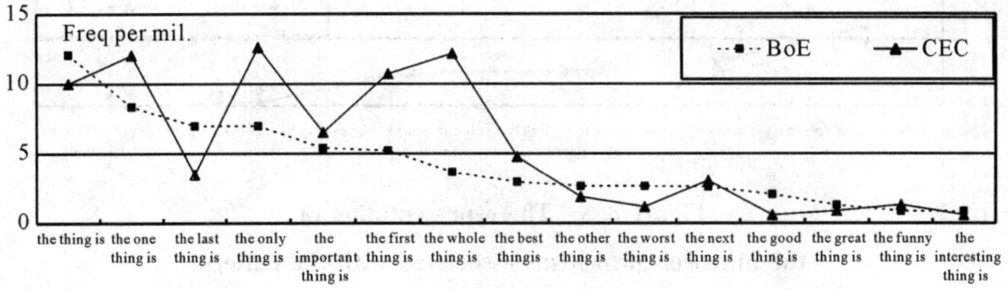

Figure 8. 7 The representation of the phraseological items associated with the pattern '*the* ADJ *thing* (*that*-cl.) *is/was*' in the BoE and in the CEC

Similarly, the phraseological items which fit the pattern '<topic> v-link ADJ *thing*' are compared between the two corpora, as shown in Table 8.8 and Figure 8.8.

Table 8.8 **The phraseological items associated with the pattern '<topic> v-link ADJ *thing*' (Section** 6.2) **in the BoE and in the CEC**

Phraseological item	BoE		CEC	
	Freq	Freq per mil.	Freq	Freq per mil.
<topic> v-link *a good thing*	2,079	4.62	41	5.94
<topic> v-link*a bad thing*	1,102	2.45	22	3.19
<topic> v-link*the* (*most*) *important thing*	1,100	2.44	18	2.61
<topic> v-link *the best thing*	1,093	2.43	17	2.46
<topic> v-link *a big thing*	504	1.12	2	0.29
<topic> v-link *a terrible thing*	342	0.76	0	0.00

It can be seen from Figure 8.8 that there is only a slight variation between the two lines. In other words, the phraseological items which fit the pattern '<topic> v-link ADJ *thing*' have similar normalised frequencies in the two corpora, which could be interpreted as a positive aspect in terms of the presentation of these phraseological items in the pedagogic corpus. However, what still appears to be problematic is that the two phraseological items in this group, '<topic> v-link *a big thing*' and '<topic> v-link *a terrible thing*', occur rarely in the CEC (see Table 8.8).

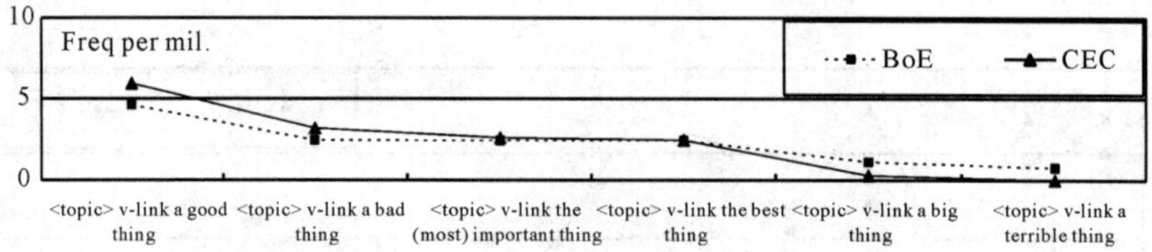

Figure 8.8 **The representation of the phraseological items associated with the pattern '<topic> v-link ADJ *thing*' in the BoE and in the CEC**

The frequently occurring phraseological items associated with a vague use, as discussed in Chapter 7, mainly include sequences such as *that sort of thing* and *this kind of thing* (see Section 7. 1. 1). These phraseological items are listed in Table 8. 9 and compared between the two corpora.

Table 8. 9 **The main phraseological items associated with a vague use in the BoE and in the CEC**

Phraseological item	BoE		CEC	
	Freq	Freq per mil.	Freq	Freq per mil.
(*and*) *that/this/the sort of thing*	5,992	13. 32	33	4. 78
that/the/this kind of thing	2,632	5. 85	18	2. 61
that/this type of thing	323	0. 72	9	1. 30
the vision thing	114	0. 25	0	0. 00
(*it's*) *a family thing*	54	0. 12	0	0. 00
(*it's*) *a long/short term thing*	51	0. 11	0	0. 00

The data show that these vague lexical items generally occur less frequently in the CEC than in the BoE. Some vague expressions, e.g. *the vision thing* and (*it's*) *a family thing* do not occur at all in the CEC (see Table 8. 9). Even though some of these items such as *a family thing* do not seem to occur very frequently in the BoE, the fact that there is no occurrence of these items in the CEC still suggests that the vague use of *thing* is 'under-represented' in the pedagogic corpus. Considering the importance of vagueness in communication and the construction of meaning in discourse, vague use should be equally incorporated in pedagogic materials. Cheng (2007: 178), for example, argues that vague use is "given too little and inadequate coverage, if any, in the textbooks". In her examination of 15 course-books which are used in Hong Kong's upper secondary schools, only 3 course-books mentioned vague language, and 2 of these 3 books actually suggested that vague language should be avoided. Similarly, Orfanò (2013) reveals that there is an 'under-representation' of vague use by university students and asserts that future teaching materials should focus more on the use of vague language.

When all the phraseological items associated with *thing* are examined using the CEC, a similar feature can be found, i.e. that there appears to be phenomena of both 'over-' and 'under-representation' of phraseological items in the CEC. As can be seen from Figure 8. 9, it seems that there is a significant variation between the 'BoE line' and the 'CEC line' regarding the normalised frequencies of the phraseological items associated with *thing*, especially when looking at the left side of Figure 8. 9.

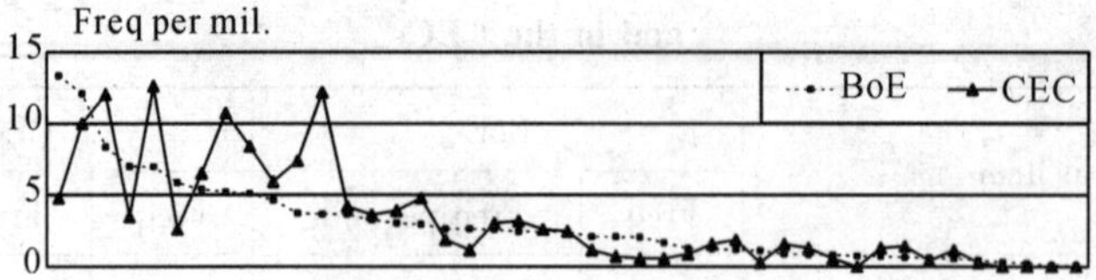

Figure 8. 9 **The overall representation of the phraseological items associated with *thing* in the BoE and in the CEC**

Therefore, to summarise the analysis of *time* and *thing*, the comparison of the frequency data of phraseological items between the BoE and the CEC suggests that there may be cases of 'over-representation' and 'under-representation' of certain phraseological items. The analysis of *time* in particular has clearly shown the significant difference between the normalised frequencies of phraseological items in the two corpora (see Figure 8. 6). Additionally, some phraseological items which are relatively frequent in the BoE were found to occur rarely in the pedagogic corpus, e.g. the sequences which are associated with a vague use (see Table 8. 9). These findings strongly indicate that there is a need for future pedagogic materials to pay more attention to the selection of phraseology, e.g. with regard to the range of phraseological items and the frequency of these items (cf. Meunier and Granger 2008).

8. 3 Presentation of phraseological items in the CEC

Since the 'frequency' approach (Section 8. 2) alone may not reveal the whole picture of the representation of phraseology in the pedagogic corpus, this study has also examined the presentation of the use of phraseology. This section will thus discuss how the use of phraseological items is represented in the CEC by looking at in detail two frequently occurring phraseological items, *at the same time* and *big time*.

8.3.1 'at the same time'

The phraseological item *at the same time* is chosen to be examined here because it occurs frequently in the BoE (56.80 times per million words). The use of this phrase represented in the pedagogic corpus, however, appears to be different from how it is represented in the BoE.

Using the BoE data, it was found that this phrase is associated with three main uses (see Section 4.3.1). To reiterate, the phrase *at the same time* can convey the sense of 'parallel time' (henceforth *at the same* $time_1$), 'in addition' (*at the same* $time_2$) and 'contrast' (*at the same* $time_3$), and each use of *at the same time* is associated with particular patterning features of this phrase.

However, when the three main uses of *at the same time* are examined in the CEC, the results show that these three usages are represented differently. In the BoE, the three uses are represented more or less equally, i.e. they occur with similar frequency. For instance, in the random sample of 100 concordance lines selected from the BoE, the use of *at the same* $time_1$ is found in 33 lines; *at the same* $time_2$ in 35 lines; and *at the same* $time_3$ in 32 lines (Section 4.3.1). In the pedagogic corpus (CEC), by contrast, the use of *at the same* $time_1$ appears far more frequently than the other two uses. In a random sample of 100 concordance lines selected from the CEC, *at the same* $time_1$ accounts for more than half of the concordance lines in the sample, as shown in Table 8.10.

Table 8.10 **The three uses of *at the same time* in the BoE and in the CEC. (**S_{100} **refers to a random sample of** 100 **concordance lines selected in each corpus.**)

	Meaning	S_{100} in BoE (%)	S_{100} in CEC (%)
at the same $time_1$	Parallel time	33	53
at the same $time_2$	In addition	35	29
at the same $time_3$	Contrast	32	18

A further analysis suggests that the fact that *at the same* $time_1$ is 'over-represented' in the CEC may be a result of the frequent occurrences of 'happen *at the same* time' which is associated with the sense of 'parallel time'. As can be seen from Table 8. 11, in the CEC the normalised frequency of this combination, i.e. when the lemma happen precedes *at the same time* within a span of 3, is 29 times more than that in the BoE (4. 20 times per million in the CEC vs. 0. 14 times per million in the BoE).

Table 8. 11 **The co-occurrence of happen and *at the same time* in the BoE and in the CEC. (The search term for this item in the BoE is 'happen@ +2at+the+same+time'.)**

Verb	Node	BoE		CEC	
		Freq	Freq per mil	Freq	Freq per mil
happen	*at the same time*	65	0. 14	29	4. 20

Therefore, this difference regarding the proportions of the three usages in the two corpora suggests thatthe English course-books included in the CEC have paid less attention to *at the same time*$_2$and *at the same time*$_3$. Furthermore, this result means that the functions which are realised by *at the same time*$_2$and *at the same time*$_3$are 'under-represented' in the pedagogic corpus. For instance, as discussed in Section 4. 3. 1, while *at the same time*$_1$ ('parallel time') is used more or less as a time adverbial phrase, *at the same time*$_2$ ('in addition') and *at the same time*$_3$ ('contrast') can also be associated with a discoursal function which contributes to the organisation of a text. Thus it is possible to argue that the discourse use of *at the same time* may have been 'under-represented' in the course-books included in the pedagogic corpus.

8. 3. 2 'big time'

The results obtained from the examination of the frequent phraseological item *big time* are also consistent with the above finding. The phrase *big time* appears to be 'mis-represented' in the CEC compared to the analysis of this phrase in the BoE.

As discussed in Section 4. 3. 2, *big time* can exhibit multiple uses in the BoE and each use is associated with a unique patterning feature of this phrase. To reiterate, when the phrase occurs in the pattern '(*hit/make*) *the big time*', it is associated with the sense of 'becoming successful' or 'reaching the top or highest level of the entertainment field'; when it occurs in the pattern '*a big time* N', it is mainly related to the state of being famous; and when it occurs in the pattern 'VP *big time*', it is similar to adverbs of degree such as *extremely* or *very much*.

However, the analysis of the phrase *big time* in the CEC shows that the presentation of its use in the pedagogic corpus seems to be rather different from its use as represented in the BoE. Firstly, this phrase appears to be 'under-represented' in the CEC because only 5 out of the 80 English course-books contain the use of *big time*. As can be seen from Figure 8.10, there are only 16 instances in total of this phrase in the CEC (some of them are also repeated occurrences in the course-books, e.g. lines 2 and 3). In other words, the normalised frequency of this phrase in the CEC (2.3 times per million words) is less than half of that in the BoE (5.7 times per million words).

1	very large number of "facts". , a. a	big-time	mobster b.. a sunshine patriot
2	bought protection in high places, and	big-time	mobsters moved in and out of co
3	bought protection in high places, and	big-time	mobsters moved in and out of co
4	looked as tough as he was. ... and	big-time	mobsters moved in and out of co
5	"bootlegging", "nightclubs" and "	big-time	mobsters "? 4) Why is Johnny co
6	term (plan), small-scale (experiment),	big-time	(mobsters), open- door (policy)
7	the marshmallow sundaes he loved. ...	big-time	mobsters moved in and out of co
8	adv. bellow /'belau/ v. belt /belt/ n.	big-time	mobster /'mobsta/ n. bill /bil/
9	he liked a good fight? 9) Why were the	big-time	mobsters able to move in and ou
10	. beyond words (L. 2) bias (L. 14) n, v.	big-time	mobster (L. 4) n. bill (L. 4) 31
11	ccessful enough to rise to the level of	big-time	college sports, the "reward" is
12	ccessful enough to rise to the level of	big-time	college sports, the "reward"
13	in any profession or occupation. So "	big-time	college sports" means "college
14	than the workforce. 5. The expression "	big-time	" is used in informal English
15	yet. [Exits] BULA: Poor, Skeeter. This	big time	newspaper business is hard on
16	This year it hit the museum scene,	big-time	, and now galleries are trying

Figure 8.10 The concordance lines of *big time* in the CEC

The results show that the most frequent use of *big time* represented in the BoE, i.e. the pattern '(*hit/make*) *the big time*' (see Section 4.3.2), does not occur at all in the CEC. On the other hand, the sequence *big time mobster* (*s*) appears very frequently in the CEC (Figure 8.10). In fact, this sequence has been considered as a key vocabulary item by one of the course-books in the CEC and is thus repeatedly shown in the exercise section and the section of vocabulary-learning. However, as suggested in Section 4.3.2, this sequence is not a frequent use of *big time*, because when *big time* occurs in the pattern '*a big time* N' (the second use as discussed above), the nouns in this pattern are often words associated with a positive or neutral sense, as in *a big time winner*, *a big time player* and *a big time rock star*. Therefore, it is argued that the frequent occurrence of *big time mobster* in the CEC is a problem or possibly a case of 'misrepresentation' of the use of *big time*.

Among the concordance lines in Figure 8.10, one example (line 14) involves the explanation of the phrase *big time* in the course-books, i.e. metalanguage used to describe *big time* in the CEC, as shown below.

14 The expression big-time is used in <u>informal</u> English to refer to <u>the highest or most important level</u> in any profession or occupation.

The first part of this explanation seems to suggest that the phrase *big time* is used only in informal English, but this is not always the case because the analysis of this phrase in the BoE shows that it can also be used in the texts related to newspapers and magazines (see Section 4.3.2). The second part in example 14 gives the meaning of *big time*; however, it only shows the meaning associated with the first use of this phrase as represented in the BoE. Thus regrettably this description of *big time* in the course-books may have only provided an incomplete (and perhaps 'misleading') explanation.

Based on the presentation of the uses of the two items, *at the same time* and *big time*, the results suggest that the CEC has only partially presented the appropriate use of these phraseological items. More specifically, the frequent use of a phraseological item may not be represented in the CEC, e.g. the first use of *big time*; or it may be represented with rare or uncommon features, e.g. the frequent occurrences of 'HAPPEN *at the same time*' and *big time mobster* in the CEC. Additionally, some of the metalanguage used in the CEC may have failed to present learners with a true picture of the use of a phraseological item, e.g. example 14 as discussed above.

8.4 Representation of phraseology in the CLEC

The investigation of the representation of phraseology in English teaching in the current study also involves an examination of the learner corpus (CLEC), because it is argued in this study that how well phraseology is represented in English teaching is also reflected in how effectively the learners use phraseological items (see Meunier and Granger 2008; Granger *et al.* 2013). Therefore, the following two sections will explore how phraseology is represented in the learner corpus (CLEC). Consistent with the investigation using the pedagogic corpus (Sections 8.2 and 8.3), the examination using the learner corpus will focus on both the selection of phraseological items (Section 8.4.1) and the presentation of the uses of phraseological items (Section 8.4.2).

8.4.1 Phraseological items used in the CLEC

To illustrate the selection of phraseological items in the learner corpus, the case of*time* will be used. As shown in Figure 8.11, the overall representation of the phraseological items associated with *time* in the CLEC is compared with that in the BoE, using normalised frequency in order to compensate to some extent for the difference in size between the two corpora.

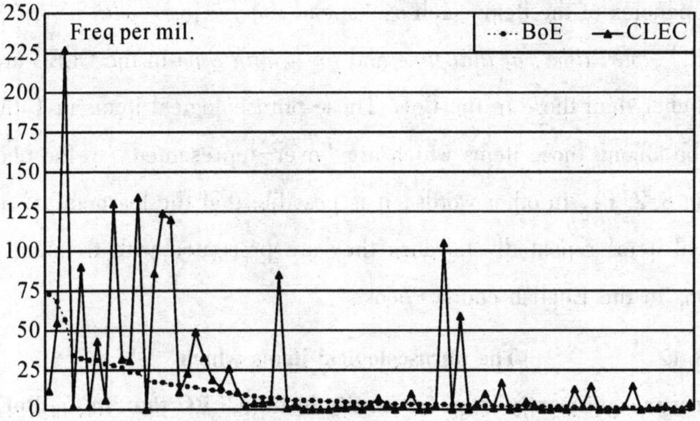

Figure 8.11 **The overall representation of the phraseological items associated with *time* in the BoE and in the CLEC**

It can be seen from Figure 8.11 that there is a huge variation between the 'BoE line' and the 'CLEC line'. It seems that this variation is even larger than the variation between the 'BoE line' and the 'CEC line' in Figure 8.6 (see Section 8.2.1). In other words, the difference between the normalised frequencies of phraseological items in the BoE and in the CLEC is even more significant than the difference between the normalised frequencies of phraseological items in the BoE and in the CEC.

What this result shows is that some phraseological items occur a lot more frequently in the CLEC than in the BoE, and the degree of 'over-representation' in the

CLEC seems to be even greater than that in the CEC (see Section 8. 2). On the other hand, many phraseological items appear to occur rarely in the CLEC (although it is admitted that this result may be influenced by the relatively small size of the CLEC). For instance, 21 phraseological items out of the 79 items under investigation do not occur at all in the CLEC, and another 12 phraseological items occur only once or twice in the CLEC. Thus this result suggests that the learners involved in this corpus tend to use a small number of phraseological items repeatedly in their writing and use the other phraseological items less frequently.

A further analysis also reveals that the repeated use of certain phraseological items in the CLEC may be the result of 'over-representation' of these items in the CEC. For instance, Table 8. 12 lists some of the phraseological items which occur significantly more frequently in the CLEC than in the BoE. It can be seen that the normalised frequencies of the items such as 'spend *time* v-ing / *with* n.', 'have *time to* -inf. / *for* n.', *part time*, *at that time* and *for a long time* in the CLEC are more than five times higher than those in the BoE. These phraseological items in Table 8. 12 also turn out to be among those items which are 'over-represented' in the pedagogic corpus (Section 8. 2. 1). In other words, it is possible that the learners are using certain phraseological items repeatedly because they are presented with frequent occurrences of these items in the English course-books.

Table 8. 12 **The phraseological items which occur significantly more frequently in the CLEC than in the BoE**

Phraseological item	BoE		CLEC	
	Freq	Freq per mil.	Freq	Freq per mil.
at the same time	25,559	56. 80	227	227. 00
all the time	14,624	32. 50	90	90. 00
spend *time* v-ing / *with* n.	12,589	27. 98	130	130. 00
have *time to*-inf. / *for* n.	10,577	23. 50	134	134. 00
part time	7,934	17. 63	86	86. 00
at that time	7,807	17. 35	124	124. 00
for a long time	7,179	15. 95	120	120. 00
have *a* ADJ *time*	6,345	14. 10	49	49. 00
from time to time	5,637	12. 53	33	33. 00

Table8. 12(continued)

Phraseological item	BoE		CLEC	
	Freq	Freq per mil.	Freq	Freq per mil.
a (*long*) *period of time*	4,644	10. 32	26	26. 00
waste *time on/in* n.	3,259	7. 24	85	85. 00
(*in*) poss. *spare time*	1,389	3. 09	105	105. 00
save *time*	1,274	2. 83	59	59. 00
time passed	985	2. 19	17	17. 00
in no time	673	1. 50	13	13. 00
time went on	563	1. 25	15	15. 00
time goes by	354	0. 79	15	15. 00

Similarly, the results show that the majority of the phraseological items which occur rarely in the CLEC are also among those items which are 'under-represented' in the CEC. For instance, 15 out of the 21 phraseological items which do not occur at all in the CLEC seem to be 'under-represented' in the CEC. These items are relatively frequent phraseological items: *half time*, *big time*, *this time around*, lose *time*, *time is running out*, *when the time comes*, buy *time*, *time is up*, etc.

Therefore, the above discussion suggests that there is a relation between the representation of phraseology in the pedagogic materials and the use of phraseology in the learners' writing. More specifically, the data indicate that the repeated use or little use of certain phraseological items in the learner corpus may be related to the 'over-' and 'under-representation' of phraseological items in the pedagogic corpus. Therefore, for the learners' benefit, it is vital that the course-book writers or material designers take into greater consideration the way phraseological items are represented in the pedagogic materials (cf. Meunier and Granger 2008; Granger *et al*. 2013).

8. 4. 2 The use of phraseological items in the CLEC

The use of phraseological items in the learner corpus is not entirely satisfactory either. Taking the phrase*from time to time* as an example, the results show that this phrase is used differently in the CLEC from how it is represented in the BoE. For instance, the BoE data suggest that it can occur in various positions of a clause or sentence, as can be seen from Table 8. 13. The phrase occurs most frequently in the middle of a sentence or clause (in 48.5% of the concordance lines); it can also occur in sentence-final position (20.3%), in sentence-initial position (17.4%) and in clause-final position (13.8%).

Table 8.13 **The flexible position of the phrase *from time to time* in sentences or utterances (data from the BoE)**

Position	Freq	%	Example
middle of a sentence or clause	2,733	48.5	*However, remind yourself from time to time that we're talking about your brain, your nervous system - and mine, too.* *You may, from time to time, be offered additional coverage at the premium rate you establish now.*
sentence-final position	1,144	20.3	*The page is constantly evolving and will only grow better with time, so make a bookmark and stop by from time to time.*
sentence-initial position	982	17.4	*From time to time, it occurs to you that wearing your new shoes was not a good idea - your feet hurt.*
clause-final position	778	13.8	*Although there have been changes from time to time, the basic design had endured since the early 1900s.*

However, the analysis of *from time to time* in the CLEC shows that the learners tend to use this phrase in the clause/sentence-final position around 90.9% of the time (30 out of the 33 instances in the CLEC). Since the position where a lexical item tends to occur in a text indicates its use in discourse or in the organisation of a discourse (see Section 7.2; also see Hoey 2005: 129-151), the use of *from time to time* by the learners may be considered as a 'mis-representation' or at least partial representation of this phrase.

The reason for this result, however, is not easily inferred. Firstly, the fact that this phrase is 'mis-represented' by the learners is not likely to be influenced by their L1, as the equivalent phraseology of *from time to time* in Chinese is seldom used in the final position of a clause or sentence (e.g. the more or less equivalent phrases such as 有时，时常 and 不时 often occur in the middle or initial position of a clause). Secondly, this 'misuse' is not related to the presentation of this phrase in the course-books, because the way the pedagogic corpus presents the phrase *from time to time* is more or less similar to the way the BoE presents this phrase. A possible reason for this partial representation by the learners then could be related to a lack of explicit teaching of this phrase. As argued by Kennedy (2008: 38–39), explicit teaching as well as implicit teaching of phraseology is required to facilitate the learning of phraseological items (cf. Boers and Lindstromberg 2008; O'Keeffe and McCarthy 2010). As a consequence, this book also proposes a few example activities which draw on the current corpus-based analysis to show one way of explicitly teaching phraseological items (see Section 8.5).

Another aspect related to the use of phraseology in the learner corpus is the error rate with phraseological items, as the error rate is also a factor that can be used to evaluate how well the learners use phraseological items in their writing (see Cross and Papp 2008; Granger *et al.* 2013). The error rate is calculated by dividing the number of concordance lines which contain the incorrect use of a phraseological item by the total number of concordance lines of that item. For instance, the verb collocation 'spend *time*' occurs in total 130 times in the CLEC. Among these concordance lines, 17 instances of the collocation are used incorrectly. Therefore, the error rate of 'spend *time*' is 13.1% (17 divided by 130).

Generally, in the case of *time*, out of the 50 phraseological items which occur at least twice in the CLEC, 19 phraseological items are associated with incorrect use. This is rather surprising because the learners involved in this corpus are all studying at the college level and a higher accuracy rate is expected from them. This result thus suggests that to achieve a 'perfect' use of phraseological items may be a challenging task for learners, regardless of their level (see Lewis 2000; Wray 2000; Schmitt 2004; Meunier and Granger 2008), and that it is essential to raise the awareness among learners and teachers with regard to the importance of the use of phraseological items (see Biber and Barbieri 2007; O'Keeffe *et al.* 2007; Kennedy 2008; Granger *et al.* 2013).

Among the phraseological items which involve an incorrect use in the CLEC, it was found that many of them, especially phraseological items with an error rate of more than 10%, are verb phrases or items which contain verbs, e.g. 'spend *time* v-ing / *with* n.', 'take *time to*-inf.', 'have *time to*-inf. / *for* n.', 'have *a* ADJ *time*', 'waste *time on/in* n.', 'save *time*', '*it* v-link *time for* n. *to*-inf.' and *time passed*. Similarly, many previous studies on learner language have suggested that learners tend to make mistakes where verbs are involved. For instance, Cross and Papp (2008) show that in three learner corpora, a German learner corpus, a Greek learner corpus and a Chinese learner corpus, verb-related errors occur more frequently than noun-related errors; and this case is particularly true for Chinese learners.

In addition, it seems that the errors in the CLEC are mainly the result of grammatical mistakes and misused collocations. In the case of 'spend *time*', for instance, the tense of *spend* may be inconsistent with the context which is a grammatical error, e.g. * *government should spent more time formatting* ... (data from the CLEC); the prepositions following 'spend *time*' can be used incorrectly, e.g. *spend time in books*, which is regarded as a collocational error.

Theseabove-mentioned items with a high error rate also appear to be those phraseological items which occur far more frequently in the CLEC than in the BoE (see Table 8.12). To some extent, it can be argued that they are used repeatedly in the learners' writing but are not necessarily used with greater accuracy.

To summarise, the above discussion shows that some phraseological items may be represented partially in the learners' writing and may involve many grammatical errors or misused collocations. It is thus suggested that there is still a need for teachers and material designers to pay more attention to the presentation of the use of phraseological items, e.g. by using corpus evidence to inform the teaching of phraseology and using a combined method of explicit and implicit teaching.

8.5 Suggestions for designing learning activities

In previous sections, it was suggested that explicit teaching of phraseology should be one important factor to be considered in future design of pedagogic materials. For instance, Section 8.3.2 has shown that the pedagogic corpus does not seem to focus on the frequent features of *big time*, but rather the infrequent or uncommon uses of this phrase. Section 8.4.2 similarly reveals that the use of the phrase *from time to time* is only partially represented in the learner corpus. Therefore, this section will propose a few learning activities which draw on the current analysis for learning these two phrases in the university classrooms.

In terms of the phrase *big time*, I have discussed in Sections 4.3.2 and 8.3.2 that this phrase can exhibit three main uses in the BoE and each use of this phrase is associated with a unique pattern. To reiterate, when the phrase occurs in the pattern '(*hit/make*) *the big time*', it is associated with the sense of 'becoming successful' or 'reaching the top or highest level of the entertainment field'; when it occurs in the pattern '*a big time* N', it is mainly related to the state of being famous; and when the phrase occurs in the pattern 'VP *big time*', it is similar to adverbs of degree such as *extremely* or *very much*. As a consequence, the objective for the design of the learning activities for *big time* should include raising the learners' awareness of the three main uses of *big time* and the association between these three uses and the three unique patterns with *big time*.

The activities that I propose for learning *big time* will consider three stages of learning this phrase: noticing the different patterns in which *big time* occurs, understanding the different uses of these patterns with *big time*, and being able to explain or use this phrase. In the first stage (see Figure 8.12), three groups of concordances which contain respectively the three patterns in which *big time* occurs will be shown to the students. They will be asked to observe the three groups of concordances, by discussing the collocates or co-texts of *big time* in different patterns.

A. Observe:
Look at the three groups of examples of *big time* below. Discuss with your partner(s) the words that appear before and after the phrase *big time*.
1) What appears before the phrase in Group 1? What kinds of topic are involved?
2) What appears before and after the phrase in Group 2? Compare the words that appear after *big time*. Are they normally used to describe a person, object or event?
3) What appears before the phrase in Group 3? Regarding these verbs orverb phrases, what trend have you noticed? Are they used to describe successful events or unsuccessful events?
Group 1:
by Frank Sinatra. Clooney, who hit the big time in the telly hospital drama ER
the boyband briefly but made the big time two years after he left jail
mind Kevin Keegan would never make the big time in football. With two years to
of Hollywood stars. Before hitting the big time, she married singer-songwriter
sister Kim. Mick has never hit the big time as a musician and runs a CD
West alight and she hopes to make the big time in the world of fashion and
The 28-year-old, who first hit the big time when she was runner-up in the
Group 2:
he's really proven himself to be a big-time Hollywood star and director.
fightback from cancer by becoming a big-time winner again. American golfer
countryman Jose Coceros became a big-time winner in April when he beat
He has proved over the years he is a big time player who rises to the big
lowered himself into the crowd like a big-time rock star. It was a real group
unless I'm being asked to take out a big-time gangster who's got a lot of
Malloy (Brando) dreams of becoming a big-time boxer while taking care of his
Group 3:
peanut business. Carmen blows it big-time in Western Australia and turns
We are all hoping he will make it big-time. Perhaps Kildare will soon
that they know they've really blown it big time. Hansen: So when you accept
part of the Honda family but blew it big time," a senior Honda executive told
the beginning of the end. He lost it big time. The more crack he took the
United Nations to tell me I messed up big-time. What is done is done but I
and we've really, really screwed up big time. Sorry, we'll try and do better

Figure 8. 12 **Part 1 of the proposed activities for the phrase *big time***

In the second stage (Figure 8. 13), an example of each use of *big time* will be looked at in detail and the features of *big time* will be elicited from the students. In the third stage (Figure 8. 13), the students can try to explain to their partners the use of *big time*. As a follow-up task, they could be asked to find examples for the three uses of *big time*, which can be done by either searching online, using concordancers or looking up dictionaries.

With regard to the phrase*from time to time*, the corpus-based analysis has shown that it can occur in flexible positions in sentences or utterances (Section 8. 4. 2) and that it can be associated with vagueness and used in business-related discourse and legal documents (Section 7. 4. 1). Therefore, the proposed tasks for learning *from time to time* shall reveal these aspects of this phrase.

B. Understand:
Now look at the following three examples of big time (respectively the first line from each group). Discuss with your partner (s) what meaning/use is associated with this phrase and whether it is different in each example.
Line 1 from Group 1:
HOLLYWOOD heart-throb George Clooney is to star in a remake of the movie "Ocean's 11" - in the role first made famous by Frank Sinatra. Clooney, who hit the big time in the telly hospital drama ER, will play Danny Ocean in the new version being directed by Steven Soderbergh.
Line 1 from Group 2:
Yeah, you know, after spending years sort of biting the dust in spaghetti movies and kind of getting not a lot of respect for Dirty Harry and things like that, he's really proven himself to be a big-time Hollywood star and director. Nice nominations. One has to assume that Unforgiven is going to do really well come March 29, when the awards are held.
Line 1 from Group 3:
Compare that to the treatment we've given Carmen Lawrence and Joan Kirner, two of the biggest losers since Jimmy Carter got out of the peanut business. Carmen blows it big time in Western Australia and turns up as a federal minister.
C. Explain:
Summarise briefly your understandings of how the phrase big time is used and share your ideas with your partner(s) or with the entire class.
D. Homework:
Find examples for big time. Provide at least one example for each use of big time. (You can search online, use concordancers, talk to native speakers, look it up in dictionaries, etc.)

Figure 8. 13 **Part 2 of the proposed activities for the phrase *big time***

Figure 8. 14 shows the first part of the activities which attempts to raise the learners' awareness about the positioning of the phrase. They will be provided with several examples of *from time to time* and also the opportunity to check with the concordancer about the positions in which *from time to time* can occur. If possible, they can check their own writing about how they used this phrase previously.

The second part of the proposed tasks, as shown in Figure 8.15, will focus on the vague use of *from time to time*. The students will be asked firstly to compare examples of *from time to time* and examples of *sometimes* and *occasionally*. The relationship between these items which involve the vague quantification of frequency will be elicited from the students. Then they will be asked to provide a few similar examples of vague use, by either searching online (e.g. facebook and twitter) or checking a corpus. The teacher will help students understand the importance of vague use in communication and why vague language should be used.

A. Positioning

1. Look at the following examples of from time to time. Discuss with your partner(s) where this phrase usually appears in a sentence or clause.

1) However, remind yourself from time to time that we're talking about your brain, your nervous system – and mine, too.

2) You may, from time to time, be offered additional coverage at the premium rate you establish now.

3) The page is constantly evolving and will only grow better with time, so make a bookmark and stop by from time to time.

4) From time to time, it occurs to you that wearing your new shoes was not a good idea – your feet hurt.

5) Although there have been changes from time to time, the basic design had endured since the early 1900s.

2. Check with the concordancer. Where does from time to time usually appear in a sentence or clause?

3. Find instances of the use of from time to time in your own writing from the past. How did you use this phrase? (The alternative is to look at the use of this phrase in others' writing.)

Figure 8.14 Part 1 of the proposed activities for the phrase *from time to time*

B. Vague use

1. Compare the following examples. Is the phrase from time to time similar in meaning (use) to sometimes, occasionally? Discuss with your partner(s).

1) I would like to see BACDS own a dance hall in the East Bay. I know that from time to time this topic has come up, but nothing to my knowledge has been done about it.

2) From time to time, it occurs to you that wearing your new shoes was not a good idea – your feet hurt.

3) But frequently, the children follow me. I sometimes ask them if I can please be alone.

4) We bought a house together and I now feel as though I am trapped. Sometimes I wonder if I will ever find happiness.

5) There are also a lot of soldiers who are heavily armed. Occasionally we hear gunfire. It's not nearby.

6) Although we occasionally run late, I enjoy working a straightforward five-day week and it's good having all my evenings and weekends free.

2. Again look at the above examples of from time to time. Do you think the phrase from time to time is related to frequency? If so, how many times do you think the phrase refers to? Is the phrase associated with vagueness?

3. Provide examples that are associated with the vague use from online (e.g. facebook or twitter) or a corpus. Discuss with your partner(s) why vagueness is used and how it might benefit the communication.

Figure 8.15 Part 2 of the proposed activities for the phrase *from time to time*

The last part focuses on the genre in which this phrase usually occurs, as shown in Figure 8. 16. The students will be looking at several examples of *from time to time* which are selected from more formal texts (e.g. business-related discourse and legal documents). They will also be given the opportunity to check the concordancer about the type of genres the phrase *from time to time* can occur in. The teacher will elicit from the students the relationship between the phrase *from time to time* and genre or between vague use and genre.

C. Text
1. Look at the following examples of from time to time. Are they from more formal texts or informal conversations? Where do you think these examples come from?
1) Foreign currency management. The Company enters into foreign exchange contracts from time to time as a hedge against accounts receivable and accounts payable denominated in foreign currencies.
2) The privileges, immunities, and powers to be held, enjoyed, and exercised by the Senate and by the House of Commons, and by the Members thereof respectively, shall be such as are from time to time defined by Act of the Parliament of Canada, but so that any Act of the Parliament of Canada defining such privileges, immunities, and powers shall not confer any privileges, immunities ...
3) The US constitution requires that the president "shall from time to time give to Congress information on the state of the Union and recommend to their consideration such measures as he shall judge necessary and expedient".
2. Check the concordance lines. What kind of texts or genres does from time to time normally appear in? Discuss with your partner(s) why this phrase can be found in these contexts, and why the vague use can be found in these contexts?

Figure 8. 16 Part 3 of the proposed activities for the phrase *from time to time*

To sum up, this section aims to provide an example for explicit teaching of phraseology. The proposed activities for*big time* and *from time to time* consider a series of aspects for learning phraseology in university classrooms. Firstly, it is necessary to raise the learners' awareness about the relationship between the language form and use, e.g. the association between the patterns with *big time* and its uses. Secondly, the learning of phraseology can incorporate the learning of other important elements of language use, e.g. the vague use and the association between phraseology and genre. Lastly, it is important that the learners are provided with the opportunity to observe and notice the language features themselves, e.g. by looking at concordance lines from a corpus or examining examples obtained from online resources.

8.6 Conclusions

In this chapter, I have investigated how phraseology is represented in English teaching in China by examining the selection of phraseological items and the presentation of their use in two corpora – a pedagogic corpus (CEC) and a learner corpus (CLEC), and four main findings emerge from the current investigation.

1) More attention should be paid to the selection of phraseology in pedagogic materials as the current analysis suggests that the criteria used for such selection in the CEC are questionable. Some phraseological items are either 'over-represented' or 'under-represented' in the CEC which means that the use associated with these items is 'over-' or 'under-represented'. For instance, the phraseological items associated with vague use occur rarely in the CEC which indicates that the course-books included in this corpus have given little coverage to vague language or failed to present vague language to learners (cf. Cheng 2007; Orfanò 2013). The metaphorical use of *time* is also represented in an unbalanced way. For example, the two particular phraseological items, 'spend *time* v-ing' and 'have *time to*-inf.', occur considerably more frequently than the other metaphorical expressions in the pedagogic corpus (Section 8.2.1). In addition, the relatively less frequent phraseological items like *what time is it* which is associated with an infrequent sense of *time* are 'over-represented' in the CEC which raises doubts as to what criteria are used to determine which phraseological items are essential to university learners or how often they should be presented in pedagogic materials (Section 8.2.1).

2) The presentation of the use of phraseological items in the course-books may be problematic. For instance, using the examples of *at the same time* and *big time*, the analysis shows that the pedagogic corpus fails to present the most frequent use of these phrases and sometimes chooses to present uncommon features to learners (Section 8.3). Thus the current study suggests that it would be valuable to use corpus evidence to inform the teaching of phraseology in pedagogic materials.

3) The presentation of phraseology in the course-books may influence how learners use phraseology in their writing. For instance, the analysis using the learner corpus reveals that the Chinese learners tend to 'overuse' certain phraseological items in their

essays and these phraseological items that they use repeatedly also turn out to be those which are 'over-represented' in the pedagogic corpus (Section 8.4.1). This result again highlights the importance for future pedagogic materials to pay more attention to the presentation of phraseology.

4) Explicit teaching of phraseology in pedagogic materials is necessary as well as implicit teaching (see Kennedy 2008). For instance, using the example of *from time to time*, the current study illustrates that even though the course-books have shown implicitly the use of this phrase in a more or less representative manner, the learners may still 'misuse' this phrase due to a lack of explicit teaching (Section 8.4.2). It is therefore recommended that a combined method of explicit and implicit teaching is used for the design of future pedagogic materials and that corpus evidence should be utilised to inform the teaching of phraseology to learners (see Section 8.5 for proposed activities to learn phraseological items).

Appendices

Appendix 1: English course-books selected for the CEC

Course-book	Author/Editor	Year	Publisher	Tokens
NewHorizon College English (1-4)	Haitang Zheng	2008	FLTRP	354,670
NewStandard College English (1-4)	Qiufang Wen	2009	FLTRP	298,835
NewVision College English (1-4)	Yan Zhou	2011	FLTRP	316,710
New College English (1-4)	Huilan Ying	2012	FLTRP	716,520
Contemporary College English (1-6)	Limin Yang	2011	FLTRP	775,513
College English (1-6)	Hu*et al.*	2004	FLTRP	531,040
Advanced English (1-2)	Hanxi Zhang	2011	FLTRP	148,101
Comprehensive College English (1-2)	Hongliu Jiang	2005	FLTRP	155,758
Zooming in: An Integrated English Course (1-8)	Xiubai Qin	2007	SFLEP	688,095
College English: Intensive reading (1-6)	Yafen Dong	2007	SFLEP	555,856
New College English: Integrated Course (1-6)	Yinhua Li	2011	SFLEP	642,000
An Integrated English Course (1-8)	Zhaoxiong He	2011	SFLEP	690,045
A New English Course (1-8)	Guanyi Li	2012	SFLEP	736,987
New College English (1-2)	Hongmei Han	2010	ESP	122,253

表(续)

Course-book	Author/Editor	Year	Publisher	Tokens
College English (1-6)	Huang*et al.*	2008	PUP	135,362
New College English (1-4)	Feng*et al.*	2011	CUPP	78,271
				Total: 6,946,016

Note: FLTRP is the initial for the publisher: Foreign Language Teaching and Research Press; SFLEP stands for Shanghai Foreign Language Education Press; ESP stands for Economic Science Press; PUP stands for Peking University Press; CUPP stands for China University of Petroleum Press.

Appendix 2: Evans's conceptual semantic network for time (Evans 2005: 52)

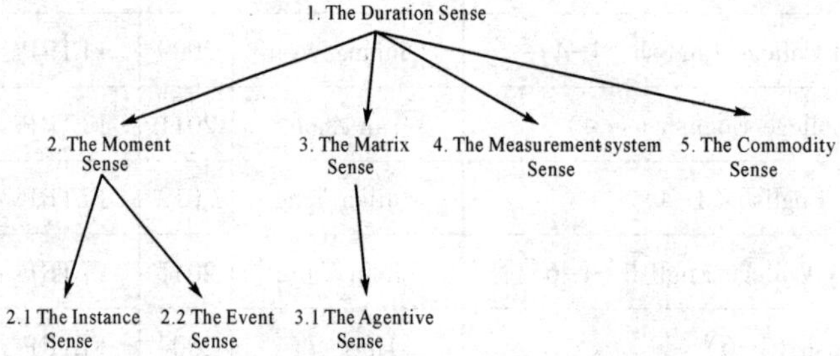

Examples given by Evans (2005):

1 The Duration Sense (similar to $time_3$ ['period'] in this study; see Table 5.1):

My headache went (away) after a short time.

2 The Moment Sense (similar to $time_2$ ['point']):

The time for a decision has arrived/come.

2.1The Instance Sense (similar to $time_4$ ['occasion']):

This time, it was a bit more serious because I got a registered letter.

2.2 The Event Sense (overlaps with $time_3$ ['period']):

The young woman's time [=labour] approached.

3 The Matrix Sense (similar to 'time as motion'):

Time flows/runs/goes on forever.

3.1 The Agentive Sense (similar to $time_8$ ['person']):

Time is the greatest innovator.

4 The Measurement-system Sense (similar to $time_1$ ['clock']):

Eastern Standard Time is five hours behind Greenwich Mean Time.

5 The Commodity Sense (similar to $time_5$ ['money']):

Remember that time is money.

References

[1] ACHARD M, NIEMEYER S. Cognitive linguistics, second language acquisition, and foreign language teaching [M]. Berlin: Walter de Gruyter, 2004.

[2] ÄDEL A, REPPEN R. Corpora and discourse: The challenges of different settings [M]. Amsterdam: John Benjamins Publishing Company, 2008.

[3] AIJMER K. English discourse particles: Evidence from a corpus [M]. Amsterdam: John Benjamins Publishing Company., 2002.

[4] AIJMER, K. Corpora and language teaching [M]. Amsterdam: John Benjamins Publishing Company, 2009.

[5] AIJMER K, ALTENBERG B. Advances in corpus-based contrastive linguistics: Studies in honour of Stig Johansson [M]. Amsterdam: John Benjamins Publishing Company, 2013

[6] AIJMER K, STENSTRÖM A. Discourse patterns in spoken and written corpora [M]. Amsterdam: John Benjamins Publishing Company, 2004.

[7] AITCHISON J. Words in the mind: An introduction to the mental lexicon. 4th edition [M]. West Sussex: John Wiley & Sons, 2012.

[8] ALTENBERG B. On the phraseology of spoken English: The evidence of recurrent word combinations [C] // A. P. COWIE. Phraseology: Theory, analysis and application. Oxford: Clarendon Press, 1998: 101-122.

[9] ANDERSON G, AIJMER K. Pragmatics of society [M]. Berlin: Walter de Gruyter, 2011.

[10] ANDERSON W. The phraseology of administrative French: A corpus-based study [M]. Amsterdam: Rodop, 2006.

[11] ANDERSON W. Language in Scotland: Corpus-based studies [M]. Amsterdam: Rodopi, 2013.

[12] ARNAUD P, BÉJOINT H. Vocabulary and applied linguistics [M]. Lon-

don: Macmillan, 1992.

[13] ARNAUD P, FERRAGNE E, LEWIS D, MANIEZ F. Adjective + Noun sequences in attributive or NP-final positions: Observations on lexicalization [C] // S GRANGER, F MEUNIER. Phraseology: An interdisciplinary perspective. Amsterdam: John Benjamins Publishing Company, 2008: 111-126.

[14] ARONOFF M, REES-MILLER J. The handbook of linguistics [M]. Oxford: Blackwell Publishing, 2003.

[15] ASHER N, BENAMARA F, MATHIEU Y. Appraisal of opinion expressions in discourse [J]. Linguisticae Investigationes, 2009, 32 (2), 279-292.

[16] BAKER G, HACKER P. Wittgenstein: Understanding and meaning [M]. Malden: Blackwell, 2008.

[17] BARCELONA A. Clarifying and applying the notions of metaphor and metonymy within cognitive linguistics: An update [C] //R DIRVEN, R PÖRINGS. Metaphor and metonymy in comparison and contrast. Berlin: Mouton de Gruyter, 2002: 207-277.

[18] BARCELONA A. Metaphor and metonymy at the crossroads: A cognitive perspective [M]. Berlin: Mouton de Gruyter, 2003.

[19] BARCELONA A, BENCZES R, RUIZ DE MENDOZA IBÁÑEZ F. Defining metonymy in cognitive linguistics: Towards a consensus view [M]. Amsterdam: John Benjamins Publishing Company, 2011.

[20] BARNBROOK G. Language and computers: A practical introduction to the computer analysis of language [M]. Edinburgh: Edinburgh University Press, 1996.

[21] BARNBROOK G. Sinclair on collocation [J]. International Journal of Corpus Linguistics, 2007, 12 (2), 183-199.

[22] BARNBROOK G, MASON O, KRISHNAMURTHY R. Collocation: Applications and implications [M]. London: Palgrave Macmillan, 2013.

[23] BAPTISTA L, RAST E. Meaning and context [M]. Bern: Peter Lang, 2010.

[24] BEDNAREK M. Evaluation in media discourse: Analysis of a newspaper corpus [M]. London: Continuum, 2006.

[25] BENCZES R, BARCELONA A, RUIZ DE MENDOZA IBÁÑEZ F J. Defining metonymy in cognitive linguistics: Towards a consensus view [M]. Amsterdam: John Benjamins Publishing Company, 2011.

[26] BESNIER N. Reported speech and affect on Nukulaelae Atoll [C] //J HILL, J IRVINE. Responsibility and evidence in oral discourse. Cambridge: Cambridge University Press, 1993: 161-181.

[27] BESSETTE J, TULIS J. The presidency in the constitutional order: An historical examination [M]. Louisiana State University Press, 2010.

[28] BIBER D. University language: A corpus-based study of spoken and written registers [M]. Amsterdam: John Benjamins Publishing Company, 2006.

[29] BIBER D, BARBIERI F. Lexical bundles in university spoken and written registers [J]. English for Specific Purposes, 2007, 26: 263-286.

[30] BIBER D, CONRAD S. Register, genre and style [M]. Cambridge: Cambridge University Press, 2009.

[31] BIBER D, CONRAD S, REPPEN R. Corpus linguistics: Investigating language structure and use [M]. Cambridge: Cambridge University Press, 1998.

[32] BIBER D, CONRAD S, CORTES V. If you look at …: Lexical bundles in university teaching and textbooks [J]. Applied Linguistics, 2004, 25 (3), 371-405.

[33] BOERS F, LINDSTROMBERG S. Cognitive linguistic approaches to teaching vocabulary and phraseology [M]. Berlin: Walter de Gruyter, 2008.

[34] BOLLY C. The acquisition of phraseological units by advanced learners of French as an L2: High-frequency verbs and learner corpora [C] //E LABEAU, F MYLES. The advanced learner variety: The case of French. Bern: Peter Lang, 2009: 199-220.

[35] BORODITSKY L. How languages construct time [C] //S DEHAENE, E BRANNON. Space, time and number in the Brain: Searching for the foundations of mathematical thought. London: Elsevier, 2011: 333-341.

[36] BOYE K. Epistemic meaning: A crosslinguistic and functional-cognitive study [M]. Berlin: Walter de Gruyter, 2012.

[37] BURGER H. Phraseology: An international handbook of contemporary research [M]. Berlin: Walter de Gruyter, 2007.

[38] BUTLER C S. Collocational frameworks in Spanish [J]. International Journal of Corpus Linguistics, 1998, 3 (1): 1-32.

[39] BUTTERFIELD J. Damp squid: The English language laid bare [M]. Oxford: Oxford University Press, 2008.

[40] BYRAM M. Teaching and assessing intercultural communicative competence [M]. Clevedon: Multilingual Matters, 1997.

[41] CADDEN M. Telling children's stories: Narrative theory and children's literature [M]. University of Nebraska Press, 2010.

[42] CALLIES M, Zaytseva E. The Corpus of Academic Learner English (CALE) - A new resource for the study and assessment of advanced language proficiency [C] //S GRANGER, G. GILQUIN, F MEUNIER. Twenty years of learner corpus research: Looking back, moving ahead. Belgium: Presses universitaires de Louvain, 2013: 49-60.

[43] CAMERON L. Confrontation or complementarity? Metaphor in language use and cognitive metaphor theory [J]. Annual Review of Cognitive Linguistics, 2007, 5 (1): 107-135.

[44] CAMERON L. Metaphor and talk [C] //R GIBBs. The Cambridge handbook of metaphor and thought. Cambridge: Cambridge University Press, 2008: 197-211.

[45] CARROLL R. Vague language in the medieval recipes of the Forme of Cury [C] // M PEIKOLA, J SKAFFAR, S TANSKANEN. Instructional writing in English. Amsterdam: John Benjamins Publishing Company, 2009: 55-82.

[46] CARTER R. Vocabulary: Applied linguistic perspectives. 2nd edition [M]. London and New York: Routledge, 1998.

[47] CARTER R, MCCARTHY M. Exploring Spoken English [M]. Cambridge: Cambridge University Press, 1997.

[48] CHANNELL J. Vague language [M]. Oxford: Oxford University Press, 1994.

[49] CHANNELL J. Corpus-based analysis of evaluative lexis [C] //S HUNSTON, G. THOMPSON. Evaluation in text: Authorial stance and the construction of discourse. Oxford: Oxford University Press, 2000: 38-55.

[50] CHARLES M., PECORARI D, HUNSTON S. Academic writing: At the interface of corpus and discourse [M]. London: Continuum, 2009.

[51] CHARTERIS-BLACK J. Corpus approaches to critical metaphor analysis [M]. London: Palgrave Macmillan, 2004.

[52] CHENG W. The use of vague language across spoken genres in an intercultural Hong Kong Corpus [C] //J CUTTING. Vague language explored. Palgrave

Macmillan, 2007: 161-181.

[53] CHENG W. What can a corpus tell us about language teaching? [C] // A O' KEEFFE, M MCCARTHY. The Routledge handbook of corpus linguistics. London: Routledge, 2010: 319-332.

[54] CONRAD S, BIBER D. Adverbial marking of stance in speech and writing [C] // S HUNSTON, G THOMPSON. Evaluation in text: Authorial stance and the construction of discourse. Oxford: Oxford University Press, 2000: 56-73.

[55] COTTERILL J. I think he was kind of shouting or something: Uses and abuses of vagueness in the British courtroom [C] //J CUTTING. Vague language explored. Palgrave Macmillan, 2007: 97-114.

[56] COWIE A P. Phraseology [C] //R ASHER. The Encyclopedia of language and linguistics [M]. Oxford: Oxford University Press, 1994: 3168-3171.

[57] COWIE A P. Phraseology: Theory, analysis, and applications [M]. Oxford: Clarendon Press, 1998.

[58] CROFT W. The role of domains in the interpretation of metaphors and metonymies [J]. Cognitive Linguistics, 1993, 4 (4), 335-370.

[59] CROFT W, CRUSE, D. Cognitive linguistics [M]. Cambridge: Cambridge University Press, 2004.

[60] CROSS J, PAPP S. Creativity in the use of verb + noun combinations by Chinese learners of English [C] //G. GILQUIN, S PAPP, M DÍEZ-BEDMAR. Linking up contrastive and learner corpus research. New York: Rodopi, 2008.

[61] CRUSE A. Meaning in language: An introduction to semantics and pragmatics. 3rd edition [M]. Oxford: Oxford University Press, 2011.

[62] CRYSTAL D, DAVY D. Advanced conversational English [M]. London: Longman, 1975.

[63] CUTTING J. Vague language explored [M]. London: Palgrave Macmillan, 2007.

[64] CUTTING J. Thingmy an aa the rest o it: Vague language in spoken Scottish English [C] // W ANDERSON. Language in Scotland: Corpus-based studies. Amsterdam: Rodopi, 2013: 189-214.

[65] DECLERCK R. The grammar of the English tense system: A comprehensive analysis [M]. Berlin: Walter de Gruyter, 2006.

[66] DEIGNAN A. A corpus-based study of some linguistic features of

metaphor [D]. Ph. D. dissertation, the University of Birmingham, 1997.

[67] DEIGNAN A. Metaphor and corpus linguistics [M]. Amsterdam: John Benjamins Publishing Company, 2005.

[68] DEIGNAN A. Corpus linguistics and metapho [C] //GIBBS. The Cambridge handbook of metaphor and thought. Cambridge: Cambridge University Press, 2008a: 280-294.

[69] DEIGNAN A. Corpus linguistic data and conceptual metaphor theory [C] //M ZANOTTO, L CAMERON, M CAVALCANTI. Confronting metaphor in use: An applied linguistic approach. Amsterdam: John Benjamins Publishing Company, 2008b: 149-162.

[70] DIRVEN R. Metaphor as a basic means for extending the lexicon [C] // W PAPROTTÉ, R DIRVEN. The ubiquity of metaphor: Metaphor in language and thought. Amsterdam/Philadelphia: John Benjamins Publishing Company, 1985: 85-119.

[71] DIRVEN R. Metonymy and metaphor: Different mental strategies of conceptualisation [C] //R DIRVEN, R PÖRINGS. Metaphor and metonymy in comparison and contrast. Berlin: Mouton de Gruyter, 2002: 75-111.

[72] DIRVEN R, PÖRINGS R. Metaphor and metonymy in comparison and contrast [M]. Berlin: Mouton de Gruyter, 2002.

[73] DORST A, KAAL A. Metaphor in discourse: Beyond the boundaries of MIP [C] //F MACARTHUR ET AL. Metaphor in use: Context, culture, and communication. Amsterdam: John Benjamins Publishing Company, 2012: 51-68.

[74] DRAVE N. Vaguely speaking: A corpus approach to vague language in intercultural conversations [C] //P PETERS, P COLLINS, A SMITH. New frontiers of corpus research: Papers from the twenty first international conference on English language research on computerized corpora, Sydney 2000. Amsterdam: Rodopi, 2002: 25-40.

[75] ELLIS N C. Phraseology: The periphery and the heart of language [C] //F MEUNIER, S GRANGER. Phraseology in foreign language learning and teaching. Philadelphia, PA: John Benjamins Publishing Company, 2008: 1-13.

[76] EVANS V. The structure of time [M]. Amsterdam: John Benjamins Publishing Company, 2003.

[77] EVANS V. The meaning of time: polysemy, the lexicon and conceptual

structure [J]. Linguistics, 2005, 41: 33-75.

[78] FAIRCLOUGH N. Analysing Discourse: Textual analysis for social research [M]. Oxford: Routledge, 2003.

[79] FAUCONNIER G, TURNER M. The way we think [M]. New York: Basic Books, 2002.

[80] FAUCONNIER G, TURNER M. Rethinking metaphor [C] //R GIBBS. The Cambridge handbook of metaphor and thought. Cambridge: Cambridge University Press, 2008: 53-66.

[81] FELDMAN J. From Molecule to Metaphor [M]. Cambridge: Bradford MIT Press, 2006.

[82] FELLBAUM C. Idioms and collocations: Corpus-based linguistic and lexicographic studies [M]. London: Continuum, 2007.

[83] FERNANDEZ J, YULDASHEV A Variation in the use of general extenders and stuff in instant messaging interactions [J]. Journal of Pragmatics, 2011, 43: 2610-2626.

[84] FERNÁNDEZ-DOMÍNGUEZ J. Productivity in English word-formation: An approach to N+N compounding [M]. Bern: Peter Lang, 2009.

[85] FIEDLER S. Phraseology in planned languages [C] //H BURGER. Phraseology: An international handbook of contemporary research. Berlin: Walter de Gruyter, 2007: 779-788.

[86] FIRTH J R. The technique of semantics [C] // J R FIRTH. Papers in linguistics 1934-1951. Oxford: Oxford University Press.. 1957: 7-33.

[87] FIRTH J R. Papers in linguistics 1934-1951 [M]. Oxford: Oxford University Press, 1957.

[88] FORCEVILLE C, URIOS - APARISI E. Multimodal metaphor [M]. Berlin: Walter de Gruyter, 2009.

[89] FRANCIS G. Anaphoric nouns [M]. Birmingham: English Language Research, 1986.

[90] FRANCIS G. A corpus - driven approach to grammar - principles, methods and examples [C] //M BAKER, G FRANCIS, E TOGNINI - BONELLI. Text and technology: In honour of John Sinclair. Philadelphia, PA: John Benjamins Publishing Company, 1993: 137-154.

[91] FREGE G. The foundations of arithmetic [M]. Oxford: Basil

Blackwell, 1978.

[92] FRONEK J. Thing as a function word [J]. Linguistics, 1982, 20: 633-654.

[93] GEE J, HANDFORD M. The Routledge handbook of discourse analysis [M]. Oxon: Routledge, 2012.

[94] GEERAERTS D. Cognitive linguistics: Basic readings [M]. Berlin: Walter de Gruyter, 2006.

[95] GEERAERTS D, CUYCKENS H. The Oxford handbook of cognitive linguistics [M]. Oxford: Oxford University Press, 2007.

[96] GENETTI C. How languages work: An introduction to language and linguistics [M]. Cambridge: Cambridge University Press, 2014.

[97] GIBBS R JR. The poetics of mind: Figurative thought, language and understanding [M]. Cambridge: Cambridge University Press, 1994.

[98] GIBBS R JR. The Cambridge handbook of metaphor and thought [M]. Cambridge: Cambridge University Press, 2008.

[99] GIBBS R JR. Evaluating Conceptual Metaphor Theory [J]. Discourse Processes, 2011, 48 (8): 529-562.

[100] GLÄSER R. A plea for phraseo - stylistics [C] //D KASTOVSKY, A SZWEDEK. Linguistics across historical and geographical boundaries. Berlin: Walter de Gruyter, 1986: 41-52.

[101] GLÄSER R. The stylistic potential of phraseological units in the light of genre analysis [C] //A P COWIE. Phraseology: Theory, analysis, and applications. Oxford: Oxford: Clarendon Press, 1998: 125-143.

[101] GOATLY A. Washing the brain: Metaphor and hidden ideology [M]. Amsterdam: John Benjamins Publishing Company, 2007.

[102] GODDARD C. Semantic analysis: A practical introduction [M]. Oxford: Oxford University Press, 1998.

[103] GOLDBERG A E. Constructions at work: The nature of generalization in language [M]. Oxford: Oxford University Press, 2006.

[104] GONZÁLVEZ-GARCÍA F, PEÑA-CERVEL M, PÉREZ HERNÁNDEZ L. Metaphor and metonymy revisited beyond the Contemporary Theory of Metaphor. Amsterdam: John Benjamins Publishing Company, 2013.

[105] GRADY E, TAUB S, MORGAN P. Compound and primitive metaphors

[C] //A GOLDBERG. Conceptual structure, discourse and language. Stanford: CSLI, 1996: 177-187.

[106] GRANGER S, MEUNIER F. Phraseology: An interdisciplinary perspective [M]. Philadelphia, PA: John Benjamins Publishing Company, 2008.

[107] GRANGER S, PAQUOT M. Disentangling the phraseological web [C] //S GRANGER, F MEUNIER. Phraseology: An interdisciplinary perspective. Amsterdam: John Benjamins Publishing Company, 2008: 27-50.

[108] GRANGER S, GILQUIN G, MEUNIER F. Twenty years of learner corpus research: Looking back, moving ahead [M]. Belgium: Presses universitaires de Louvain, 2013.

[109] GREAVES C, WARREN M. What can a corpus tell us about multi-word units? [C] //A O' KEEFFE, M. MCCARTHY. The Routledge handbook of corpus linguistics. London and New York: Routledge, 2010: 212-226.

[110] GRIES S. Phraseology and linguistic theory: A brief survey [C] //S GRANGER, F MEUNIER. Phraseology: An interdisciplinary perspective. Amsterdam: John Benjamins Publishing Company, 2008: 3-16.

[111] GROOM N. Closed-class keywords and corpus-driven discourse analysis [C] //M BONDI, M SCOTT. Keyness in texts. Amsterdam: John Benjamins Publishing Company, 2010: 59-78.

[112] HALLIDAY M A K. An introduction to functional grammar. 2nd edition [M]. Oxford: Blackwell, 1994.

[113] HALLIDAY M A K, HASAN R. Cohesion in English [M]. London: Longman, 1976.

[114] HANDFORD M. The language of business meetings [M]. Cambridge: Cambridge University Press, 2010.

[115] HANDL S. Essential collocations for learners of English: The role of collocational direction and weigh [C] //F MEUNIER, S GRANGER. Phraseology in foreign language learning and teaching. Amsterdam: John Benjamins Publishing Company, 2008: 43-66.

[116] HANKS P. Metaphoricity is gradable [C] //A STEFANOWITSCH, S T GRIES. Corpus-based approaches to metaphor and metonymy. Berlin: Mouton de Gruyter, 2006: 17-35.

[117] HANKS P. 2013. Lexical analysis: Norms and Exploitations. Cambridge:

MIT Press.

[118] HARVEY K, KOTEYKO N. Exploring health communication: Language in action [M]. Oxon: Routledge, 2013.

[119] HASER V. Metaphor, metonymy, and experientialist philosophy: Challenging cognitive semantics [M]. Berlin: Walter de Gruyter, 2005.

[120] HASSELGÅRD H. Thematic choice and expressions of stance in English argumentative texts by Norwegian learners [C] //K AIJMER. Corpora and language teaching. Amsterdam: John Benjamins Publishing Company, 2009: 121-139.

[121] HENKIN H. Drafting engineering contracts [M]. Essex: Taylor & Francis, 2005.

[122] HERBST T, FAULHABER S, UHRIG P. The phraseological view of language: A tribute to John Sinclair [M]. Berlin: Walter de Gruyter, 2011.

[123] HERMAN D, JAHN M, RYAN M. Routledge encyclopedia of narrative theory [M]. Oxfordshire: Routledge, 2005.

[124] HOEY M. Lexical priming: A new theory of words and language [M]. London and New York: Routledge, 2005.

[125] HOFFMANN S, EVERT S, SMITH N, LEE D, PRYTZ Y. Corpus linguistics with BNCweb: A practical guide [M]. Frankfurt am Main: Peter Lang, 2008.

[126] HOOVER D, CULPEPER J, O'HALLORAN K. Digital literary studies: Corpus approaches to poetry, prose, and drama [M]. New York: Routledge, 2014.

[127] HOWARTH P A. Phraseology in English academic writing: Some implications for language learning and dictionary making [M]. Tübingen: Max Niemeyer Verlag, 1996.

[128] HUNSTON S. Corpora in applied linguistics [M]. Cambridge: Cambridge University Press, 2002a.

[129] HUNSTON S. Pattern grammar, language teaching, and linguistic variation: Applications of a corpus-driven grammar [C] //R REPPEN, S FITZMAURICE, D BIBEr. Using corpora to explore linguistic variation. Amsterdam: John Benjamins Publishing Company, 2002b: 167-183.

[130] HUNSTON S. Phraseology and system: A contribution to the debate [C] // G THOMPSON, S HUNSTON. System and corpus: Exploring connections.

London: Equinox, 2006: 55-80.

[131] HUNSTON S. Starting with the small words: Patterns, lexis and semantic sequences [J]. International Journal of Corpus Linguistics, 2008, 13 (3), 271-295.

[132] HUNSTON S. How can a corpus be used to explore patterns [C] //A O'KEEFFE, M MCCARTHY. The Routledge handbook of corpus linguistics. London and New York: Routledge, 2010: 152-166.

[133] HUNSTON S. Corpus approaches to evaluation: Phraseology and evaluative language [M]. New York: Routledge, 2011.

[134] HUNSTON S, FRANCIS G. Pattern grammar: A corpus-driven approach to the lexical grammar of English [M]. Philadelphia, PA: John Benjamins Publishing Company, 2000.

[135] HUNSTON S, SINCLAIR J. A local grammar of evaluation [C] //S HUNSTON, G THOMPSON. Evaluation in text: Authorial stance and the construction of discourse. Oxford: Oxford University Press, 2000: 74-101.

[136] HUNSTON S, THOMPSON G.. Evaluation in text: Authorial stance and the construction of discourse [M]. Oxford: Oxford University Press, 2000.

[137] HYLAND K, TSE P. Metadiscourse in academic writing: A reappraisal [J]. Applied Linguistics, 2004: 25, 156-176.

[138] JI, M. Phraseology in corpus-based translation studies [M]. Bern: Peter Lang, 2010.

[139] JOHN S, LASO N J. A corpus-based analysis of the collocational patterning of adjectives with abstract nouns in medical English [C] // VERDAGUER, N J LASO, D SALAZAR. Biomedical English: A corpus - based approach. Amsterdam: John Benjamins Publishing Company, 2013: 55-70.

[140] JOHNS T, KING P. Classroom concordancing [J]. English Language Research Journal, 1991: 4, 1-16.

[141] JUCKER A H, SMITH S W, LÜDGE T. Interactive aspects of vagueness in conversation [J]. Journal of Pragmatics, 2003, 35: 1737-1769.

[142] KENNEDY G.. Phraseology and language pedagogy: Semantic preference associated with English verbs in the British National Corpus [C] //. Meunier, S Granger. Phraseology in foreign language learning and teaching. Philadelphia, PA: John Benjamins Publishing Company, 2008: 21-41.

[143] KNOWLES M, MOON R. Introducing metaphor [M]. London and New York: Routledge, 2006.

[144] KOESTER A. Investigating workplace discourse [M]. Oxon: Routledge, 2006.

[145] KOESTER A. 'About twelve thousand or so': Vagueness in North American and UK offices [C] //J CUTTING. Vague language explored. Palgrave Macmillan, 2007: 40-61.

[146] KOESTER A. Workplace discourse [M]. London: Continuum, 2010.

[147] KÖVECSES, Z. Language, mind, and culture: A practical introduction [M]. Oxford: Oxford University Press, 2006.

[148] KÖVECSES Z. Metaphor: A practical introduction [M]. Oxford: Oxford University Press, 2010.

[149] KREUZ R, CAUCCI G. Social aspect of verbal irony use [C] //H PISHWA. Language and social cognition: Expression of the social mind. Berlin: Walter de Gruyter, 2009: 325-347.

[150] LAKOFF G. The contemporary theory of metaphor [C] // A ORTONY. Metaphor and thought. Cambridge: Cambridge University Press, 1993: 202-251.

[151] LAKOFF G. The neural theory of metaphor [C] //R GIBBS. The Cambridge handbook of metaphor and thought. Cambridge: Cambridge University Press, 2008: 17-38.

[152] LAKOFF G., JOHNSON M. Metaphors we live by [M]. Chicago: University of Chicago, 1980a.

[153] LAKOFF G, JOHNSON M. Conceptual Metaphor in everyday language [J]. The Journal of Philosophy, 1980b, 77 (8): 453-486.

[154] LAKOFF G, JOHNSON M. Philosophy in the flesh: The embodied mind and its challenge to western thought [M]. New York: Basic Books, 1999.

[155] LAKOFF G, JOHNSON M. Metaphors we live by [M]. London: The University of Chicago Press, 2003.

[156] LANGACKER R. Grammar and Conceptualisation [M]. Berlin: Mouton de Gruyter, 2000.

[157] LEMKE J. Resources for attitudinal meaning: Evaluative orientations in text semantics [J]. Functions of Language, 1998, 5 (1): 33-56.

[158] LEWIS M. Teaching collocation: Further developments in the lexical ap-

proach [M]. Boston: Thomson Heinle, 2000.

[159] LI S. A corpus-based analysis of metaphorical uses of the high frequency noun time: Challenges to Conceptual Metaphor Theory [C] //. ROMERO-TRILLO. Yearbook of corpus linguistics and pragmatics 2014: New empirical and theoretical paradigms. Springer International Publishing Switzerland, 2014: 79-96.

[160] LIANG M. Sparing a free hand: context-based automatic categorisation of concordance lines. Paper presented at the 7th International Corpus Linguistics Conference (CL2013) [R], Lancaster University, Lancaster, 2013.

[161] LINDQUIST H. Corpus linguistics and the description of English. Edinburgh [M]: Edinburgh University Press, 2009.

[162] LITTLEMORE J. Applying cognitive linguistics to second language learning and teaching [M]. Basingstoke: Palgrave Macmillan, 2009.

[163] LITTLEMORE J, LOW G. Figurative thinking and foreign language learning [M]. London: Palgrave Macmillan, 2006.

[164] LITTLEMORE J, TAGG C. Metonymy in text messaging (or The role of metonymy in a corpus of British text messages) [R]. Unpublished presentation given at the ELR seminar at University of Birmingham, 2014.

[165] LÖBNER S. Understanding semantics. 2nd edition [M]. London: Routledge, 2013.

[166] LOUW B. Irony in the text or insincerity in the writer? - The diagnostic potential of semantic prosodies [C] //M BAKER, G FRANCIS, E TOGNINI-BONELLI. Text and technology: In honour of John Sinclair. Philadelphia, PA: John Benjamins Publishing Company, 1993: 157-176.

[167] LOW G., DEIGNAN A., CAMERON L, TODD Z. Researching and applying metaphor in the real world [M]. Amsterdam: John Benjamins Publishing Company, 2010.

[168] LYBBERT E K. Substitutes as 'replacements' [M]. Linguistics, 1972, 91: 5-16.

[169] LYONS J. Semantics: Volume 2 [M]. Cambridge: Cambridge University Press, 1977.

[170] MACARTHUR F, ONCINS-MARTÍNEZ J, SÁNCHEZ-GARCÍA M, PIQUER-PÍRIZ A. Metaphor in use: Context, culture, and communication [M]. Amsterdam: John Benjamins Publishing Company, 2012.

[171] MAHLBERG M. English general nouns: A corpus theoretical approach [M]. Amsterdam: John Benjamins Publishing Company, 2005.

[172] MAHLBERG M. But it will take time…points of view on a lexical grammar of English [C] // A RENOUF, A KEHOE. The changing face of corpus linguistics. New York: Rodopi, 2006: 377-390.

[173] MAIENBORN C, VON HEUSINGER K, PORTNER P. Semantics: An international handbook of natural language meaning [M]. Berlin: Walter de Gruyter, 2011.

[174] MARCO M. Collocational frameworks in medical research papers: a genre-based study [J]. English for Specific Purposes, 2000, 19: 63-86.

[175] MARTIN J. Beyond exchange: Appraisal systems in English [C] //S HUNSTON, G. THOMPSON. Evaluation in text: Authorial stance and the construction of discourse. Oxford: Oxford University Press, 2000: 43-175.

[176] MARTIN J. Sense and sensibility: Texturing evaluation [C] //J FOLEY. Language, education and discourse: Functional approaches. London: Continuum, 2004: 270-304.

[177] MARTIN J, WHITE P. The language of evaluation: Appraisal in English [M]. London: Palgrave, 2005.

[178] MARTIN W. A unified approach to semantic frames and collocational patterns [C] //S GRANGER, F MEUNIER. Phraseology: An interdisciplinary perspective. Amsterdam: John Benjamins Publishing Company, 2008: 51-66.

[179] MCCARTHY M. Vocabulary [M]. Oxford: Oxford University Press, 1990.

[180] MCENERY T, HARDIE A. Corpus linguistics: Method, theory and practice [M]. Cambridge: Cambridge University Press, 2012.

[181] MCENERY T, XIAO R, TONO Y. Corpus-based language studies: An advanced resource book [M]. Oxon: Routledge, 2006.

[182] MCGLONE M. What is the explanatory value of a conceptual metaphor? [J]. Language & Communication, 2007, 27: 109-126.

[183] MEUNIER F, GOUVERNEUR C. The treatment of phraseology in ELT textbooks [C] // E HIDALGO, L QUEREDA, J SANTANA. Corpora in the foreign language classroom. Amsterdam: Rodopi, 2007: 119-139.

[184] MEUNIER F, GRANGER S. Phraseology in foreign language learning

and teaching [M]. Philadelphia, PA: John Benjamins Publishing Company, 2008.

[185] MEUNIER F, DE COCK S, GILQUIN G, PAQUOT M. A taste for corpora: In honour of Sylviane Granger [M]. Amsterdam: John Benjamins Publishing Company, 2011.

[186] MIHATSCH W. Nouns are THINGS: Evidence for a grammatical metaphor? [C] //K PANTHER, L THORNBURG, A BARCELONA. Metonymy and metaphor in grammar. Amsterdam: John Benjamins Publishing Company, 2009: 75-95.

[187] MILLER D, JOHNSON J. Evaluative phraseological choice and speaker party/gender: A corpus-assisted comparative study of 'register-idiosyncratic' meaning in Congressional debate [C] //G THOMPSON, L ALBA-JUEZ. Evaluation in context. Amsterdam: John Benjamins Publishing Company, 2014, 345-366.

[188] MILLER J. An introduction to English syntax [M]. Edinburgh: Edinburgh University Press, 2002.

[189] MINDT I. Adjective complementation: An empirical analysis of adjectives followed by that-clauses [M]]. Amsterdam: John Benjamins Publishing Company, 2011.

[190] MOON R. The analysis of meaning [C] // J SINCLAIR. Looking up. London: Collins, 1987: 86-103.

[191] MOON R. Textual aspects of fixed expressions in learners' dictionaries [C] //P ARNAUD, H BÉJOINT. Vocabulary and applied linguistics. London: Macmillan, 1992: 13-27.

[192] MOON R. Fixed expressions and idioms in English: A corpus-based approach [M]. Oxford: Oxford University Press, 1998.

[193] MOON R. What can a corpus tell us about lexis? [C] //A O' KEEFFE, M MCCARTHY. The Routledge handbook of corpus linguistics. London and New York: Routledge, 2010: 197-211.

[194] MURPHY B. Corpus and sociolinguistics: Investigating age and gender in female talk [M]. Amsterdam: John Benjamins Publishing Company, 2010.

[195] NATTINGER J R, DECARRICO J S. Lexical phrases and language teaching [M]. Oxford: Oxford University Press, 1992.

[196] NERLICH B, TODD Z., HERMAN V, CLARKE D. Polysemy: Flexible patterns of meaning in mind and language [M]. Berlin: Mouton de Gruyter, 2003.

[197] NESI H, BASTURKMEN H. Lexical bundles and discourse signalling in academic lectures [C] //J FLOWERDEW, M MAHLBERG. Lexical cohesion and corpus linguistics. Amsterdam: John Benjamins Publishing Company, 2009: 23-43.

[198] NESSELHAUF N. Collocations in a learner corpus [M]. Amsterdam: John Benjamins Publishing Company, 2005.

[199] NIDA E. The molecular level of lexical semantics [J]. International Journal of Lexicography, 1997, 10 (4): 265-274.

[200] O' KEEFFE A, MCCARTHY M, CARTER R. From corpus to classroom: Language use and language teaching [M]. Cambridge: Cambridge University Press, 2007.

[201] O' KEEFFE A, MCCARTHY M. The Routledge handbook of corpus linguistics [M]. London and New York: Routledge, 2010.

[202] ONGLEY J, CAREY R. Russell: A guide for the perplexed [M]. London: Bloomsbury Academic, 2013.

[203] ORFANÒ B. Analysing the use of vague language in spoken interlanguage: A corpus-based study of a group of Brazilian university students learning English as a second language [C] //S GRANGER, G GILQUIN, F MEUNIER. Twenty years of learner corpus research: Looking back, moving ahead. Belgium: Presses universitaires de Louvain, 2013: 367-376.

[204] OSBORNE J. Phraseology effects as a trigger for errors in L2 English: The case of more advanced learners [C] //F MEUNIER, S GRANGER. Phraseology in foreign language learning and teaching. Philadelphia, PA: John Benjamins Publishing Company, 2008: 67-83.

[205] OVERSTREET M. Vagueness and hedging [C] ///G ANDERSON, K AIJMER. Pragmatics of society. Berlin: Walter de Gruyter, 2011: 293-317.

[206] PANTHER K, RADDEN G. Metonymy in language and thought [M]. Amsterdam: John Benjamins Publishing Company, 1999.

[207] PANTHER K, THORNBURG L, BARCELONA A. Metonymy and metaphor in grammar [M]. Amsterdam: John Benjamins Publishing Company, 2009.

[208] PAPROTTÉ W, DIRVEN R. The ubiquity of metaphor: Metaphor in language and thought [M]. Amsterdam/Philadelphia: John Benjamins Publishing Company, 1985.

[209] PAQUOT M. Exemplification in learner writing: A cross-linguistic per-

spective [C] //F MEUNIER, S GRANGER. Phraseology in foreign language learning and teaching. Philadelphia, PA: John Benjamins Publishing Company, 2008: 101-119.

[210] PARTINGTON A. Linguistics of laughter: A corpus-assisted study of laughter-talk [M]. Oxon: Routledge, 2006.

[211] PATTERSON K. The identification of metaphor using corpus methods: Can a re-classification of metaphoric language help our understanding of metaphor usage and comprehension? [R]. Paper presented at the 7th International Corpus Linguistics Conference (CL2013), Lancaster University, Lancaster, 2013.

[212] PATTERSON K. The analysis of metaphor: To what extent can the theory of lexical priming help our understanding of metaphor usage and comprehension [J]. Journal of Psycholinguistic Research, 2014, DOI 10. 1007/s10936-014-9343-1.

[213] PAVIČIĆ TAKAČ V. Vocabulary learning strategies and foreign language acquisition [M]. Clevedon: Multilingual Matters, 2008.

[214] PAWLEY A. Developments in the study of formulaic language since 1970: A personal view [C] //P SKANDERA. Phraseology and culture in English. Berlin: Walter de Gruyter, 2007, 3-45.

[215] PAWLEY A, SYDER F. Two puzzles for linguistic theory: nativelike selection and nativelike fluency [C] //J RICHARDS, R SCHMIDT. Language and communication. London: Longman., 1983.

[216] PÉREZ HERNÁNDEZ L. Metaphor - Based Cluster Models and Conceptual Interaction: the Case of 'Time' [J]. Atlantis, 2001, 23 (2): 65-81.

[217] PHILIP G. Collocation and connotation: A corpus-based investigation of colour words in English and Italian [D]. PhD thesis submitted to the University of Birmingham, 2003.

[218] PHILIP G. Reassessing the canon: 'Fixed' phrases in general reference corpora [C] // S GRANGER, F MEUNIER. Phraseology: An interdisciplinary perspective. Amsterdam: John Benjamins Publishing Company, 2008: 95-108.

[219] PHILIP G. Colouring meaning: Collocation and connotation in figurative language [M]. Amsterdam: John Benjamins Publishing Company, 2011.

[220] PIIRAINEN E. Figurative phraseology and culture [C] //S GRANGER, F MEUNIER. Phraseology: An interdisciplinary perspective. Philadelphia, PA: John Benjamins Publishing Company, 2008: 207-228.

[221] PRAGGLEJAZ GROUP. MIP: A method for identifying metaphorically used words in discourse [J]. Metaphor and Symbol, 2007, 22 (1): 1-39.

[222] RADDEN G. How metonymic are metaphors? [C] //R DIRVEN, R PÖRINGS. Metaphor and metonymy in comparison and contrast. Berlin: Mouton de Gruyter, 2002: 407-434.

[223] RADDEN G. The ubiquity of metonymy [C] //J CAMPO, I FERRANDO, B FORTUÑO. Cognitive and discourse approaches to metaphor and metonymy. Castelló de la Plana: Publicacions de la Universitat Jaume I, 2005: 11-28.

[224] RADDEN G, KÖPCKE K, BERG T, SIEMUND P. Aspects of meaning construction [M]. Amsterdam: John Benjamins Publishing Company, 2007.

[225] RENOUF A. Explorations in corpus linguistics [M]. Amsterdam: Rodopi, 1998.

[226] RENOUF A, BAUER L. Contextual clues to word-meaning [J]. International Journal of Corpus Linguistics, 2000, 5 (2): 231-258.

[227] RENOUF A, SINCLAIR J. Collocational frameworks in English [C] //K AIJMER, B ALTENBERG. English corpus linguistics. New York: Longman, 1991: 128-143.

[228] REPPEN R. Using corpora in the language classroom [M]. Cambridge: Cambridge University Press, 2010.

[229] RICKHEIT G, STROHNER H. Handbook of communication competence [M]. Berlin: Walter de Gruyter, 2008.

[230] RIEMER N. The semantics of polysemy: Reading meaning in English and Warlpiri [M]. Berlin: Mouton de Gruyter, 2005.

[231] RIEMER N. Introducing semantics [M]. Cambridge: Cambridge University Press, 2010.

[232] RÖMER U. Progressives, patterns, pedagogy: A corpus-driven approach to English progressive forms, functions, contexts and didactics [M]. Amsterdam: John Benjamins Publishing Company, 2005.

[233] RÖMER U. Pedagogical applications of corpora: Some reflections on the current scope and a wish list for future developments [J]. Zeitschrift für Anglistik und Amerikanistik, 2006, 54 (2): 121-134.

[234] RÖMER U, SCHULZE R. Exploring the lexis-grammar interface [M]. Amsterdam: John Benjamins Publishing Company, 2009.

[235] RÖMER U, SCHULZE R. Patterns, meaningful units and specialized discourses [M]. Amsterdam: John Benjamins Publishing Company, 2010.

[236] RONZITTI G. Vagueness: A guide [M]. London and New York: Springer Science & Business Media, 2011.

[237] RUIZ DE MENDOZA IBÁÑEZ F J, PÉREZ HERNÁNDEZ L. The Contemporary Theory of Metaphor: Myths, Developments and Challenges [J]. Metaphor and Symbol, 2011, 26 (3): 161-185.

[238] RUSSELL B. Vagueness [C] //R KEEFE, P SMITH. Vagueness: A reader. Cambridge: MIT Press, 1997, 3: 61-68.

[239] SAKA P. How to think about meaning [M]. The Netherlands: Springer, 2007.

[240] SARDINHA T. Metaphor probabilities in corpora [C] //M ZANOTTO, L CAMERON, M CAVALCANTI. Confronting metaphor in use: An applied linguistic approach. Amsterdam: John Benjamins Publishing Company, 2008: 127-147.

[241] SCHMID, HANS-JÖRG. English abstract nouns as conceptual shells: From corpus to cognition [M]. Berlin: Mouton de Gruyter, 2000.

[242] SCHMITT N. Formulaic sequences: Acquisition, processing, and use [M]. Amsterdam: John Benjamins Publishing Company, 2004.

[243] SCOTT M. WordSmith Tools version 6 [M]. Liverpool: Lexical Analysis Software, 2013.

[244] SEMINO E. Metaphor in discourse [M]. Cambridge: Cambridge University Press, 2008.

[245] SEMINO E, DEIGNAN A, LITTLEMORE J. Metaphor, genre and recontextualization [J]. Metaphor and Symbol, 2013, 28 (1): 41-59.

[246] SIEPMANN D. Phraseology in learners' dictionaries: What, where and how? [C] //F MEUNIER, S GRANGER. Phraseology in foreign language learning and teaching. Philadelphia, PA: John Benjamins Publishing Company, 2008: 185-202.

[247] SINCLAIR J. 1987. Looking up. London: Collins.

[248] SINCLAIR J. Corpus, concordance, collocation [M]. Oxford: Oxford University Press, 1991.

[249] SINCLAIR J. The search for units of meaning [J]. Textus, 1996, 9 (1): 75-106.

[250] SINCLAIR J. Reading concordances: An introduction [M]. London: Pearson, 2003.

[251] SINCLAIR J M. Trust the text: Language, corpus and discourse [M]. London and New York: Routledge, 2004a.

[252] SINCLAIR J M. How to use corpora in language teaching [M]. Amsterdam: John Benjamins Publishing Company, 2004b.

[253] SINCLAIR J, JONES S, DALEY R. English collocation studies: The OSTI report [M]. London: Continuum, 2004.

[254] SINDONI M G. Spoken and written discourse in online interactions: A multimodal approach [M]. New York: Taylor & Francis, 2013.

[255] SKANDERA P. Phraseology and culture in English [M]. Berlin: Walter de Gruyter, 2007.

[256] SMITH N. Vagueness and degrees of truth [M]. Oxford: Oxford University Press, 2008.

[257] STAHL S, NAGY W. Teaching word meanings [M]. New Jersey: Lawrence Erlbaum Associates, 2006.

[258] STEADMAN J. Drafting legal documents in plain English [M]. Milano: Giuffrè Editore, 2013.

[259] STEEN G. Finding metaphor in grammar and usage [M]. Amsterdam: John Benjamins Publishing Company, 2007.

[260] STEEN G. The paradox of metaphor: Why we need a three-dimensional model of metaphor [J]. Metaphor and Symbol, 2008, 23 (4): 213-241.

[261] STEEN G, DORST A, HERRMANN J, KAAL A, KRENNMAYR T, PASMA T. A method for linguistic metaphor identification: From MIP to MIPVU [M]. Amsterdam: John Benjamins Publishing Company, 2010.

[262] STEFANOWITSCH A, GRIES S T. Corpus - based approaches to metaphor and metonymy [M]. Berlin: Mouton de Gruyter, 2006.

[263] STEWART D. Semantic prosody: A critical evaluation [M]. New York, NY: Routledge, 2010.

[264] STENSTRÖM A, ANDERSEN G, HASUND I. Trends in teenage talk: Corpus compilation, analysis and findings [M]. Amsterdam: John Benjamins Publishing Company, 2002.

[265] STUBBS M. Words and phrases: Corpus studies of lexical semantics

[M]. Oxford: Blackwell, 2001.

[266] STUBBS M. Two quantitative methods of studying phraseology in English [J]. International Journal of Corpus Linguistics, 2002, 7 (2): 215-244.

[267] STUBBS M. Notes on the history of corpus linguistics and empirical semantics [C] //M Nenonen, S Niemi. Collocations and idioms. Joensuu: Joensuun Yliopisto, 2007a: 317-329.

[268] STUBBS M. An example of frequent English phraseology: Distribution, structures and functions [C] // R Facchinetti. Corpus linguistics 25 years on. Amsterdam: Rodopi, 2007b: 89-105.

[269] STUBBS M. On texts, corpora and models of language [C] //M HOEY, M MAHLBERG, M STUBBS, W TEUBERT. Text, discourse and corpora: Text and analysis. London: Continuum, 2007c: 127-161.

[270] STUBBS M. Memorial article: John Sinclair (1933-2007) The search for units of meaning: Sinclair on empirical semantics [J]. Applied Linguistics, 2009a, 30 (1): 115-137.

[271] STUBBS M. Technology and phraseology: With notes on the history of corpus linguistics [C] //U RÖMER, R SCHULZE. Exploring the lexis-grammar interface. Amsterdam: John Benjamins Publishing Company, 2009b: 15-31.

[272] STUBBS M. A tribute to John McHardy Sinclair (14 June 1933 - 13 March 2007) [C] //T HERBST, S FAULHABER, P UHRIG. The phraseological view of language: A tribute to John Sinclair. Berlin: Walter de Gruyter, 2011.

[273] SVENSSON M H. A very complex criterion of fixedness: Non-compositionality [C] //S GRANGER, F MEUNIER. Phraseology: An interdisciplinary perspective. Amsterdam: John Benjamins Publishing Company, 2008, 81-93.

[274] TEUBERT W. Meaning, discourse and society [M]. Cambridge: Cambridge University Press, 2010.

[275] TEUBERT W. Building onto the corpus-driven approach: A wider look on meaning [R]. Unpublished presentation given at the ELR seminar at University of Birmingham, 2015.

[276] TEUBERT W, ČERMÁKOVÁ A. Directions in corpus linguistics [C] //MAK HALLIDAY, W TEUBERT, C YALLOP, A ČERMÁKOVÁ. Lexicology and corpus linguistics. London: Continuum, 2004: 113-166.

[277] THOMPSON G, HUNSTON S. System and corpus: Two traditions with a

common ground [C] //G THOMPSON, S HUNSTON. System and corpus: Exploring connections. London: Equinox, 2006: 1-14.

[278] TOGNINI-BONELLI E, DEL LUNGO CAMICIOTTI G. Strategies in academic discourse [M]. Amsterdam: John Benjamins Publishing Company, 2005.

[279] UNGERER F. 1997. "Emotions and emotional language in English and German news stories". In: S. Niemeyer and R. Dirven (eds), The language of emotions. Amsterdam: John Benjamins Publishing Company, 307-328.

[280] VALLÉE R. Holism, semantic and epistemic [C] //A BARBER, R STAINTON. Concise encyclopedia of philosophy of language and linguistics. Oxford: Elsevier, 2010: 295-297.

[281] VINCENT B. Investigating academic phraseology through combinations of very frequent words: A methodological exploration [J]. Journal of English for Academic Purposes, 2013, 12: 44-56.

[282] WAGNER A. Interpretation, law and the construction of meaning: Collected papers on legal interpretation in theory, adjudication and political practice [M]. The Netherlands: Springer, 2007.

[283] WALKER C. Factors which influence the process of collocation [C] //F BOERS, S LINDSTROMBERG. Cognitive Linguistic Approaches to Teaching Vocabulary and Phraseology. Berlin: Mouton de Greyer, 2008: 291-308.

[284] WALKER C. A corpus-based study of the linguistic features and processes which influence the way collocations are formed: Some implications for the learning of collocations [J]. TESOL Quarterly, 2011, 45 (2): 291-312.

[285] WALKER C. At the same time: A case of lexical congruency [J]. The Language Teacher, JALT, 2014, 38 (4): 30-32.

[286] WALSH S, O' KEEFFE A, MCCARTHY M. '... post-colonialism, multi-culturalism, structuralism, feminism, post-modernism and so on and so forth': A comparative analysis of vague category markers in academic discourse [C] //A ÄDEL, R REPPEN. Corpora and discourse: The challenges of different settings. Amsterdam: John Benjamins Publishing Company, 2008: 9-29.

[287] WANG A. When precision meets vagueness: A corpus-assisted approach to vagueness in Taiwanese and British courtrooms [R]. Paper presented at the 7th Biennial Conference of International Association of Forensic Linguists, Cardiff, 2005.

[288] WARREN M. Features of naturalness in conversation [M]. Amsterdam:

John Benjamins Publishing Company, 2006.

[289] WIKBERG K. Phrasal similes in the BNC [C] //S GRANGER, F MEUNIER. Phraseology: An interdisciplinary perspective. Amsterdam: John Benjamins Publishing Company, 2008: 127-142.

[290] WILLIAMSON T. Vagueness [M]. London: Routledge, 1994.

[291] WILLIS J D. Grammar and lexis: Some pedagogical implications [C] // J SINCLAIR, G FOX, M HOEY. Techniques of description. New York: Routledge, 1993: 83-93.

[292] WILLIS D. Rules, patterns and words: Grammar and lexis in English language teaching [M]. Cambridge: Cambridge University Press, 2003.

[293] WRAY A. Formulaic sequences in second language teaching: Principle and practice [J]. Applied Linguistics, 2000, 21 (4): 463-489.

[294] WRAY A. Formulaic language and the lexicon [M]. Cambridge: Cambridge University Press, 2002.

[295] ZANOTTO M, CAMERON L, CAVALCANTI M. Confronting metaphor in use: An applied linguistic approach [M]. Amsterdam: John Benjamins Publishing Company, 2008.

Dictionaries

[296] Collins COBUILD Advanced Learner' s English Dictionary 5th edition (CALD) 2005. Harper Collins Publishers.

[297] Collins English Dictionary 10th edition (CED) 2010. Harper Collins Publishers.

[298] Oxford Advanced Learner' s Dictionary 8th edition (OALD) 2010. Oxford University Press.

[299] Oxford English Dictionary 7th edition (OED) 2012. Oxford University Press.

Notes

1 The term "discourse" in this study is used broadly to refer to both the linguistic aspect of discourse (language form, e.g. a piece of written or spoken text, or a certain register) and the social aspect of discourse (the meaning beyond lexis, e.g. the evaluative, metaphorical, interpersonal or ideological use of an utterance). The use of "discourse" here relates to the linguistic aspect, i.e. texts in general. A more detailed discussion of this term can be seen in Pennycook 1994.

2 "Institutionalisation" refers to the integration of a lexical item into the existing stock of vocabulary as generally acceptable by a certain language community; while "lexicalisation" refers to a gradual historical process, involving graphemic, phonological and semantic changes and the loss of motivation (cf. Fernández-Domínguez 2009: 92).

3 More information about the Bank of English is available at the website: http://www.titania.bham.ac.uk/

4 More information about BNCweb can be found at the website http://www.lancaster.ac.uk/fss/courses/ling/corpus/blue/bncweb_top.htm or in the book Corpus linguistics with BNCweb: A practical guide by Hoffmann et al. (2008).

5 Permission to use these course-books for research purposes was sought from their publishers. The majority of publishers have replied and granted permission. However, in a few cases, no response has yet been received.

6 Hoey (2005) proposes the theory of "lexical priming" which suggests that "words are 'primed' for use through our experience with them, so that everything we know about a word is a product of our encounters with it" (2005: i).

7 The capitalised form of domains (e.g. TIME and MONEY) or conceptual metaphors (e.g. TIME IS MONEY) is different from that of a lemmatised word (or lemma). The lemma of an item stands for all word forms of this word (e.g. SPEND for all

word forms of the verb spend) and is usually written with small capitals in this thesis (see Section 4. 3. 3).

8 As explained in the conventions for this thesis, the capitalised form of time in this thesis (TIME) refers to the conceptual domain; the italicised form of time, i.e. time, refers to the word under analysis; and the normal form with single quotation marks, 'time', is also used sometimes to refer to the concept.

9 The notion of "adjectives" for the pattern 'the ADJ thing (that-cl.) is/was' is used more broadly to include numerals such as first, last and one which can also act as premodifiers of the noun thing in the pattern.

10 "Linguistic competence" relates to the knowledge of the system of linguistic rules, e.g. the ability to produce and interpret meaningful utterances in accordance with the rules of language (see Byram 1997: 48). "Communicative competence" relates to the effectiveness in communication, e.g. when it is appropriate to speak and how (see Rickheit and Strohner 2008).